Travels in
Northern Mongolia

Travels in Northern Mongolia

DON CRONER

Library of Congress Number: 2003099383
ISBN: Hardcover   1-4134-4275-7
                 Softcover   1-4134-4274-9

This book was printed in the United States of America.

To order additional copies of this book, contact:
Xlibris Corporation
1-888-795-4274
www.Xlibris.com
Orders@Xlibris.com
23230

Contents

PART III

The Birthplace of the Mongols

PART I

The Source of the Ider

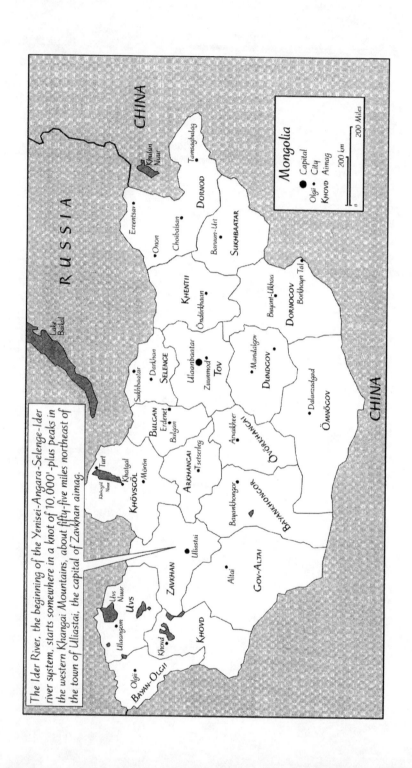

The Ider River, the beginning of the Yenisei-Angara-Selenge-Ider river system, starts somewhere in a knot of 10,000'-plus peaks in the western Khangai Mountains, about fifty-five miles northeast of the town of Uliastai, the capital of Zavkhan aimag.

Mongolia

- ● Capital
- • *Olgii* City
- KHOVD Aimag

200 km
200 Miles

CHINA

RUSSIA

Lake Baikal

Khulan Nuur

Tsagaanhulag

DORNOD

Baruun-Urt

SUKHBAATAR

Ereentsav

Onon

Choibalsan

Borhoyn Tal

Bayant-Uhaa

DORNOGOV

KHENTII

Öndörkhaan

Mandalgov

DUNDGOV

Darkhan

SELENGE

Sukhbaatar

Ulaanbaatar

Zuunmod

TOV

ÖVÖRKHANGAI

Arvaikheer

Dalanzadgad

ÖMNÖGOV

Erdenet

Bulgan

BULGAN

Tsetserleg

ARKHANGAI

Khatgal

Khövsgöl Nuur

Turt

KHÖVSGÖL

Mörön

CHINA

Uliastai

Bayankhongor

BAYANKHONGOR

ZAVKHAN

Altai

GOV-ALTAI

Uvs Nuur

UVS

Ulaangom

Khovd

Khovd

KHOVD

Olgii

BAYAN-ÖLGII

Ulaan Baatar

I ARRIVED IN Ulaan Baatar, the capital of Mongolia, at 2:18 P.M., exactly fifteen hours and twenty-six minutes after leaving Anchorage. The once weekly flight from Seoul, where I had laid over for four hours while changing planes, was only about half full–perhaps sixty people–and about half of those were Americans. From what I could gather from a few conversations in the Seoul departure lounge, most of the Americans were oil guys from Dallas. According to the buzz Mongolia is the next Alaska in terms of oil, and the Zuunbayan and Tsagaan Els fields of Dundgov aimag (*aimag* = province) in the Gobi Desert are the next Prudhoe Bay. Shortly after takeoff I pried myself out of my assigned seat between beefy guys with Texan accents and went to the back of the plane where I claimed a whole row of seats to myself. I was soon absorbed in the book *The Great Wall of China* in which Arthur Waldron describes the nearly 2,000 years of almost continuous struggle between the dynasties of China and the nomadic tribesmen of the Mongolian Plateau and the consequent construction of the many walls by which the Chinese sought to define their borders. I couldn't help but wonder whether the existence of huge oil deposits in the Gobi Desert so close to the Chinese border might result in a new chapter to this saga.

Heavy cloud cover obscured the ground for the first two hours of the flight. About an hour out of Ulaan Baatar holes opened in the clouds, revealing the sere grasslands, grayish sands, and reddish gravels of the Gobi. A half hour out of Ulaan Baatar the sky cleared completely and below could be seen the completely treeless undulating ridges of central Mongolia stretching off in all directions for hundreds of miles before disappearing beyond the curvature of the earth. Although it was near the middle of June and the hills should have been green with fresh grass, most were still buckskin tan. Only the northern slopes of some bore a greenish tinge.

Then ahead and to the right appeared a huge flat-topped mountain almost completely covered with forest—the first trees we have seen since the clouds cleared. This was Bogd Khan Uul (*uul* = mountain), the massif which looms over the southern edge of Ulaan Baatar. We flew west past Bogd Khan Uul and then made a big loop around to the east for the approach to Buyant-Ukhaa Airport. The ground temperature was a balmy 78°F. "Welcome to the blue skies of Mongolia," the flight attendant intoned in English over the intercom as we taxied to the unloading gate. This was followed by an instrumental version of "I Left My Heart in San Francisco." Thus began my third trip to Mongolia.

During the three years I lived in Irkutsk, the city of 650,000, seated on the banks of the Angara River about thirty miles downstream from the outlet of Lake Baikal—the huge expanse of water that dominates East Siberia—I had often wanted to visit Mongolia, whose border was only about a hundred and thirty miles to the south. My immediate interest was Mongolia's Lake Khövsgöl, just south of 11,450-foot Munku-Sardik—the highest peak in the East Sayan Mountains—whose summit lies exactly on the border between Siberia and Mongolia. Situated at an altitude of 5,379 feet, eighty-four miles long and up to twenty-four miles wide, Khövsgöl drains via the Egiyn River into the Selenge River, the largest tributary of Lake Baikal, and is known in Siberia as "Baikal's Little Brother." The summer before I had flown from Irkutsk, about 325 miles south to Ulaan Baatar, where I met up with a group of Americans who were headed for Khövsgöl. With them I traveled along the entire east coast of the lake by horse, kayak, and four-wheel drive truck.

Then the following February I returned to Ulaan Baatar. The center line of the total eclipse of the sun scheduled for March 9 was passing near the city of Darkhan 136 miles north of Ulaan Baatar and I planned to be there. Along with some 1,600 other foreign visitors I traveled north to the center line only to be disappointed by a fierce snowstorm which blew in the night before and almost completely blotted out any view of the eclipse. For several weeks after the eclipse I stayed on in Ulaan Baatar, walking the length and breadth of the city, exploring its attractions, and making preliminary plans for the coming summer.

Now I am back again. The passport control official stamps my Mongolian visa without even looking at the picture page of my passport and the customs woman waves me through without glancing at my bags. In the reception area I am greeted by Ganaa, a cab driver I had met on my first trip to the city. He was also the very first person I bumped into outside of customs on my second trip. This time he is waiting for me, knowing that I am arriving by Korean Air in the first or second week of June. Fifty-six years old, with straggly shoulder-length hair, Ganaa claims to have learned English in the last couple of years with the help of his daughter, a graduate of the Mongolian Institute of Foreign Languages. She originally had studied Russian, and had lived in Alma Ata, in the old Soviet Union, for several years, but now, as with so many Mongolians, her interest has switched to English. His youngest daughter, Ganaa tells me, also studied English and has just been accepted into a one-year economics course in England. She plans to work for a bank when she returns to Mongolia. Ganaa was a high school mathematics teacher in Ulaan Baatar for many years but quit because of poor pay and working conditions ("very hard job, Mongolian kids not interested in mathematics," he says) and now is a full-time cab driver. His long hair makes him look like an aging hippie, an impression enhanced by his predilection for 1960s folk music. His favorite song is "Where Have All the Flowers Gone"–for which he made me write down all the words on my previous trip–"Green Fields" by the Kingston Trio, and Peter, Paul, and Mary's version of "Blowin' in the Wind." I present him with a small gift–a tape of Peter, Paul, and Mary's greatest hits.

When I left Ulaan Baatar at the beginning of April Ganaa assured me that when I returned in early June the steppe would be carpeted with green grass and ablaze with wild flowers. Now, though the grasslands on both sides of the road on the ten-mile drive into town are a parched tan nowhere is there enough vegetation to hide a golf ball.

Yet Ganaa assures me there has been rain—on the first of June it even snowed several inches in Ulaan Baatar and up to a foot on the higher slopes of Bogd Khan Uul just to the south. Just one more good rain, Ganaa insists, and the grasslands so crucial to Mongolia's subsistence economy would bloom again, but in the meantime the cows wandering across the road and halting traffic to and from the airport look pitifully thin.

I am soon ensconced in the Geegee Hotel, located on a hillside a half mile east of the city center, in what is known as the Sansar District. The hotel is an old Soviet-style apartment building and for my ten bucks a night I get what is essentially an efficiency apartment—big living room opening onto a balcony, bath with intermittent supplies of hot water, and a small kitchen from which stove and refrigerator have been removed. If you have ever been in cheesier examples of Khrushchev-era Soviet apartments, you get the idea. I will stay here for a few days while I complete arrangements for several trips into the countryside I have planned for the upcoming summer.

In 1993 a party of seven Russians—members of a rafting club in the East Siberian city of Angarsk—and four Americans, myself included, decided to float the headwaters of the 2,728-mile-long Lena River—according to Soviet geographers the longest single river in all of Russia. The Lena River begins on the western slopes of the Baikal Ridge, the towering rampart bordering the northwest shore of East Siberia's vast Lake Baikal. From its source, less than eight miles from the shoreline of Baikal but over 2,500 feet above the lake's surface, the river flows north for twelve miles, coming to within five miles of the shoreline of the lake, but still over 2,000 feet higher, then turns and flows away to the west. Eventually it trends north again and begins its long journey to the Laptev Sea, bordering on the Arctic Ocean.

The northwest coast of Baikal where the Lena begins is remote wilderness accessible only by chartered boat or helicopter. We chartered a fifty-foot steel-hulled boat and from Listvyanka, a small village at the outlet of Lake Baikal, cruised northward 195 miles to Pokoyniki, a tiny settlement consisting of a ranger station serving the Baikal-Lena Preserve, a protected area encompassing the headwaters of the Lena, and three or four other buildings. From Pokoyniki we lugged our gear and inflatable rafts up 2,200 vertical feet and inland five miles through a gap in the Baikal Ridge to the put-in point on the Lena River, just twelve miles from its actual source.

After six days of floating we arrived in the tiny ranger station of Chanchur, not far from the western edge of the Baikal-Lena Preserve. We spent the night there and over tea were debriefed by the head ranger, a short, wiry man in his fifties named Vladimir Petrovich Trapeznikov. The next day we floated on to Biryulka, on the road system, where we had arranged for a bus to take us back to Irkutsk.

While living in Irkutsk the following winter I got a telephone call from Vladimir Petrovich. He wondered if I would be interested in accompanying him on a trip from Chanchur to the actual source of the Lena. He explained that he had pioneered a new route to the source of the Lena bypassing the rugged thirty mile-long canyon on the upper Lena which made upstream travel by boat or foot impossible via the river itself. Using this route we would go part way up the Lena by boat, hike overland to the source of the Lena, and then walk downstream to the rafting put-in point where we would take the trail to Pokoyniki on the shores of Baikal. This fifty-mile overland route he had dubbed the "Wolf Path to Baikal." I agreed to go with him.

The next June we drove to Biryulka, then took Vladimir Petrovich's outboard-powered aluminum river boat four hours upstream to his house in Chanchur. The next morning we motored up the Lena another four hours. At the Wolf Path trail head—an unmarked spot that only Vladimir Petrovich knew—we tied up the boat and walked overland seven miles across a rugged forested ridge to the banks of the Little Anai River. Here we spent the night in a tiny log patrol cabin that Vladimir Petrovich had built. The next day we hiked eleven miles up the Little Anai and spent the night in yet another patrol cabin. The next morning we headed up a small tributary of the Little Anai which we tracked to its source high in the mountains. By early evening we had emerged above timberline. Topping a barren ridge we saw before us the small lake where the Lena River begins. We scrambled down to the lake and were soon standing at its four-foot wide outlet. Vladimir Petrovich nailed up a sign officially designating the spot the "Source of the Lena," then turned to me: "You know, very few Russians have ever stood here at the source of Russia's longest river, and according to the records of the Baikal-Lena Preserve you are the very first American. Congratulations."

The next day, as we trudged twenty miles down the Lena valley and over the Baikal Ridge to Pokoyniki, my thoughts turned to the other great river systems which drain northern Asia: the Yenisei, the Ob, the Irtysh, and the Amur. Where were their sources, and who had first found them? Was it possible for me, an American, to visit the sources of all these rivers? I didn't know, but I was determined to find out. Back in Irkutsk I began extensive research on these river systems. My attention soon focused on the Yenisei. With an average flow of 19,800 cubic meters of water per second at its mouth, the Yenisei, measured by volume, is the largest river in Russia and Siberia and also the largest of any of the earth's river flowing north into the Arctic Ocean Basin. The only other river in Russia which comes close is the Lena, with a flow of 17,000 cubic meters of water per second at its mouth.

The river bearing the name Yenisei begins at the confluence of the Ka Khem and the Biy Khem rivers near the city of Kyzyl in the Autonomous Republic of Tuva, now part of the Russian Federation. From here it flows 2,161 miles to the Kara Sea, which ranks it fourth in length among Siberia's rivers after the Lena, the Irtysh, and the Ob. This, of course, was not the source of the Yenisei I was looking for. I wanted to locate the ultimate source, which I realized must lie at the headwaters of either the Ka Khem or the Biy Khem. A check of various reference books found them almost evenly divided on which of these rivers constituted the real source of the Yenisei. I turned to Dr. Leonid Korytny, chief researcher at Irkutsk's Institute of Geography, a branch of the Russian Academy of Sciences, for clarification. In a lengthy memorandum Dr. Korytny weighted all the relevant factors and finally concluded that the beginning of the Biy Khem was the source of the Yenisei. He added, "The Biy Khem begins on the western slopes of the Pogranichny Ridge, at the foot of one of the highest points of the Sayan Mountains—Peak Topograf—on the border between the autonomous republics of Tuva and

Buryatia. It is true that this is a very hard area to reach. I wish you the best of luck in finding the source of the Yenisei."

It took fourteen days to get from Irkutsk to the source of the Yenisei and back. From the end of the road system I and two Russian companions had to hike a total of about ninety miles, but we did finally find the beginning of the Biy Khem–the source of the Yenisei–at the outlet of a small pond in a cirque beneath the massif of Peak Topograf. From here the Biy Khem-Yenisei flows north 2,537 miles to the Kara Sea.

From a hydrological point of view the drainage of the Yenisei basin is, however, extremely complicated. The Angara River, the tributary of the Yenisei which drains Lake Baikal, is in fact considerably larger than the Yenisei where the two come together. At the confluence of the two rivers the Angara is a mile wide, with an annual average flow of 123 cubic kilometers of water, while the Yenisei is only a half-mile wide, with an annual flow of 100 cubic kilometers. Thus the Angara could be considered the main trunk of the river system which occupies the Yenisei basin. This trunk of the river system does not end at the outlet of Lake Baikal, the beginning of the Angara. It also includes the largest tributary of Lake Baikal, the Selenga River. The Selenga (or Selenge, as it is spelled in Mongolia) in turn starts at the confluence of the Delger Mörön and Ider rivers in Mongolia. Since the Ider is the bigger of the two its beginning constitutes the ultimate source of the Yenisei-Angara-Selenge-Ider river system, which according to Russian sources measures 3,683 miles in length. The National Geographic *Atlas of the World* gives the length of the Yenisei-Angara (it's not clear whether this includes the Selenge and Ider) as 3,432 miles. In either case it would rank, according to the *Atlas of the World*, as the fifth longest river system on earth, after the Nile, Amazon, Yangtze, and Mississippi-Missouri.

Finding the source of the Yenisei-Angara-Selenge-Ider river system is the first of my goals for the summer. The Ider River, the beginning of the system, starts somewhere in a knot of 10,00-foot-plus peaks in the western Khangai Mountains, about fifty-five miles northeast of the town of Uliastai, the capital of Zavkhan aimag.

Uliastai

DURING MY VISIT to Mongolia the previous April I had met with S. Batchuluun, who, in addition to being one of the leaders of the post-communist democratic movement in Mongolia, has in recent years become a tourism magnate, leading horseback riding groups, rafters, and kayakers to various locations throughout Mongolia. I explained to him that I was not interested in accompanying a group but wished to organize my own expedition to the source of the Ider. As it turned out, Batchuluun was born and raised in Zavkhan aimag and thus knew, as he put it, all the "big potatoes"–i.e., important people–in the region. Batchuluun is somewhat of a big potato himself; not only is he a panjandrum in the ruling Democratic Coalition but he also weighs in at over 250 pounds, and with his massive head and long shaggy black locks, has an uncanny resemblance to a yak. He readily agreed to provide me with contacts near the village of Ider where I could rent horses for the trip up the Ider Valley.

When I returned to Ulaan Baatar in June I met again with Batchuluun and nailed down the final plans. Also, one of the translators who worked for Batchuluun recommended as a translator for my trip a friend of his who had just graduated from the Foreign Languages Institute a week earlier. This was Shandas, a crew-cut young man who, when I first met him, was wearing a brand-new cap emblazoned with a Nike swoosh sign, which unfortunately gave me a somewhat poor initial impression. He readily admitted that this would be his very first paid translation job. Also, I was a bit disconcerted by his further admission that he had only ridden a horse "once or twice in my childhood," as he put it. His English was passable, however, and he seemed personable enough, so I hired him and together we bought airplane tickets from Ulaan Baatar to Uliastai for June 26.

The plane was supposed to leave at 8:40 A.M. but the weather did not cooperate. All of western Mongolia was socked in with heavy cloud cover. The domestic terminal was jammed with passengers on grounded flights to Uliastai and the aimag capitals of Khovd and Olgii, farther on out west. Every hour on the hour from 9:00 A.M. the takeoff time for these three flights was postponed yet another hour. If the planes could not fly by four in the afternoon the flights would have to be postponed to the next day. Finally at 4:00 P.M., after I had spent almost eight hours sitting on the concrete floor of the terminal, all three flights were called for boarding.

For two hours we flew over immense cloud banks which billowed and mushroomed far above the altitude of our plane. Finally we emerged from the clouds and circled over a broad green valley dotted with white gers (the circular tents in which many Mongolians live) and herds of livestock. Along the northeastern edge of this lush valley though rose stark cliffs and rocky ramparts almost totally devoid of vegetation. At the base of one of the cliffs were a couple of streets lined with buildings and small apartment blocks—this was downtown Uliastai—and creeping up the nearby ravines and the less steep hillsides were several ger settlements—crowded collections of white tents surrounded by high wooden fences. One standard source gives the population of Uliastai as 20,500, but given my initial impression from the air I would have guessed no more than four or five thousand.

We landed at the dirt airstrip just across the Bogdyn River from downtown. At the terminal we were confronted by a short, trim man in his thirties dressed in leather cap and coat, pink shirt, and dark blue crushed velvet pants. From his appearance I thought he might be the town pimp trying to drum up some business, but he turned out to be Batchuluun's acquaintance, a man named Oingerel. He lives in the Ider Valley and is a sheep herder by profession, but apparently he has his own ideas about what constitutes town wear.

We took a cab—a Russian jeep, of which there appeared to be several dozen at the airport—and were soon ensconced in the town's only working hostelry, a dilapidated dump called, predictably, the Uliastai Hotel, which we soon discovered had neither hot nor cold running water. The management, however, was friendly enough, and a cheerful woman soon appeared at our door with a thermos of hot tea and asked if we would like dinner. They had a cook on duty till ten who could rustle up something for us if we wished. We wished—Shandas and I had both skipped breakfast and had eaten nothing all day at the airport. A half hour later the cook knocked on our door and we followed her to the small upstairs dining room, which, oddly enough, was decorated with large color murals of Banff National Park in Canada. We were the only diners; in fact, we appeared to be the only guests in the hotel. When the cook brought our plates of fried mutton and noodles (2,500 tögrögs = $3.22 total for three people, with second helpings included), she apologized profusely because there were no vegetables. From this I gathered that she had had some experience with Americans, who are always whining about the lack of vegetables. Yes, in fact, some Peace Corps people were here the week before and there was a lot of grousing over the unavailability of salads. Over dinner Oingerel and I, with Shandas translating (to my disappointment Oingerel did not speak more than a few words of Russian) made plans for the next day. In the morning we would buy twenty kilos of potatoes—Oingerel confirmed that these were the only vegetables currently available in Uliastai—charter a Russian jeep, and drive fifty-three miles north to the Ider Valley, where Oingerel and his family lived. We would spent the night in his ger and continue by horse up the Ider the next day. After dinner Oingerel excused himself and went to line up a jeep charter. Shandas and I went back to our room where I read the Russian ethnologist A. M. Pozdneev's description of Uliastai in the 1890s until eleven o'clock, when the electricity was shut off in the entire hotel. Uliastai, now one of the least visited and more remote of Mongolia's aimag capitals, once vied with Ulaan Baatar (then known as Urga, at least among foreigners) as the most important town in Mongolia. As Pozdneev noted in 1892:

> Although Uliastai is the second among the cities of
> northern Mongolia in size and area . . . it must necessarily
> be regarded as the chief city of Khalka [eastern and central
> Mongolia], as a consequence of its administrative position.
> Uliastai is in direct contrast with Urga. The latter, as the
> residence of the supreme Buddhist pontiff of the Mongols,
> is nothing more than an enormous monastery. Uliastai, on
> the other hand, is the central point of Chinese
> administration in Mongolia and is chiefly a military
> fortress . . . for the quartering of defense garrisons of Manchu
> troops.[1]

The present-day visitor to Uliastai may well wonder why this seemingly out of-the way place was chosen as the Manchu headquarters in Mongolia. The answer lies in the town's position on the western edge of the Khangai Mountains, close to the boundary between the Eastern (Khalkha) Mongols and the Western (Oirat) Mongols. From the Uliastai fortress the Manchus could both administer Khalkha Mongolia and maintain a military presence against the Oirats, who stubbornly refused to acknowledge Manchu suzerainty long after the Khalka Mongols had become more or less loyal Manchu partisans.

The Oirats were originally a forest people who dwelt in the taiga and mixed steppe-woodlands west of Lake Baikal and around Lake Khovsgol. With the rise of Chingis Khan, they, like so many other peoples of Inner Asia, fell under his banner and served as auxiliaries in the great military campaigns of the Eastern Mongols. They remained more or less subordinate to the Chingis Khanites until after the fall of the Yüan Dynasty founded by Khubilai Khan and the expulsion of the Mongols from China in 1368.

The Chingis Khanite Mongols, shorn of their Chinese empire, regrouped around their ancient capital of Kharkhorum on the Orkhon River. In 1370 and again in 1388, huge armies mustered by the Ming, who had replaced the Mongols as rulers of the Celestial Empire, crossed the Gobi Desert into Mongolia, hoping to stamp out any chance of a Chingis-Khanite revival. The 1388 invasion, consisting of over 100,000 Chinese troops, crushed the Mongols in a decisive battle south of the

Kherlen River, after which the reigning khan, Toquz Temur, was assassinated by a disgruntled relative. Bereft of leadership, many of the Mongol tribes, including the Oirats, claimed autonomy, each jockeying for position as the new rulers of Mongolia.

By 1434, after half a century of inter-Mongol warfare, the Oirats had gained control of most of Mongolia. Then in the 1550s Eastern Mongols, united once again under the Tümed chieftain Altan Khan, who claimed legitimacy as a descendant of Chingis, drove the Oirats out of the capital of Kharkhorum and back into the Khovd region west of the Khangai Mountains. Continued pressure by the Eastern Mongols at the beginning of the seventeenth century drove the Oirats still farther west, beyond the Altai Mountains into the valleys of the Black Irtysh, Ili, and the Imil, and north into the upper Yenisey basin. Thus it was in 1616 that the Torgut chief Khu Urluk went even farther, leading his people on a great migration westward, finally settling in the lower Volga basin, where he recognized the suzerainty of the Russians.

By 1635 a series of strong Oirat leaders had regrouped the Western Mongols then living on the fringes of Khalka Mongolia and created the Jungarian empire. Consisting of four major tribes—the Dörvöt, Torgut, Khoshot, and Choros—the Four Confederates, as they were also called, controlled Mongolia west of the Khangai Mountains to the Altai Mountains, the eastern Kazakhstan steppes beyond the Altai, and the deserts north of the Tian Shan Mountains in China.

The Jungarian khanate reached its zenith under the command of the charismatic warlord, Galdan. Born in 1644, Galdan was the grandson of Khara Khula, the founder of the Jungarian empire. At the age of six he was sent to Tibet where he was educated under the supervision of the Dalai Lama. He took monastic vows and seemed destined for a religious life. Then in 1671 Galdan's two half-brothers, Sechen and Jobta, killed his older brother, Sengge, in an attempt to gain control of the Jungarian empire. Galdan received a canonical dispensation from the Dalai Lama, which freed him from his religious vows, and returned to Mongolia seeking revenge for the murder of his brother. He had Sechen and Jobta assassinated and declared himself the ruler of Jungaria. Once in power his ambitions escalated. Eventually he hoped to conquer Khalka Mongolia and then, with all Mongols reunited, sweep off the

Mongolian Plateau and reclaim the throne of China held by the Manchu upstarts who had overthrown the Ming Dynasty in 1644. The Manchus, after all, were descendants of the Jurchid, a tribe earlier vanquished by Chingis Khan. "Are we to become the slaves of those who were once at our command?" Galdan thundered. "The empire [of China] is the heritage of our forebears!"[2]

Starting in 1688 Galdan, hoping to defeat the Khalkha Mongols and place them under his banner, launched a series of raids into the valleys of the Orkhon, Tuul, and Kherlen rivers. Instead of submitting, the Tüsheet Khan and other Khalka princes decamped into northeast China where they sought the protection of the energetic and charismatic Manchu emperor, Kang Hsi. In 1690 Kang Hsi sent an army, by then armed with muskets and cannons, into central Mongolia. This new firepower proved too much for Galdan, and he and his forces soon fled back into western Mongolia. In 1691 Zanabazar, who, as the first Bogd Gegen of Mongolia, was the undisputed religious leader of the country, brokered a deal whereby the Tüsheet Khan, Setsen Khan, and other Khalkha princes recognized Manchu suzerainty in exchange for protection against the Western Mongols. Galdan again invaded Khalka in 1695, but in 1696 another Manchu army slaughtered his forces near the present city of Ulaan Baatar and even managed to kill his wife. Yet another Manchu campaign was planned against the remainder of Galdan's army when he suddenly committed suicide on May 3, 1697. His dream of restoring Mongols to the throne lost by the descendants of Chingis Khan came to naught; instead, he drove the Khalkha Mongols into the arms of the Manchus. This marked the end of Mongolia's independence and the beginning of Manchu rule, which lasted until 1911, when the Manchu dynasty had almost collapsed.

Yet the Western Mongols were hardly finished off. Galdan's nephew, Tsewang Rabdan, assumed leadership of the Oirats and patiently began plotting his next move against the Manchus. His chance came when the Manchu emperor Kang Hsi, meddling in the affairs of Tibet, attempted to nominate a new Dalai Lama and install a pro-Manchu faction in Lhasa, the Tibetan capital. Incensed by this Manchu incursion into Lhasa, the wellspring of Lamaism, the religion of Mongolia, Tsewang Rabdan launched a daring raid across the formidable Kun Lun Mountains and the high, desolate Tibetan Plateau beyond. On December 2, 1717, Tsewang Rabdan's army, under the command of his brother, Tsereng Dondub, entered the Holy City of Lhasa and massacred the Manchu faction. Unfortunately, his troops then pillaged the Potala, the Dalai Lama's palace, and ransacked numerous temples in search of idols and artwork to take back to Mongolia as war booty. Kang Hsi soon organized an expeditionary army to oust the Oirats from Lhasa, and by 1720 they were forced to decamp back to Mongolia. A Chinese administration was then installed in Lhasa; in effect, the Chinese have been there ever since.

Tsewang Rabdan's son, Galdantseren, continued the battle against the Manchus and the Khalkha Mongols, who were now allied. In the early 1730s he sent several raiding parties as far east as the Tuul River. The Eastern Mongols fought back and massacred a large band of Oirats near Kharkhorum. Pressing the advantage, a Manchu army pushed the Oirats back to the west of the Khangai Mountains, and in 1733 the Manchus established the fortress-city of Uliastai at the confluence of the Chigesteyn and Bogdyn rivers. From here they hoped to keep the Oirats at bay in the west of Mongolia.

I awake in the Uliastai Hotel at 6:30 A.M. the next day. There is still no running water, hot or cold. Shandas is still asleep when I set out for an early morning walk. Our hotel is located on a small square at the western end of the town. The main street heading eastward from the square is pleasantly lined with poplars. (The name "Uliastai" is derived from *ulias*, or "poplar," signifying a city with poplar trees.) A couple of housewives are taking the early morning air on benches in front of their small, one-story houses, but otherwise the street is deserted. Off on side streets squat a few small three-, four-, and five-story Soviet-style apartment blocks. About a quarter mile from the hotel, the main street ends at the base of a rocky spine leading up to the cliffs behind the town. I climb the spine to a rock knob surmounted by a small pagoda. Mounted on boulders just below the pagoda are life-sized concrete statues of an elk, a wild sheep, and an ibex. From the inside of the pagoda, which is littered with empty beer cans and bottles, candy wrappers, and used condoms, I get a panoramic view of the environs.

To the east, emerging from between high barren ridges, is the Bogdyn River, which originates about fifty miles eastward on the slopes of 13,149-foot Otgon Tenger Mountain, the highest peak in the Khangai. To the north is the broad valley of the Chigesteyn River, its lush green banks contrasting with the stark, sere, stony ridges on either side. Just on the other side of the rocky spur from downtown a sizable ger community, each cluster of gers surrounded by a wooden fence, creeps up the side of the hill. Directly below me, near where the Bogdyn and the Chigesteyn meet, is supposedly the location of the old Manchu fortress. As far as I could see no trace of it remains.

The original Manchu fortress, started in 1733, was enlarged in 1748, and again in 1765, when formidable walls of earth packed between two rows of log palings were constructed. By the late nineteenth century the garrison numbered between 800 and 3,500 men, depending on the needs of the moment. A Chinese trade quarter, with the standard name of Maimaicheng, just as Chinese trade quarters in other Mongolian cities, including Urga, were named, soon sprang up around the fortress. By the time of Pozdneev's visit in the early 1890s the Chinese trade quarter consisted of 180 to 200 houses and numerous stores and trading posts. Pozdneev found for sale brick tea, flour, vegetable oil, rice, wines and beers, cotton cloth from the United States; Russian calico and leather goods; Chinese silk, chinaware, tobacco, pipes and snuff boxes, needles, thread, and a host of other knickknacks. Meat, firewood, and lumber were sold almost exclusively by the Mongols who lived in gers on the nearby hillsides, presumably in the same areas occupied by ger settlements today. Their women, noted Pozdneev—an impartial recorder of details—almost universally engaged in prostitution.

While there may be very few vegetables in Uliastai at present, in the nineteenth century they were quite common. The Chinese settlers, indefatigable agrarians, established farms along the Bogdyn River using river water for irrigation, and in addition to considerable amounts of wheat and barley, they grew potatoes, carrots, radishes, cabbages, pumpkins, onions, and other greens in profusion. Pickled vegetables from Uliastai were even exported to western China, where they were traded for raisins, dried peaches and apricots, and melons. The Chinese have long since departed, and there is no trace of their fields visible from my aerie in the pagoda. When sunlight has finally flooded the entire valley of the Bogdyn River I slowly head back toward the hotel, keeping an eye out along the way for traces of the old Manchu fortress.

In 1911, when the Manchu dynasty was in its death throes, Mongolia declared its independence and a monarchy ruled by the Eighth Bogd Gegen was created. The Bogd Khan, as the Bogd Gegen was now titled, immediately issued orders expelling the Manchu officials and troops from Uliastai and the fortress-city of Khovd farther west. The military governor of Uliastai gave up without a fight (unlike the military governor of Khovd) and along with his troops was given safe passage out of the country. Presumably most of the Chini|e settlers and traders, now foreigners in a hostile country, also chose to leave. The Mongols eventually razed the fortress, which stood as a symbol of Manchu oppression, along with most of the buildings used by the Manchu administration.

In 1915, however, independent Mongolia, squeezed between the demands of its two immense neighbors, was forced to accept the so-called Tripartite Agreement adopted by Russia and China during a meeting of the three countries at Kyakhta on the Mongolian-Russian border. By the terms of this accord Mongolia would remain an autonomous power, but under the suzerainty of China. The Chinese government stationed four military governors and supporting troops in Urga, Kyakhta, Khovd and Uliastai, and Chinese traders and merchants were allowed to resume their activities, most importantly the collection of the huge debts with which they had saddled the Mongolian people prior to 1911 and on which compound interest was rapidly accruing.

Then in the autumn of 1918 more Chinese troops arrived in Mongolia, partly on the pretext of protecting it from the newly minted Bolshevik armies which had appeared to the north in Siberia after the Russian Revolution. Faced with the de facto military occupation of their country, Mongolian leaders, including the Bogd Khan, were pressured into negotiations to once again accept Chinese sovereignty. Then in late 1919 a still larger Chinese army, led by General Hsü Shu-teng, arrived in Urga. The dictatorial Little Hsü, as he was known, forced the Mongolian leadership to accept the revocation of Mongolian autonomy and declared that the country was once again part of China. During the ceremony to hand over power to the Chinese, which took place in February of 1920, Mongolian officials were made to kowtow to Little Hsü, and the Bogd Khan had to display obeisance to the Chinese flag. The Chinese were back with a vengeance.

It was under these unsettled conditions that the Polish scientist and adventurer Ferdinand Ossendowski arrived in Uliastai in 1921. Ossendowski had sided with the White Russian regime in Siberia, and when the Bolsheviks achieved dominance he, like thousands of others, was forced to flee south to Mongolia. He soon holed up in Uliastai with other exiles who were plotting escapes either to China or over the Tibetan Plateau and the Himalayas to the safety of British-controlled India. Uliastai at that time was an extremely dubious refuge. "When we arrived in that town," Ossendowski wrote, "we were at once in the sea of political passions. The Mongols were protesting in great agitation against the Chinese policy in their country; [and] the Chinese raged and demanded from the Mongolians the payment of taxes for the full period since the autonomy of Mongolia had been forcibly extracted from Peking . . ."[3] The situation was further complicated by bands of White Russian desperadoes and Russian Bolshevik spies and provocateurs who swarmed through the countryside terrorizing the populace.

Not long after their arrival in Uliastai, Ossendowski and a companion made a reconnaissance in search of Red Army detachments which were rumored to be approaching from the west. It was on this scouting mission that Ossendowski claims to have met the notorious bandit-warlord, Dambijantsan, also known variously as the Ja Lama, Tushegoun Lama, and the Avenger Lama, although it's not precisely clear if he ever was in fact a lama. A Kalmuk Mongol born in the Volga region of Russia, Dambijantsan returned to Mongolia and eventually became a living legend renowned and feared for his ruthlessness and allegedly supernatural powers. According to one version of the many legends swirling about him he was the grandson of Amarsanaa, the Oirat warlord who staged one of the last great uprisings against Manchu rule in

Mongolia. This was highly unlikely, however, since Amarsanaa died in 1757. According to a variant of this legend he was simply the reincarnation of Amarsanaa. In any case, he strove to advance Amarsanaa's cause: the expulsion of all Manchus and Chinese from Mongolia.

While visiting with Ossendowski in a ger Dambijantsan performed one of those magical feats for which he was renowned all over Mongolia. Taking out his knife, Dambijantsan ordered one of the Mongolian men in the ger to stand up. According to Ossendowski:

> When the shepherd had risen, the Lama quickly unbuttoned his coat and bared the man's chest. I could not yet understand what was his intention, when suddenly the Tushegoun with all his force struck his knife into the chest of the shepherd. The Mongol fell over covered with blood, a splash of which I noticed on the yellow silk of the Lama's coat . . . With a few strokes of the knife he opened the chest of the Mongol and I saw the man's lungs softly breathing and the distinct palpitations of his heart. The Lama touched these organs with his fingers but no more blood appeared to flow and the face of the shepherd was quite calm . . . As the Lama began to open his abdomen, I shut my eyes with fear and horror; and when I opened them a little while later, I was still more dumbfounded at seeing the shepherd with his coat still open and his breast normal, quietly sleeping on his side and the Tushegoun Lama sitting peacefully by the brazier, smoking his pipe and looking into the fire in deep thought.[4]

Ossendowski came to believe that what he had seen was merely a vision induced by hypnosis and that Dambijantsan had never actually cut the man open. For his part, Dambijantsan downplayed the whole incident, calling it a "futile demonstration" and intimating that he was capable of much greater feats.

Back in Uliastai events had taken an even more ominous turn. The Chinese merchants had distributed weapons to their staffs and organized an armed militia among the transient Chinese laborers in the city. "This trash of China," as Ossendowski termed the militia, "now felt themselves strong, gathered together in excited discussions and evidently were preparing for some outburst of aggression."[5] Apprised that the Chinese were gathering one night in the Maimaicheng to organize a pogrom against the Mongols and Russians in the city, Ossendowski and some companions, hoping to overhear their plans, sneaked up to the walled enclosure. "In the courtyard was a great hubbub," wrote Ossendowski. "About two thousand men were shouting, arguing and flourishing their arms about in wild gesticulations. Nearly all were armed with rifles, revolvers, swords, and axes."[6] After announcing that he would present local officials with an ultimatum not to interfere with the planned pogrom the leader of the Chinese mob left the compound on horseback. At that moment a man on horseback–Ossendowski believed it was Dambijantsan–appeared out of the shadows and stealthily followed the Chinese agitator. Not long afterwards the lone horseman returned and riding close by the Maimaicheng flung the head of the agitator over the wall into the midst of the Chinese throng. As Ossendowski put it, "This event terrorized the Chinese and calmed their heated spirits."

The very next day the situation was completely reversed. A messenger riding by horseback the whole way from Urga arrived in town and headed straight for the marketplace where many Mongolians were assembled. Without dismounting he shouted:

> "Urga has been captured by our Mongols and Chiang Chün Baron Ungern. Bogd Hutuktu is once again our Khan! Mongols, kill the Chinese and pillage their shops! Our patience is exhausted!"[7]

The messenger was referring to Baron Roman von Ungern-Sternberg, a former Russian Army officer who had organized an army of White Russians and Mongolians with the intention of expelling the Chinese and Bolsheviks from Mongolia and setting up an independent Buddhist monarchy. When the "Bloody Baron," as he was known, seized Urga from the Chinese in early February of 1921 and reinstated the Bogd Gegen as monarch many Mongolians viewed him as a liberator, although he was soon revealed as a murderous psychopath. In Uliastai the news of his victory over the Chinese caused a sensation. The Chinese militia disbanded and disappeared from sight; the local civil authorities urged calm among Mongolians who wanted to take action against the Chinese; and armed patrols of White Russian exiles roamed the streets attempting to maintain order among the various opposing factions. Mongolian officials and the Chinese authorities, with Ossendowski acting as a go-between, soon reached an agreement by which the Chinese would be given safe passage to China if they agreed to leave peacefully. The Chinese evacuated Uliastai on March 12, 188 years after the Uliastai fortress had been founded. This time they would not return.

On my circuitous walk back to the hotel I could find no trace of either the Chinese fortress or the Maimaicheng. Chinese influence has not entirely disappeared however. The city is littered with hundreds of empty beer bottles from a brewery in Urumchi, in western China. Shandas is up and stirring when I return and we retire to the upstairs dining room for breakfast—big bowls of mutton and noodle soup and tea (960 tögrögs = $1.24 for two). This morning a few Mongolian families and the town's chief of police are in the dining room and all are noisily slurping soup. Oingerel is supposed to meet us at nine o'clock, so we take our bags and go out to the benches in front of the hotel to wait for him (room for two: 4800 tögrögs = $6.20). At nine the temperature is already in the eighties.

Three codgers are also taking the sun in front of the hotel and I ask them if they know where the old Manchu fortress was located. One claims it was located right here at the site of the hotel. Behind the hotel, he says, are some small vegetable gardens which originally had been used by the soldiers of the fort. If I go back and root around in the weeds I might find a brick or two from the fortress; otherwise nothing remained. About the Maimaicheng they were less sure. They seem to think there were a couple Mai-maichengs, one on this side of the river and another on the other side. The three of them get into a lengthy dispute about this which eventually veers off into unrelated matters. From what I can gather no trace of any of the old Chinese trading quarters remains.

Oingerel finally shows up at eleven o'clock. First he had trouble chartering a jeep and then finding potatoes, but now we are ready to drive to the Ider Valley–after buying gas at the gas station in the ger settlement behind the town. Here we are besieged by a horde of people cadging free rides. We already have four in the little jeep but manage to squeeze in one rather hefty woman dressed incongruously, for a dusty jeep ride, in an attractive and well-cut pants suit of lightweight purple wool. She is going the whole way to the Ider Valley, where she lives with her family in a ger.

Valley of the Ider

ACCOMPANIED BY OUR driver's cassette player blasting a Spice Girls tape, which had somehow washed up in Uliastai, we head north up the Chigesteyn Valley. The road is unpaved, but not terribly rough, at least in its initial stages. Off to the right, surprisingly numerous white gers and huge herds of sheep and yaks dot the broad green river bottom for the first ten miles out of town. According to Oingerel, Zavkhan has more sheep than any other aimag in Mongolia (1,257,031 in 1993, according to published figures). The high ridges beyond the river to the right are mantled with thick forests of larch, but to our left are bleak, rocky hills with very little vegetation.

After seventeen miles the Chigesteyn River curves off to the east. The road continues straight ahead up the valley of a small tributary of the Chigesteyn, Khatavch Creek. This valley quickly narrows and grades sharply upward as we approach Zagastayn Pass. About halfway to the pass the tape player mercifully breaks, allowing me to get in a few words. I ask if anyone has heard of Dambijantsan; surprisingly, our driver, Shandas, and Oingerel have all heard of him. A few years before there was a movie about Dambijantsan which was shown all over Mongolia and which even now is occasionally aired on Mongolian TV. Shandas has also heard the story about how, when he was finally executed by the Bolsheviks, Dambijantsan's head was chopped off and carried by his assassins first to Uliastai and then to Urga as proof they had indeed killed the supposedly invincible warlord and magician. He has heard too that the head was eventually taken to Moscow and placed in a museum where to this day it is kept preserved in a big bottle of formaldehyde. He got this story partly right. Actually Dambijantsan's head is preserved in the Peter the Great Museum of Anthropology and Ethnography in St. Petersburg. Then our woman passenger, apparently bored by the turn of the conversation, starts singing lovely Mongolian songs. Our driver and Oingerel soon join in and accompanied by these melodies—superior, in my opinion, to those of the Spice Girls—we slowly climb toward Zagastayn Pass.

Ferdinand Ossendowski, getting restless during his stay in Uliastai, decided to travel north by horseback to Khatgal, at the southern end of Lake Khövsgöl, which was one of the rallying points of White Russians in Mongolia—the Russian border is just a few miles from the northern end of the lake. He used the very road we were on, and as he approached Zagastayn Pass he noticed his Mongol guides growing increasingly nervous and fearful. Questioning them, he discovered that they believed the pass was inhabited by an evil demon.

It happened that long before, when the Mongols ruled China, the Chinese revolted and assassinated one of their Mongol khans. They also tried to kill his family, but with the help of an old lama the khan's wife managed to escape with her tiny son, a descendant of the line of Chingis Khan. On camels the three fled from China across the Gobi Desert into Mongolia. Chinese mandarins offered a reward for their capture and a strong detachment of three hundred mounted troops soon sniffed out their trail. Once the troops almost caught up with them, but the lama called down from Heaven a deep snow which stopped the horses of the Chinese but not their own camels. But as they approached Zagastayn Pass the Chinese horsemen were once again in close pursuit. The princess and the lama could hear the soldiers shouting triumphantly as they rode up the valley, already anticipating their reward for bringing back the heads of the Mongols. At the top of the pass the old lama, completely exhausted, laid down and died. The young princess, at wit's end, took her tiny baby in her arms and raised him to the sky. "Earth and Gods of Mongolia!" she shouted. "Behold the offspring of the man who has glorified the name of the Mongols from one end of the earth to the other! Allow not this very flesh of Chingis Khan to perish!" At that moment a tiny white mouse appeared beside her. "I am sent to help you," said the mouse in a low, quiet voice. "Go calmly and do not fear. Those who pursue you and your son, who is destined to a life of great glory, have come to the last bourne of their lives." The princess looked down at the mouse and with a disdainful voice scoffed, "How can you, a tiny little mouse, stop three hundred horsemen?" Suddenly a thunderous boom shook the mountain and a huge section of the cliff above the trail leading to the pass broke off, sweeping the horsemen away to their deaths. Then the tiny mouse jumped up on a rock and in a much different voice roared, "I am the demon of Zagastayn Pass. I am mighty and beloved of the gods but, because you doubted the powers of the miracle-speaking mouse, from this day the pass of Zagastayn will be dangerous for the good and the bad alike."[8]

Travelers learned to fear Zagastayn Pass. Many were the tales of horrific winds which suddenly swept through here, carrying before them fist-sized rocks which maimed and even killed unwary travelers and horses. Pozdneev, who came this way in 1892, noted, "When we entered Dzagasutain davaa [Zagastayn Pass], a terrible and cold wind came up." Before Pozdneev reached the top four inches of snow had fallen, and he and his companions were forced to walk their camels in order to keep warm.[9] Naturally I was eager to see this pass. It was, however, not as I expected. Instead of a distinct mountain pass with towering crags on either side it was simply a deep dip in a long, steppe-covered, east-west trending ridge. I don't doubt that ferocious winds are sometimes funneled through this pass from the large valley systems on either side, but as we approach it is perfectly calm. At the very top is an immense ovoo draped with hundreds, perhaps thousands, of khadags–prayer scarves–offered up by travelers who have crossed the pass safely. My altimeter gives the altitude at 8,360 feet, not terribly high as passes in Mongolia go. On the hillside about 200 feet to the right of the ovoo are some granite tors. I walk by myself to these and sit quietly for a few moments, half-hoping that the miracle-speaking mouse would appear, but of course I am disappointed. Just as we were pulling away, a group of six horsemen approach from the other side of the pass. They dutifully circle the ovoo clockwise three times on their horses, then a couple of them dismount and place cigarettes on the rocks–placations to the notorious demon of Zagastayn Pass–before continuing on.

This pass is also of some geographical interest, marking as it does the Continental Divide of Inner Asia. Little Khatarch Creek, which we had followed toward the pass, flows into a river system draining westward into one of the salt lakes of the Great Lakes Depression, none of which have an outlet to the ocean. On the north side of the pass begins Zagastayn Creek, which flows into the river systems eventually draining into the Arctic Ocean thousands of miles to the north. To find the source of the greatest of these river systems, the Yenisei-Angara-Selenge-Ider, is of course the raison d'être of this trip.

From Zagastayn Pass the road drops quickly via a couple of hairpin turns to the valley of Zagastayn Creek. When Ossendowski and his companions were descending from the pass they discovered the dead bodies of a man and his horse, neither of which showed any signs of wounds or injuries. Perplexed, Ossendowski wondered how they died. "Our Mongol bowed his head in anxiety," reported Ossendowski, "and said in hushed but assured tones: 'It is the vengeance of Jagastai [Zagastayn]. The rider did not make sacrifice at the southern obo [ovoo] and the demon has strangled him and his horse.'"[10]

We continue on down the Zagastayn Valley thirteen more miles without incident–apparently the rocks we added to the ovoo at the top of the pass have mollified the demon–then turn off the main road onto a dirt track which goes eleven miles to the village of Ider, the administrative center of Ider sum (sum = rough equivalent of an American county). Entering the Ider Valley we pass a small monastery which Oingerel promises we will visit before heading out on horses. A mile down the valley is Ider village, a small huddle of one-story buildings. We head upstream a half mile to six gers grouped together on a perfectly flat expanse of land near the bank of the Ider. This is where Oingerel lives.

After I pay the driver (24,000 tögrögs = about $33.00) Oingerel ushers me into his ger. Near the back wall is a small white table where Oingerel places a stool and invites me to sit. This, for the moment, is the place reserved for guests. From a cupboard along the side of the ger he produces a big plate stacked over a foot high with large homemade rectangular biscuits and topped with slices of homemade cheese, öröm (dried milk foam), and store-bought hard candies. This, I am made to understand, is more or less a ceremonial offering. A smaller plate of fried bread, cheese, and öröm is placed nearby. This is for snacking. An elderly woman, Oingerel's mother-in-law (his wife, who has an administrative job in the nearby sum center, won't be home till evening) hands me a bowl of milk tea. This standard tea of the countryside is made from a weak decoction of low-grade tea heavily laced with milk—in this case yak's milk—and seasoned with salt. I take the bowl in my right hand, at the same time touching my right elbow with the fingers of my left hand in the accepted manner. I quickly slurp this down, and Oingerel's mother-in-law, hovering nearby, pours me another. Oingerel's six-year-old daughter, Tuvshin, sits quietly on a bed, intently staring at me.

For the benefit of those who have never been in one, I will digress here a bit on gers, the ubiquitous dwellings which differentiate the *esgiy tuurgatan* ("people of the felt tents"—Mongols, Kazakhs, Kirghis, etc.) from other peoples and which serve as the micro-center of their domestic life. Gers vary somewhat in size but are usually from 20 to 25 feet in diameter. They have one low door—always facing to the south—about five feet high and often colorfully painted, and no windows. The walls, about six feet high, consist of sections of wooden latticework. The size of the ger is determined by the number of these sections—thus there may be three-, four-, and five-section gers. From the tops of the walls closely spaced wooden roof poles converge on a cartwheel-shaped wooden ring, known as a *toono*, which rests on two vertical posts placed in the center of the ger. The walls and roof are generally covered with inner layers of felt and nowadays, an outer layer of canvas. The toono, which is five or six feet in diameter, is usually kept open during the day, but has a flap which can be adjusted by ropes from outside the ger to keep out rain and cold. The stove is in the middle of the ger, between the posts supporting the toono. The stove pipe which runs up through the toono is often taken down at night when the stove is not in use.

The interior furnishings of gers are arranged according to the strict dictates of custom. Apart from a few minor idiosyncrasies of the individual inhabitants, the interior of every ger is laid out in almost exactly the same fashion, and it can be said with some truth that if you have been in one ger you have been in them all. Upon entering a ger one must never step on the wooden threshold, an act which can precipitate bad luck, and you should also be careful not to bang your head on the top of the door frame, a faux pas I have committed numerous times. Visitors are expected to move around a ger clockwise. Just to the left of the door is usually a storage area where various items for use outside—saddles, saddle blankets, axes, water buckets, and whatnot—are kept. Often these items are concealed by large decorated clothes hanging from the roof. Next to this, on the left side of the ger, is a narrow bed or sofa on which people sit during the day and sleep at night. As a general rule, any items which you are carrying—packs, hand bags, coats, etc.—should be placed on a bed and not on the floor. An eight-to-ten inch-wide strip of cloth colorfully decorated with hand-embroidered birds, fish, animals, and geometric designs is often draped along the ceiling above the bed. There is sometimes a curtain, a couple of feet or so in width, which can be pulled across the front of the bed to provide a modicum of privacy at night. Next to the bed, still in the left side of the ger, are sets of dressers or chests where the family keeps its clothes and other personal belongings. In the back of the ger are more and larger dressers or chests, or, as in the case of Oingerel's ger, another bed-sofa arranged exactly like the one on the left. In the back right side are still more dressers and chests. On top of these various chests and dressers are mirrors, mounted family photographs spanning several generations, and often a small altar with incense burner, printed depictions of various gods from the Lamaist pantheon, and perhaps a photograph of the Dalai Lama. On the right side of the ger is still another bed-sofa, a mirror image of the one on the left. Next to this, just to the right of the entrance, are shelves and cupboards containing kitchen implements, household stores of flour, tea, etc., buckets of milk and cream awaiting processing, and prepared food. Most countryside gers have earth floors covered with carpets except for bare areas by the entrance and around the stove. The men routinely toss spent matches and cigarette butts on this ground floor around the stove, and the women later dispose of them.

Oingerel had informed me that the locals were eagerly awaiting the visitor from exotic America. News of my arrival has spread and we were soon besieged with visitors. First was a passel of children, including tiny babies toted by young girls, an assortment of crawlers, toddlers, tots, a couple of completely naked four- and five-year-old boys, and some young teenagers. These children aligned themselves on the beds and stared at me wide-eyed. Then came two old men, relatives of Oingerel. One offered me a jade snuff bottle. This I took and attempted to sample the contents. The bottle is in fact empty; the gesture is ceremonial only. Now I am left-handed, so without thinking I handed the bottle back to him with my left hand, even though from my previous trips I knew that this was a serious breach of etiquette. He hesitated for a split second and then took it from my hand. Around the ger everyone's eyes seemed to get wider. Shandas, who up until then had proffered no advice or criticism, now admonished me, "Please do not take or give things back with your left hand."

Oingerel's mother-in-law offered tea to the adult visitors, and Oingerel now thought it appropriate to break out a bottle of arakh, homemade moonshine made from milk. He half filled a small china pitcher and sat it in front of me. "This is for you alone; help yourself as you wish," he said, then poured some into a bowl for his guests. One of the two old men accepted the bowl. After dipping a ring finger into it and flicking three droplets–offering to the gods of the sky, the air, and the earth–he took a small polite sip and handed it back. Oingerel then filled the bowl to the brim and gave it back to the old man. This time he finished it off. The whole procedure was repeated with the other old man.

Up until then the guests had been mostly members of Oingerel's extended family. Now visitors from up and down this section of the valley started arriving. Oingerel broke out a bottle of store-bought Russian vodka and every visitor had to have at least one drink. Meanwhile his mother-in-law mixed up some khaimag, a special treat often served to guests. First she heated four or five pounds of butter in the big woklike pan which fits into the top of the wood stove, then carefully dipped out the clear, clarified oil which emerged. This she poured into bottles. Into the remaining butter solids she thoroughly blended flour and finally added sugar, then ladled the whole mixture into a big bowl, stuck half a dozen big spoons into it, and placed the bowl on the table. Anyone who wanted some was free to dig in.

Probably twenty to twenty-five adults traipsed in and out of the ger that afternoon. At some point I was introduced to Amardavaa, a short guy in his early thirties who lived in the ger to the right of Oingerel's, and to Purevbazar, a tall, thin man in his late twenties who lived in the ger to the left. These two would be making the horseback trip with us. In the lull between guests we discussed our provisions for the trip. From Ulaan Baatar I had brought only three kilos of dry sausage, a kilo of cheese, black tea, sugar, and as treats two cans of pineapple and a kilo of raisins. In Uliastai we added twenty kilos of potatoes. Now Oingerel proposed killing a sheep to add to our larder. We went outside to where the younger teenaged girls were milking the sheep and goats. The rest of the flock, several hundred in all, was milling around a pen in which the lambs were kept. Oingerel waded into the flock and, after thoroughly feeling up the legs and saddles of numerous sheep, finally picked out one which was especially fat. This sheep Amardavaa collared between his legs and led to a small storage ger where it was to be slaughtered. Oingerel insisted that I return to his ger to drink more arakh, so I did not witness the preparation of the sheep, but I had seen the process before and will describe it here.

The sheep is thrown down on its back and held by two or three men. One man makes a four- or five-inch incision in the rib cage above the stomach and inserts his arm. Reaching in up to the elbow he locates the main artery leading from the heart and squeezes it shut (some people reportedly squeeze the whole heart in their fists). The sheep dies almost immediately with surprisingly little fuss. Then the incision is stitched shut with coarse twine or a length of tree branch or root so that no blood is lost. The carcass is then skinned. When the hide is completely removed, the abdomen and chest cavity are opened. By now the blood is congealed into a fairly thick mass. This is ladled out with a dipper into a bucket, taking care not to spill a single drop. I have heard it said that part of the reason for this method of slaughter is the Buddhist prohibition against shedding blood—indeed no blood ever touches the ground—but I have been unable to confirm this. (Chingis Khan, on his great military campaigns, observed the same fastidiousness toward high-ranking royalty that he captured. Rather than shed their blood he had them rolled up in thick carpets and trampled to death by horses.) Then the various innards are removed. The stomach and intestines are carefully cleaned and washed out. The accumulated blood is poured into the stomach, which will be cooked to make blood sausage. The cut-up offal, along with chunks of fat, is stuffed into the intestines for more sausage. The sausages and remaining offal will be eaten as soon as they are cooked. The front and hind quarters, ribs, and neck are set aside for later use.

By early evening Oingerel's wife, Oyunchimag, had returned from her job in the sum center. She changed out of her well-cut wool pants suit—she could have worn it to any office job in America—into a deel, and quickly pitched in to help prepare the sausages. Soon a huge basin of coiled intestines, stuffed stomach, and other indefinable body parts was boiling away on the stove top. The host of discalsed dandiprats, who for the most part had left after getting bored with the strange foreigner, now reassembled, lured by the smells issuing from this bubbling cauldron.

Dinner was finally ready. Oingerel cut a small piece of sausage and tossed it into the stove—an offering to the gods of fire—then cut another piece and placed it into a small brass bowl. This bowl he placed in front of a photograph of a tiny boy on one of the drawers. I had seen this picture earlier, the centerpiece of what looked like a small altar, and wondered about it. Now it turned out that the little boy was Oingerel's son who had died of some childhood ailment. The sausage was an offering to his spirit. "You see," noted Shandas, "the little boy is a god now too."

Then Oingerel, Shandas, and I huddled around the table and Oyunchimag placed the big basin of sausages and whatnot in front of us. We each took knives and dug in. There were a few chunks of meat floating among the intestines and soft parts and I concentrated on these. While we were gorging ourselves, Oingerel's mother-in-law came over and cut thick slices of the blood sausage. She topped each with a big chunk of white fat and handed them to the young boys lolling around the edge of the ger. This, she said, would make them grow up big and strong. After devouring several pounds of sausage and meat and downing numerous bowls of broth, we men had our fill. The tub was then passed to the women and girls who had assembled on their haunches around the fire. Before starting to eat, Oingerel's daughter, Tuvshin, cut off a small chunk of sausage and placed it in the brass bowl on the dresser top–an offering to her lost little brother. After eating, Oyunchimag began to fill smaller basins with sausages, meat, fat, and broth. These would be sent to the five neighboring gers, as was the custom after killing a sheep. She was careful that each basin had a good mixture of everything in the large cooking pot since, as Shandas explained, if one family felt they had been shortchanged they would send the basin back to be refilled.

After more milk tea and arakh it was finally time to turn in. I was offered the bed on the right of the ger, and Oyunchimag began to lay out blankets. Don't bother, I said, pulling my sleeping bag out of my pack. Oyunchimag and Oingerel had never seen an American sleeping bag before and, kneeling down on their knees, both stroked the smooth nylon cover, plumped the fill, and carefully examined the zippers. Finally, after taking down the stove pipe, Oyunchimag went outside and closed the flap over the toono. A candle flickering in front of the altar on the dresser was blown out. Thus ended another day on the Mongolian steppe.

When I awake the next morning the sun has still not risen, but the cover of the toono has been thrown back, the stove pipe is in place, and Oyunchimag is on her knees by the stove starting a fire. Oingerel and his daughter are still asleep on the back bed. Sluggardly, I lie in bed until Oyunchimag has prepared hot milk tea. When I finally rise she offers to pour some water from a plastic jug over my hands and face. This is the extent of my morning ablutions. Outside, I spend half an hour watching the young girls and women milk the cows, yaks, and khainags (cow-yak crosses). Nearby, calves are tied to ropes strung along the ground. Several of the women motion me over and demonstrate their milking technique. They also want me to take photos of them. One, a tall, attractive round-faced young woman with a thick braid of black hair reaching down almost to her waist, breaks into a few words of English. She is eighteen, she says, and a student of economics at the institute in Uliastai. She has also taken a course in English but has never before had a chance to chat with a native speaker of the language. The day before I had seen this young woman constantly carrying an infant, but this, it turns out, is the child of her sister, the wife of Purevbazar. She herself is unmarried. Now, of course, she is on summer vacation but will be returning to Uliastai in the fall. Soon the milking is done and the cows are reunited with their calves. Later the boys and younger men will drive the livestock out to pasture for the day.

Oingerel calls me back into the ger for breakfast and once again we men sit down around the big wash tub, now only a quarter full of cold sausage and meat. Oingerel cuts up some cold mutton and fat and places it in his bowl, adds some crumbled biscuits and slices of cheese, then pours hot milk tea over the whole mixture. While not particularly appetizing in appearance, this breakfast does seem to cover several of the major food groups. Over breakfast we discuss our plans. Eventually we must pack our gear and provisions, cut out horses from the herd and saddle them, and load our pack horse, but first we will witness a horse race and then go to the monastery. Oingerel informs Shandas that he will not start out on a journey without first paying a visit to the lamas.

Near Amardavaa's ger eight race horses are tethered to a rope stretched between two ten-foot-high posts. These horses, Oingerel explains, are the encampment's contenders in the upcoming Naadam races, which will be held in about two weeks. Naadam, which means "games," is held in July every year and features the three sports of wrestling, archery, and horse racing. The National Naadam in Ulaan Baatar is of course the best known, attracting people from all other the country and a horde of foreign spectators, but each provincial capital and many sum centers like Ider have their own scaled-down versions. The competition is no less keen in these local naadams, and up and down the Ider Valley each encampment is carefully preparing its horses.

In the days leading up to Naadam the horses are fed very little, or nothing at all. Leanness, it is believed, will make them run faster. The horses, two- and three-year-olds, are surprisingly small. Their riders, five- to nine-year-old boys, mount them barebacked. Slowly riding the horses in an oval around the hitching posts the boys wail a special song which is supposed to inspire both themselves and their mounts. The entire encampment has assembled to witness this ceremony which takes place daily during the last weeks leading up to Naadam. Finally, the boys ride to the starting point across the Ider River. They will race about four miles up the valley, circle a landmark, and return to the starting point. We stay by our position near the hitching posts where Oingerel and several other men follow the course of the race through binoculars, closely watching each rider and horse as they try to decide which will eventually be entered in the Naadam races. Afterwards the boys walk their mounts back to the hitching posts, then sit around discussing the race among themselves. This is of course just a warm-up contest and there is no special prize for the winner.

Then Oingerel, Shandas, and myself ride down the valley to the monastery, which is about mile upstream from the sum center. This consists of a single small temple surrounded by a wall and a couple of outbuildings. The head lama greets us at the door. Inside three lamas are chanting their morning services. Showing us around, the head lama explains that this temple was just built in 1990, when religious freedom was reestablished in Mongolia. This I find surprising, since both the interior and the exterior have already acquired the patina of age. On a table in the back left corner of the temple is a small intricately detailed scale model of another monastery farther on up the Ider Valley which had been destroyed by the communists during the anti-religion campaigns of the 1930s. It has been faithfully constructed with the help of old-timers in the valley who remember the original monastery and a few old black-and-white photographs. Oingerel informs me that we will pass the site of the former monastery when we ride up the valley that afternoon.

This was the "Monastery of the Lama Who Separated Milk from Water." As the head lama told the story, there was once a small boy living here in the Ider Valley who, goofing around in his family's ger one day, poured water into a bucket of milk. Scolded by his mother, the little boy proceeded to separate the water from the milk, something which Mongolian housewives maintain cannot be done. This was taken as a sign that the boy had miraculous powers; indeed, he grew up to be a powerful and respected lama. The so-called "Separator Lama" lived at the monastery which bore his name until the late 1930s, when he was arrested by the communists. Like thousands of other lamas he then simply disappeared; apparently he was executed or died in a prison camp. Had he not met an unnatural death, the head lama tells us, the Separator Lama could still be alive today, although a very old man.

Along the back wall of the temple are shelves stacked with what looks to me like a rather large collection of xylographs, Tibetan and Mongolian scriptures block printed on long rectangular sheets of paper, each bundle wrapped in cloth and tied with a string. I opine that a good number of these obviously very old books have survived. Not so, says the head lama; the vast majority was destroyed in the 1930s or had gotten lost or damaged since. What remain are mere remnants, and not very important ones at that.

In front of the main altar at the back of the temple juniper incense slowly rises from a brass bowl. Oingerel touches his forehead to the front of the altar, then wafts some incense smoke over himself. Shandas, a college-educated city kid who obviously spends a lot more time in nightclubs than temples, hesitates for a moment, then does the same. In the spirit of ecumenicalism so do I. On a side altar smolders another brass incense burner with a short chain attached to the handle. This Oingerel picks up and passes three times around his body. The enveloping smoke is supposed to purify one's aura (according to one interpretation) and is considered especially beneficial before starting out on a journey. Shandas and I dutifully perform the same ritual.

In the back right corner of the temple is a scale model of yet another large monastery which was destroyed in the 1930s. This is the Khamba Monastery, which was located somewhere downstream on the Ider. About the exact location, indeed about anything else concerning this monastery, the head lama is maddeningly vague; the only certain thing is that it no longer exists. At the front right corner of the temple sits a young lama who hands us small hand-wrapped packets of juniper incense. We can use this as an incense offering the next time we visit a Lamaist temple.

As is the case with most Lamaist monasteries photography is not permitted inside this temple. Few object to outdoor photos, but when we step outside and I ask the head lama if I may photograph the exterior of the temple he is clearly not pleased. He is of the old school, for whom monasteries and temples are not tourist attractions to be photographed. He does, however, walk us the entrance gate and wish us a safe journey.

Back at Oingerel's ger it seems the entire encampment has been mobilized to get us packed, mounted up, and underway. Thirty-some horses have been herded into a makeshift corral of several ox-carts arranged in a "V." At the opening of the "V" two old men and a flock of kids stand waving their arms, keeping the horses corralled. Half a dozen break out anyhow and gallop off to their grazing grounds near the river, having escaped, for the moment, an encounter with bridle and saddle. Armed with an *uurga*, a long pole with a loop of rope at the end which is used as a lasso, Oingerel's father-in-law wades into the herd. Although of course broken the horses are definitely not eager to be singled out. When he finally lassos one he leads it to one of the other older men who slowly approaches the skittish horse and very cautiously slips on the bridle. Finally succumbing to the inevitable, the horse settles down and is led off by one of the kids to Purevbazar, who saddles it up. Finally six horses had been singled out, five for riding and one as a pack horse.

Meanwhile Oingerel's mother-in-law–his wife is at work–scurries around his ger packing pails and sacks with butter and other dairy products, flour, tea, and rock salt. From another ger emerges a huge wash basin of freshly made fried bread which is dumped into a burlap bag. Various other womenfolk scamper forth with bed rolls, cooking pots, and utensils. Oingerel hacks up the front and hind quarters of our sheep into manageable pieces and packs them in cloth bags. Then we load the pack horse, a complicated procedure which requires the concentrated efforts of Oingerel's father-in-law, Purevbazar, and

Amardavaa, all hefting gear and heaving on ropes, accompanied by the advice of half a dozen bystanders.

Oingerel, Purevbazar, and Amardavaa slip into *deels* (*deel* = robe worn by Mongolian men and women) and Oingerel's mother-in-law produces a deel for Shandas. There is an awkward moment when he doesn't know how to tie the sash—perhaps it is the first deel he has ever had on—and one of the women had to help him. Oingerel then gives him a Chinese army surplus cap to wear, replacing his Nike swoosh cap. I am greatly relieved—I thought I was going to have to have a talk with him about that cap. By noon we are ready to pull out. My horse seems calm and experienced, and in deference to my height it is bigger than the average size. Shandas, with very little riding experience, seems likewise firmly ensconced on a well-mannered mount. Thus our small procession crosses the Ider and with Purevbazar leading the way heads up the east side of the valley. We will spend the night, Oingerel has informed us, at Nogoon Nuur.

Nogoon Nuur

THE PART OF the Ider Valley where Oingerel lives is perhaps a mile wide. Downstream just below the settlement of Ider and upstream several miles from Oingerel's encampment encroaching ridges pinch off the valley, creating a large, partially enclosed basin. The right side of this basin–facing upstream–where Oingerel lives, is known as Tavan Tolgoi. In addition to Oingerel's encampment this area is occupied by three or four other groups of gers, each with its own herds of horses and cattle and flocks of sheep and goats. The left side of the valley, known as Nomkhon, also hosts four or five encampments. The Ider, where we forded it, is much smaller than I expected–only about sixty feet wide and nowhere more than a foot deep. Batchuluun, back in Ulaan Baatar, had told me that the river was teeming with grayling, *lenok*, and the elusive *taimen*, much sought after by sports fishermen, but this section of the river was nothing but rock-strewn riffles which seemed to offer very little suitable habitat for fish.

As we slowly walked our horses up the valley I tried to find out from Oingerel about previous foreign visitors to the Ider. Batchuluun had once brought a small group of Americans to Ider on a horseback riding tour, but apparently they had only rode around this lower part of the valley, and he later returned with a rafting-fishing group which had floated a short distance on homemade log rafts when the river was considerably higher after hard rains. Then that spring a foreign trophy hunter intent on wolves appeared in the village of Ider but after a day or two, for reasons unclear, suddenly decamped back to Ulaan Baatar

without firing a shot. In any case, Oingerel believed that no foreigners–
with the possible exception of Russian geologists–had ever been in the
valley of the Ider above Tavan Tolgoi-Nomkhon.

According to my woefully inadequate maps–a Mongolian map of
the entire Zavkhan province (scale-1:1,000,000) and another from a
series produced by the U.S. Defense Department by satellite imagery
and subject–as I knew from previous experience–to curious inaccuracies
(scale-1:500,000), we had to travel about fifty to sixty miles up the Ider
to reach its source. Oingerel had a map of Ider sum in a better scale
(1:140,000) but it did not have contour lines, and it showed the uppermost
reaches of the Ider merely as a dotted blue line which eventually petered
out indistinctly in a large knot of mountains indicated by symbols.
Purevbazar and Amardavaa had both made several hunting trips to the
headwaters of the Ider, but neither could say exactly where the source
was; indeed, it was unclear if they even understood the concept of a
river's source in the strict geographical sense. Clearly we were venturing
into terra incognita.

After walking our horses a few miles we broke into a trot and
crossed a series of low ridges which marked the upper limit of the basin
where Oingerel lived. On the other side of these ridges we emerged in
another, even larger basin at least two miles wide and stretching off
upstream for five or more miles. This was called the Darkhan basin,
after a conspicuous mountain on the left side of the valley. We soon
rode up on a small encampment of three gers where yet another horse
race was in preparation. As in Oingerel's camp the young horses were
tethered to a rope stretched between two ten-foot-high posts. Just as
we approached, the young boy-jockeys mounted up and began slowly
riding around the posts while wailing their characteristic song. About
thirty men from various encampments in this part of the valley watched
from horseback. After warming up the horses the boys rode them
down to the starting point close by the river. It was decided that we
would accompany the thirty or so men to the finishing line near a high
hill at the upper edge of the basin. The whole group of spectators,
ourselves included, charged out of the encampment at full gallop and
fanned out across the steppe.

After a mile or so, crossing a particularly flat patch of ground,

Oingerel and Shandas rode up beside me and we slowed to a trot. Here, Oingerel indicated, was the site of the Monastery of the Lama Who Separated Milk from Water. Amidst the stubbly grass only a barely noticeable line of stone blocks inset in the ground marked the foundation of the main temple. Nearby are a few lines of cut stone indicating the foundations of other buildings and temples. I probably would have not noticed any of these remnants had not Oingerel pointed them out. Oingerel also mentioned that the basin in which the monastery was situated was surrounded by four mountains: Sebjin Balbor Uul on the south, Bitüüdü Uul on the west, Khandu Uul on the north, and Darkhan Uul on the east. Local people, he said, still make annual sacrifices of tea and dairy products to an ovoo on top of Darkhan Uul.

The mention of Darkhan Uul jarred something loose in my mind. Was this monastery also known as the Ilaguksan Monastery? I asked. Yes, Oingerel said, staring at me as if unable to figure how I knew this bit of trivia; he had heard it called that by some old people of the valley. I now realized that this was the monastery which had been visited by Pozdneev in 1892.

In Pozdneev's time it was the home of the Ilaguksan Khutagt (*khutagt* = having fortune or sanctity, blessed one, or holy one; Ilaguksan Khutagt could be translated as the "Khutagt who has been victorious," i. e., achieved enlightenment). He was one of the thirteen khutagts of Mongolia who were officially recognized by the Manchu government as "Living Buddhas." Like the Bogd Gegen of Mongolia, he was thought to be a reincarnation of one of Buddha Shakyamuni's original five hundred disciples. The next ten reincarnations appeared in India and Tibet. Starting with the eleventh, they began appearing in Inner Mongolia; but as to how many incarnations were born there is unclear. Later the Ilaguksan Khutagts appeared in northwest Mongolia; since then there had been four reincarnations, including the one met by Pozdneev in 1892.

Little is known about the first of these Mongolian reincarnations. The second appeared in Khovd, where he was appointed the head of the Shara Temple. He later founded his own monastery of Ebügen Khüree (*khüree* = monastery), ten miles west of Uliastai. When he died his mummified remains were preserved there in a golden *suburgan*. The next reincarnation was the brother of one of the hereditary princes who ruled the upper Ider Valley—the Dalai Wang. This highly revered reincarnation made five trips to Beijing where he served tours of duty in the Manchu court and received numerous honors and titles. He was still the head lama at Ebügen Khüree but was granted permission to start a new monastery here on the Ider in 1867. He died in 1880 at the age of 63, and a new reincarnation appeared in 1881. A year later he was recognized by the Bogd Gegen of Mongolia and was officially confirmed as the Ilaguksan Khutagt by the Manchu emperor in 1886. He was eleven years old when Pozdneev met him.

The monastery had at least six temples. The main temple was devoted to the worship of Geser of Ling, the legendary Tibetan king and warrior. In addition to his other distinguished predecessors, the Ilaguksan Khutagt was also thought to be a reincarnation of one of Geser's thirty-two heroes who had accompanied him on his campaigns against the forces of Evil. (Geser, known in Chinese as Huang Ti, was also venerated by the Manchus.) In another temple was an immense forty-foot-high statue of Maitreya, the coming Buddha. In still another was a suburgan containing the mummified body of the previous Ilaguksan Khutagt which had been gilded, dressed in the robes of a lama, and placed in an upright sitting position. The suburgan itself was constructed with twenty-eight pounds of silver. About two hundred lamas were enrolled at the monastery. The monastery itself maintained a herd of 3,000 horses, and the Ilaguksan Khutagt had his own herd of 3,000—by tradition, all chestnuts—plus another herd of 2,500 of mixed colors. These were watched over by nearby herdsmen in exchange for a portion of the mare's milk, and also for the manes, tails, and horse hair which were sold to Chinese merchants.

But how did the history of the Ilaguksan Khutagt fit in with what we had been told at the temple in Ider about the Lama Who Separated Milk from Water? Obviously the monastery of the Ilaguksan Khutagt and the monastery of this lama were one and the same. The Lama Who Separated Milk from Water lived in the twentieth century. Was he a later reincarnation of the Ilaguksan Khutagt or a different personage altogether? If the latter, why do local people now associate the monastery with him and not the Ilaguksan Khutagt? Oingerel could only shrug; he had no answers.

In any event the temples, the statue of the Maitreya, the silver suburgan, the mummified remains of the Ilaguksan Khutagt, and all other traces of the monastery with the exception of a few foundation blocks have long since disappeared. This was one of the more than seven hundred monasteries destroyed by the communists during the anti-religion campaigns of the late 1930s. The thousands of lamas who were imprisoned, or shot, or simply disappeared included the Lama Who Separated Milk from Water. The fate of the Ilaguksan Khutagt–assuming he was a different person–is unknown.

Galloping again, we soon arrived at the high hill near the upper end of the basin near where the horse race was to conclude. From here the assembled horsemen were able to follow almost the entire five mile-long race through binoculars. One boy broke into an early lead and easily won by over a quarter of a mile. Again there were no special accolades for the winner; this was merely a warm-up event for the Naadam races.

Our little group continued on across some low ridges and into a small pocket of flat land occupied by an encampment of four gers. This place, Oingerel informed me, was called the Two Trees Ford, after two lone trees on the riverbank which indicated a crossing point. Here his brother lived, and we must stop and pay a visit. In his brother's ger we sipped hot milk tea while an old woman whipped up a batch of khaimag. Here, however, they had no sugar to add. The entire encampment filed through the ger for a bowl of tea and a look at the strange guest. One old man informed me that he was a wolf hunter. He had already killed two that year and would have gotten more, but he had a very poor rifle, an ancient single-shot .22, and very little time to spare on hunting. Why don't foreigners come here to hunt wolves? he wondered; they would be doing the locals a big favor by keeping down the wolf population. For a moment I considered telling him that wolf hunting was now frowned upon by many in America, where efforts were actually being made to reintroduce wolves in some areas, but then realized that this point would probably be lost on this nomadic sheep herder, whose perspective on the subject was obviously quite different from that of Western environmentalists. After some more chitchat, mainly about the prospects of various wrestlers in the upcoming Naadam, Oingerel informed his brother that we must move on and would pay a longer visit on the way back.

Not far upstream from the Two Trees Ford the valley suddenly narrowed, with high ridges crowding in on either side. Larch forests crept down the hillsides and on the valley bottom majestic cottonwoods and thickets of willows alternated with damp, lush meadows of high, thick grass. In one small meadow grazed a herd of horses belonging to Oingerel's brother. This meadow grass was so good that later on in the summer men would come here, cut it with scythes, and dry it for winter forage.

In the lower basin the river had been out of sight, but here the trail, still a rough jeep track, followed its left bank. To my surprise, the Ider, which had seemed merely a stream near Oingerel's encampment, here appeared to be a river of considerably larger size. When I pointed this out to Oingerel he explained that this was indeed the case and that downstream from here part of the river drained away into the gravels of the valley bottom. Not only was the river bigger, but as it snaked through the narrow valley it formed deep, tree-lined pools and smooth runs and riffles which appeared to be perfect fish habitat. Indeed, numerous fish could be seen feeding off the surface as we passed. Oingerel agreed that the river was chock-full of fish, but added that neither he nor anyone he knew had ever fished in it. To do so, he explained, would irreparably anger the river gods. Thus no one in the valley ever ate fish. Apparently no foreigner had ever fished in this upper part of the river either, but Oingerel maintained that the locals would not object if they did. If the river gods chose to punish the foreigners it was not a local problem.

At one point we rode through a particularly thick stand of larch. How would I like to ride through here at night? Oingerel wondered. Apparently he himself considered this a frightening prospect. When I said that I wouldn't find it a problem he stared at me dubiously. This gloomy stretch of woods had apparently affected someone else. On a tree trunk were nailed three shoulder blades of sheep. On the shoulder blades were painted inscriptions in Tibetan. Oingerel studied these bones intently. They must have been placed there by lamas, the only locals who knew Tibetan, but he said he didn't have a clue as to what they signified.

After a few miles the trail climbed a rounded ridge which ran perpendicular to the valley. On the opposite side of the valley the river cut through a narrow slot in the ridge. On the upstream side of this ridge nestled a small lake. This was Nogoon Nuur–Green Lake. Here, Oingerel announced, we would spend the night. Not counting our various breaks, we had only ridden about four hours, and it seemed early to stop, but he insisted that this was an auspicious place to camp. Nogoon Nuur is considered a sacred place by the local lamas, who periodically come here to make offerings. The lake, which covers three or four acres, is fed by several springs, and it is these water sources which the lamas sanctify. There were fish rising on the surface and Oingerel assured me that the lake contained some unusually large specimens. The lamas have prohibited fishing in the lake, however, and unlike the river this ban applies to both locals and–should any come here and attempt it– foreigners. Of course, this was a religious prohibition only and not, as I understood it, an enforceable law, but it was clear that Oingerel, for one, would not like to see it ignored.

Between the lake and river was a flat grassy spot which showed the traces of previous campsites. Purevbazar and Amardavaa flew into action and within minutes our horses, except for Amardavaa's, were unsaddled and staked out on long tethers. Now, as we had passed through the encampments in the Darkhan part of the valley that afternoon I had gotten a suspicion that these people would be unable to resist the temptation of visiting our camp that night. Sure enough, a group of four horsemen arrived at Nogoon Nuur just minutes after us, followed by another group of three a little later. They sat down, lit up hand-rolled cigarettes, and watched attentively as we set up the two tents I had brought from America. My sleeping bag and air mattress received especially close scrutiny. Oingerel was really taken by the air mattress. "Just like a sofa!" he exclaimed. But what really grabbed their attention was the big wooden strike-anywhere kitchen matches I had brought from America. They themselves had only cheap Chinese safety matches, about half of which won't light. They were amazed when I lit one on a rock, and truly stunned when, showing off, I lit another on my front tooth. Several asked for matches and attempted to duplicate this simple feat.

Amardavaa had brought along a .22 rifle, and after camp was set up he rode off to hunt for marmots. He had told us several times during the day that he was determined to have marmot for dinner. A pack of cards materialized from somewhere and Oingerel, Shandas, Purevbazar, and the visitors soon fell into a spirited card game. I set off on a walk.

Not far upstream from our camp the river split into two branches, one of which went straight ahead while another elbowed to the left. I had assumed that the Ider went straight ahead, but according to Oingerel's map the fork to the left was the Ider. Viewing the confluence of the two forks I could see that the left one was indeed the main trunk of the river system. The smaller fork which went straight ahead was called Tsagaan Gol–White River.

Turning back downstream I realized that the high bank which ran across the valley in front of Nogoon Nuur was in fact a moraine left by a receding glacier. During the Pleistocene a glacier had swept down one or both of these valleys, pushing in front of it a wall of boulders and gravel which remained here after the glacier had receded. I knew from my earlier investigations that little, if any, research has been done on the Pleistocene glaciation of the Khangai Mountains, so it is difficult to say exactly when this moraine was created. The last Ice Age ended about ten thousand years ago, so it was before then.

Just to the right of Nogoon Nuur, facing downstream, looms a distinctive mountain known as Ovoot Uul–Ovoo Mountain. Not only is the entire mountain itself shaped like an ovoo, but its treeless sides are also strewn with dozens of natural rock formations which assume the shape of ovoos. Just opposite, on the left side of the river, rises an equally distinctive pyramid-shaped peak, partially mantled with larch, known as Tusgalt Uul–Reflection Mountain. Presumably it got its name from the fact that its reflection can be seen in Nogoon Nuur when traveling on the horse path. These two distinguishing mountains no doubt contribute to the belief that Nogoon Nuur is a sacred and auspicious spot.

The visitors had left by the time I returned to camp. A fire had been started and a tin pail of tea–salted but with no milk–prepared. Amardavaa had not returned with the promised marmot, so Purevbazar had gone ahead with dinner. A large slab of homemade unsalted cheese and a bag of fried bread had already been laid out. Chunks of mutton simmered away in a large heavy wok supported by three stones. Kneeling by the fire, Purevbazar patiently rolled out dough on a thin piece of plywood and cut it into fine strips. Then he diced up a few potatoes. After blowing up the fire, he threw the dough strips and potatoes into the bubbling cauldron. Before the soup was done Amardavaa rode in with a dead marmot swinging from a saddle strap. No problem, said Oingerel, we would have the marmot as a midnight snack, and as a special treat for me they would prepare it in the traditional way–cooked in its own skin.

Over dinner Oingerel, Amardavaa, and Purevbazar got into a long discussion accompanied by much laughter. What were they talking about? I asked Shandas, who was remaining silent. Oh, nothing important, he maintained. Tell me, I insisted. After some more coaxing he finally explained that Oingerel had often noticed that Europeans, or as in my case Americans of European descent, almost always had hair on the back of their hands and on their arms and chests. Mongolians, Oingerel pointed out, had very little, if any, body hair. He therefore concluded, and Amardavaa and Purevbazar agreed, that on the scale of evolution Europeans were not that far removed from animals, while Mongolians, on the other hand, were obviously much more highly developed human beings.

I had to laugh at that. I suspected that most European or American visitors in Mongolia, no matter how liberal-minded and free from cultural prejudices they considered themselves, simply assumed that they, who have flown in by jet from the highly developed civilizations of the West armed with cameras, video recorders, and all the other trappings of the modern world, were more "advanced" than these countryside Mongolians who lived in tents with no electricity, TV, or telephones. How many realized that these Mongolians might be thinking of them as underdeveloped human beings, who, for reasons unclear, possessed a surfeit of shiny and novel toys? How many of these supposedly advanced people knew, after all, how to cook a marmot in its skin?

It was almost dark by the time Amardavaa got around to skinning the marmot. After making an incision the whole way around its throat he pulled the hide off the entire carcass, very carefully removing the leg bones, so that when he was finished he had a fur-covered sac open only at the neck. From this sac dangled four little paws. Then he cut up the legs, carcass, and selected innards into bite-sized pieces. Meanwhile Purevbazar had heated eight or ten lemon-sized stones in the fire. Taking the ax, he fashioned a crude pair of tongs out of two pieces of firewood. While Amardavaa held the neck of the skin sac open, Purevbazar, using the tongs, dropped in two hot rocks. An amazingly loud wheezing sound issued from the skin sac as the hot rocks came in contact with the fatty interior. Amardavaa called this phenomena "the marmot's last whistle." Purevbazar threw in a handful of cut-up meat, tamping it into the skin sac with a stick, then added more hot rocks. He kept alternating levels of meat and hot rocks until the skin sac was almost completely full and finally poured in a little water. Clouds of steam bellowed from the neck of the sac.

Purevbazar cut a bundle of hair from the long tail of one of our horses and Amardavaa twisted it into a small rope which he loosely wrapped around the neck of the sac. Into this looped rope he inserted a short stick. By twisting the stick he could open and close the neck opening. This was necessary to let out entrapped steam. He explained that the skin of a marmot is very thin at this time of the year, and that if one wasn't very careful the sac could explode, spewing bystanders with hot meat and boiling broth. I automatically took a step or two backwards.

For about half an hour the contents of the sac stewed from the heat of the hot rocks. Then Amardavaa held the sac over the fire and singed the fur. This burnt fur he rubbed off with a stick. Purevbazar had earlier found a flat piece of scrap iron near one of the old campsites and this he now heated till it was red hot. With this iron he continued to rub the exterior of the sac until the last vestige of fur was removed. The sac, which now resembled an overinflated balloon with four tiny claws attached, was placed on the hot rocks at the very edge of the fire. Amardavaa explained that the whole process was complete when the furless hide turned a yellowish color and began to ooze fat from the inside.

Venus had already risen and sunk again in the northwest sky and Jupiter was directly overhead by the time the marmot was finally done. Slicing open the sac, Amardavaa threw one piece of meat into the air–an offering to the gods of the sky–and another into the fire–an offering to the fire gods–then proudly handed me a meaty leg bone. While watching the entire preparation I had make up my mind that I wasn't going to eat any of the meat, but realizing now how much effort Amardavaa and Purevbazar had expended preparing this treat, I decided it would be churlish to refuse. To my surprise the meat was quite tasty, though dry and chewy, and when Amardavaa offered me a second and third piece I took them without hesitation. The broth from the skin sac was, however, very fatty, and I took only a few sips. As we ate Amardavaa explained that marmot cooked in its own skin was a favorite meal of sheep herders moving their herds for long distances. It was not necessary to take along any food or even a pot. All you needed was a marmot.

Tsagaan Nuur

W HEN I ROSE the next morning half a dozen upland buzzards were wheeling in the sky over our camp. They were cleaning up the remains of our feast. As I watched one swooped down and plucked a marmot bone out of the grass. Even after we had a fire going and were sitting around with bowls of tea they kept diving all around us, approaching so close I could feel the wind from their wings brush my cheeks.

It was a warm morning, 42°F at 7:30, and not a wisp of cloud marred the robin's egg blue sky. By ten o'clock we were back on the trail. Instead of continuing up the Ider Valley, the rough jeep track we had been following turned off into the valley of Tsagaan Gol. There were, Oingerel said, a few gers on up the Tsagaan Gol valley, but no more upstream on the Ider. My USDOD map actually indicated the jeep track, and showed it continuing to the head of the Tsagaan Gol valley and crossing a pass to the headwaters of Rashaan Gol, a tributary of the Bogdyn Gol, then following the Bogdyn on downstream the whole way to Uliastai. Pozdneev, back in 1892, described this as an alternate route from Uliastai to the Ider Valley and the Ilaguksan Monastery. Even then, however, it was too rocky for camels and could be used only by horses. Oingerel just shook his head when I showed him the map. Years ago a few jeeps may have taken this route, but then, he claimed, the water table somehow changed and the highlands between Tsagaan Gol and the Rashaan Gol turned into treacherous bogs. Now it's dangerous to take even horses through this area. Apparently, however, the old trail still showed up on the satellite photos used to produce the USDOD maps.

Veering to the left, we take the horse trail up the Ider Valley, which soon doglegs around again to the southeast. Ahead and to the right is a conspicuous mountain topped by a dramatic collection of granite tors. For some reason I can't take my eyes off these tors; they seem to form a kind of natural amphitheater on the very summit of the mountain. This, says Oingerel, is Sevren Uul. He adds that just behind this mountain is Tsagaan Nuur, which drains into Tsagaan Gol. Tsagaan Nuur is considered even more sacred than Nogoon Nuur. Just that spring a big delegation of lamas convened at an ovoo on its shores and made offerings to the particularly propitious gods which they believed resided in the lake. These ceremonies had been conducted regularly in the old days, but the practice had been abandoned during most of the communist era. Not far up the Ider Valley it is possible to cross a low pass and reach this lake. If I am interested, says Oingerel, we could make a detour and visit it. I am interested. The trail to the pass is a half hour or so ahead.

Meanwhile Amardavaa, a small bundle of barely containable exuberance, keeps galloping off into the hills by himself. He is hunting for more marmots and also for shed deer antlers. These can be sold for up to 6,000 tögrögs a kilo, and one big antler may weigh up to four or five kilos. Coming around a corner we find him kneeling on the ground. At his feet is a small marmot, not yet half grown. He says he saw a buzzard swoop down and snatch it, then losing its grasp of the struggling animal, drop it from a height of about twenty feet. Amardavaa's appearance prevented the buzzard from making another attempt. The marmot is still alive but stunned and bleeding from the nose. Amardavaa is convinced it will survive, and he carefully picks it up and places it inside a nearby marmot hole where the buzzard can't get it.

Soon Oingerel points to a dip in the ridge line to the right. "There is the pass to Tsagaan Nuur," he says. "It takes an hour to get to the lake from here." He tells Purevbazar to continue upstream with the pack horse to a lake in the Ider Valley where we will camp for the night while the rest of us go to Tsagaan Nuur. The steep ridge which rises abruptly from the flat valley floor is mantled with larch. A faint trail switchbacks up through the thick forest and emerges on the rim of a high barren tableland where we get a good view across the Khangai Mountains. The Khangai are not fault block mountains with their characteristic sharp peaks and ridge lines. Rather, they are the result of the ancient upwelling of an immense oblong dome stretching almost 250 miles east-to-west and 100 miles north-to-south. Rivers have cut out deep valleys through this dome, leaving between them relatively flat tablelands like the one we are standing on. From our aerie these elevated tabletops can be seen rearing up in all directions. In this part of the Khangai they are at an elevation of 8,500 to 9,500 feet, or 1,000 to 2,000 feet above the valley floor of the Ider where we left it. Above these tablelands distinct massifs do rise, most notably 13,149-foot Otgon Tenger Uul thirty miles to the south and 11,873-foot Öndör Ölziit Uul at the head of the Ider Valley. It is on the flanks of Öndör Ölziit Uul that I hope to find the ultimate source of the Yenisei-Angara-Selenge-Ider river system.

One would think these tabletops would be well drained. They are not. Oingerel points out that most of these highlands are wet and boggy and dangerous to travel across by horse. Here the morasses are interspersed with nasty boulder fields. Amardavaa leads the way, continually yelling back warnings to us greenhorns, Shandas and myself, about some particularly treacherous spot. After a mile or so of this, we cross a low rise and there below us, like an immense turquoise gemstone set among the tor-topped ridges, is Tsagaan Nuur. On the far side of the lake is a narrow notch in the ridges through which the lake drains into Tsagaan Gol. Just to the right of the notch can be seen the ovoo which the local lamas have consecrated. Dismounting to rest and take in the scene, I ask Oingerel why the lamas worship this lake in particular. Like Nogoon Lake, he explains, it is completely spring-fed–indeed, not even a rivulet can be seen running into it–and such water sources, which are fed from deep underground, are considered the abodes of the gods who rule the earth. This lake is especially important, he adds, because it is considered one of the sources of the Ider Gol. Perhaps one of the sources, I point out, but not the ultimate source, which must be at the headwaters of the Ider. Shrugging, he admits that he really doesn't know where the ultimate source is, and I suspect he does not understand what I mean by the source of a river in the strict geographical sense. In a spiritual sense, perhaps, Tsagaan Nuur does qualify as one of the sources of the Ider.

We pick our way back across the boulders and mires and drop back down to the Ider Valley, walking our horses down the steepest parts of the trail. Moving upstream Amardavaa keeps calling out the names of the surrounding mountains and the few tiny creeks flowing out of the hills. Almost every feature of the landscape appears to have a name, even though this part of the valley is frequented only by hunters. On the left appears Dood Bayan Uul (Lower Rich Mountain) and then Deed Bayan Uul (Upper Rich Mountain). Topping a small rise we see two lakes, a smaller one called Bayan Nuur (Rich Lake) and above it the larger Gyagaryn Nuur (Smooth Lake). As we approach two huge pure white whooper swans taxi off of Bayan Nuur. On a grassy ridge between the two lakes Purevbazar has set up our tents and has a fire going. Three o'clock in the afternoon seems to me a bit early to stop, but camp is already made and Oingerel is adamant about staying here. Apparently there are auspicious camping spots approved by long use and custom and this is one of them. "It's a beautiful place," he observes.

I agree. Directly in front of our camp is six-to-eight-acre Gyagaryn Nuur, its mirror-calm surface reflecting the surrounding ridges. Several large flocks of ducks dot the lake, and a hundred yards away a dozen or more big gray herons trod the bank. Above the lake the valley divides—this fork is not shown on either of my maps—with the Ider going to the left and the Gyagaryn Gol going to the right. Between the forks soar barren ridges which I know must hide the source of the Ider. Just below our camp is Bayan Nuur, connected to Gyagaryn Nuur by a short stretch of river which is dimpled by dozens of fish feeding off the surface. As I watch the two whooper swans we had seen earlier circle and land on the small lake. On the grassy steppe between the lakes wander two pairs of elegant demoiselle cranes.

Despite the attractiveness of the surroundings these lakes are not considered sacred. Unlike Nogoon Nuur and Tsagaan Nuur, which are fed by springs and thus sources of water themselves, Gyagaryn Nuur and Bayan Nuur are simply dammed up sections of the Ider. As a camping spot the only drawback here is the lack of wood. The nearest trees creep down the ridge on the other side of the Ider, a half mile away, and Purevbazar has had to fetch firewood by horseback.

After we refresh ourselves with tea, fried bread, cheese, and cold mutton I announce that I am going to climb the high ridge to our left, which is too steep and rock-strewn to ascend with horses. From near the top I think I might get a glimpse of the source of the Ider. To my surprise both Oingerel and Shandas, neither of whom up until now has shown any particular enthusiasm for hiking, insist on coming along. Under the cloudless skies the sun pounds down relentlessly and by late afternoon the temperature has soared into the high eighties. Picking our way up the steep slope we have to stop every ten minutes to pant for breath and wipe our brows. My altimeter gives the elevation of Gyagaryn Nuur as 7,848 feet, and we climb about a thousand vertical feet above this. We finally top the crown of the ridge only to find Amardavaa and Purevbazar lounging on a bed of moss, calmly puffing on cigarettes. Nearby are their hobbled horses. They had ridden up-valley a couple miles, found a negotiable ravine which led to the top of the ridge, then followed the ridge line back to here. And Amardavaa had found a big deer antler weighting four or five kilos. The exhausted Oingerel shakes his head ruefully. I have a feeling this would be his last hike.

We are, however, rewarded with a splendid panorama. At what looks like the head of the Ider Valley stands a huge massif which I assume is 11,873-foot Öndör Ölziit Uul, the second high peak in the Khangai Mountains, on whose slopes I believe the Ider finds its source. Through binoculars I can see a huge cirque with a back wall of a thousand feet or more. Below this cirque a long alluvial fan of yellowish gravel leads down to the valley of the Ider. Amardavaa, looking through Oingerel's binoculars, notices this same patch of yellow gravel, which stands out distinctly from the surrounding grays, and excitedly announces that this has to be the source of the Ider. Our view of part of the upper Ider Valley is blocked by an intervening ridge, but I carefully scan that part which we can see and there appears to be no obstacles to reaching the alluvial fan or the cirque above it. The next day we will ride to a convenient spot near the head of the valley, make camp, and the following day locate the actual source. That decided, the others are eager to return to camp, but I decide to stay here by myself awhile longer.

I was elated. I had planned this trip for over a year and now it seemed my goal was finally in sight. I thought back to two years ago when, after a trek of over fifty miles over brutally difficult terrain, I had finally reached the true source of the Lena River, and about how the following year I had traveled to the East Sayan Mountains in Buryatia, just north of Mongolia, where two Russian companions and I hiked a total of ninety miles to reach the source of the 2,537 mile-long Yenisei-Biy Khem river system, the other great branch of the Yenisei. Now within two days I should be standing at the source of the Yenisei-Angara-Selenga-Ider, the longest north-flowing river system on earth and the fifth longest of all the earth's river systems.

Reaching into my coat pocket for a handkerchief, I find myself holding the small packet of incense the lama at the Ider temple had given me. It seems an appropriate moment to make a small incense offering to the gods which have allowed me to come this far. Gathering up a handful of dry grass I place it on a rock and light it with one of my kitchen matches. Most dry grass almost explodes in a quick short burst of hot flame, but this grass only smolders fitfully. When I sprinkle the weak flames with incense they die out completely. I try again, and again the flames go out the moment I sprinkle them with incense. Perplexed, I try a bigger handful of grass and get the same result. Soon I have used all the incense, most of which is scattered unburned on the rock. This ineffectual offering nags at my thoughts the whole way back to camp.

That night we had boiled sheep ribs for dinner. I gnawed away at mine but seemed to be leaving a lot of meat on the bone. Noticing this, Oingerel showed me how to cut open the cartilage at the end of the rib and then strip it and all the attached meat off, leaving the bone cleaner than a hound's tooth. Surprised that I didn't know how to do this, he asked Shandas, "Don't people eat sheep ribs in America?"

It was almost dark by the time we finished dinner. Amardavaa and Purevbazar roused themselves from the campfire and went to water the horses before turning in for the night. They returned in a few moments. Two of the horses, they announced, had slipped their hobbles and were gone. Oingerel jumped up, muttering under his breath. Amardavaa and Purevbazar, whose job it was to take care of the horses, stood there sheepishly. Oingerel explained that when horses ran off like this they would often attempt to go back to where they came from—in this case his encampment over thirty miles down the valley. It was imperative to find them tonight, before they had a chance to get too far. Oingerel, who owns the horses, and Amardavaa would go look for them, even though by then it was almost completely dark. Oingerel and Amardavaa had just finished saddling their horses when from a high ridge about a mile down the valley came the long drawn-out howl of a wolf. Oingerel spat out a curse and jumping into their saddles, he and Amardavaa pounded off into the darkness.

Now I have spent a lot of time in wolf country in Alaska and Siberia and I have seen numerous wolves in the wild. At no time did I ever think there was any real reason to fear them. In Alaska people go to great lengths to see wolves and consider themselves fortunate just to get a glimpse of one. I was surprised, then, to see how rattled Shandas and Purevbazar became. Shandas, muttering "This is really scary," threw a big arm load of wood into the fire. Purevbazar grabbed Amardavaa's rifle and shot three rounds into the air. As if in defiance the wolf answered with an even longer ululation. Our remaining two horses neighed loudly and jerked at their tethers. Standing in the small circle of light cast by the fire, we three silently stared off into the darkness down the valley for over an hour. Shandas and Purevbazar said they were staying up until the other two returned, but finally I crawled into my tent. Lying in the dark, I remembered that Ferdinand Ossendowski had encountered numerous packs of wolves in the Ider Valley. His Mongol guides had assured him that they were servants of the Demon of Zagastayn, sent to perform its mischief in the material realm. With these gloomy thoughts I drifted off to sleep.

The camp was completely silent when I woke at the late hour of nine the next morning. During the night I dreamed that the stray horses had returned. This dream seemed so real that I was actually not sure if they had come back or not. A quick check on our horses revealed that they had not. Now what? We did not have enough horses to move our camp forward, and a day trip to the source and back was probably impossible from here. And then how would all five of us and our gear get back down the valley? Someone would have to go back for more horses and after this delay there might not be time to continue upstream. Yesterday the source of the Ider had appeared so close; now it seemed to have receded far into the distance. My thoughts went back to the incense which wouldn't burn. Had the gods of the river and the surrounding mountains withdrawn their favor? Or was it the Demon of Zagastayn?

Hoping to raise my spirits I fired up my little backpacking stove and made some instant coffee I had been hoarding. Amardavaa poked his head out of his tent and I waved him over. He sipped hesitantly at the strange coffee, his usual ebullience muted by our predicament. One by one the others assembled by my tent. Oingerel was clearly not a happy camper. After coffee–which he pronounced was much too "bitter"–he sent Purevbazar down the valley to look again for the horses. The night before, he reported, he and Amardavaa had ridden at least six or seven miles down the trail without seeing any sign of the horses. They had heard more wolves, members of what he believed was a pack of at least eight or ten. There was a very real possibility that this pack was now hunting the horses. From what I had seen of their speed and stamina I doubted that wolves could ever catch a Mongolian horse. Not so, claimed Oingerel. Spooked by wolves, a horse would bolt off running wildly. Part of the pack would take short cuts and head it off, while the rest of the pack would follow up from behind. Finally encircling the horse, they would badger it until they brought it down. Horses, he assured me, were no match for wolves.

So as not to waste time waiting for Purevbazar to return Oingerel proposed making an exploratory trip up the valley of Gyagaryn Gol, which forked off to the right just above our camp. The previous afternoon we had gotten a good view up this valley from our vantage point on the ridge above our camp, and Oingerel had pointed out that the right flanks of the lower valley were thickly forested with larch. I suspected that the real reason for this jaunt was to look for deer antlers in the woods. I was not adverse, however, since at the head of this valley were several attractive peaks separated by passes which I knew lay right on the continental divide of inner Asia. I was eager to take a closer look at this area. We would leave right after lunch. Shandas, who was suffering from saddle sores, would hold down the fort.

Meanwhile, I decided to freshen up a bit. I heated water on my little stove, washed my hair and shaved. I was lolling on the grass with yet another cup of coffee when looking up I saw Purevbazar riding into camp with the two stray horses in tow. Oingerel saw them at the same time and barked out a sharp laugh. Around the campfire lanky Purevbazar explained in his laconic fashion that he had spotted the horses halfway up the ridge just a mile to two below our camp. Oingerel opined that they had headed down the trail until spooked by the howling of the wolves and then bolted up the hillside. Apparently the pack had not pursued them.

Deciding it was too late to break camp, we stuck to our original plan of exploring the Gyagaryn Gol. We rode up-valley for about ten miles to where the river forked and followed the left branch. At about 8,800 feet we entered classic alpine tundra–dwarf birch, labrador tea, and reindeer moss. Every time a rivulet entered the creek Oingerel pointed at it and asked in Russian, "*istok* (source)?" I said no and pointed straight ahead. Finally at 9,600 feet we found ourselves in a small cirque. Just to the left of the cirque was a pass which marked the continental divide. The opposite side of this pass drains into the Buyant River, which eventually flows into the sump of the Great Lakes Depression. From the back wall of the cirque tumbled numerous runnels which collected into a small pool. From the outlet of the pool flowed a foot-wide stream. Pointing to this outlet I pronounced *istok*! Up until then, as I had suspected, my companions had only a hazy idea of what I meant when I said I was looking for the source of the Ider. Now they understood what I meant by the source of a river in its geographical sense. We shared a cup of water from the rivulet and Amardavaa built a small rock cairn to mark the spot. Lazing on a flat patch of reindeer moss we lunched on cheese, sausage, and fried bread. Soon we were all sound asleep.

An hour and a half later, refreshed, we started back downstream. The Mongols were exuberant. The thin mountain air rang with their seemingly endless supply of Mongolian songs. At the confluence of the two forks Amardavaa and Purevbazar rode off by themselves to look for antlers. Oingerel and I went on ahead down the valley. Side by side, our stirrups jangling together, we galloped nonstop the last three or four miles into camp. When I finally dismounted my legs were so rubbery I could barely stand. Oingerel laughed uproariously as I wobbled up the campfire. In all we had ridden twenty-eight miles, our longest day so far.

Source of the Ider

UNDER SLATE GRAY skies the next morning we continued up the valley. Above Gyagaryn Nuur the Ider took a dogleg turn to the left, then back again to the right. In the crook of the first turn, which was hidden in shadow for most of the day, the river was lined by deep, hard-packed drifts of old snow, even though the temperatures were reaching the low eighties every afternoon. Coming around the second dogleg I saw that the Ider forked yet again, but the mountains at the head of these two branches were hidden in gray-black masses of roiling storm clouds. The yellow alluvial fan which we thought was the source of the Ider was nowhere to be seen. On a grassy bench still three miles before the fork Purevbazar and Amardavaa dismounted and began to unload the pack horse. We had ridden for only a little over three hours and I thought we should continue on. Shandas was still nursing his saddle sores and Oingerel had been lagging behind with him, but when they caught up I explained that we should ride up to the fork, determine which was the main branch of the Ider, and continue upstream some way before stopping for the day. But Oingerel was adamant. The two forks were in the rain shadow of the mountains, he explained, and we would have a wet camp; indeed, as we talked a hard rain could be seen falling near the fork of the river, only three miles away. Also, there was plentiful grass here for the horses, and farther up there might not be any. Neither of these two arguments was entirely convincing, but all three Mongols apparently had other indefinable ideas about what constituted a good campsite. This place meets their criteria, and it was clear they would not go on without an argument. Anyhow, Oingerel insisted, the source of the river, whichever fork it was on, could not be far off. After setting up camp and having tea we would make a reconnaissance upriver. If it appeared possible to reach the source that day we would continue on. If not we would make a long day trip the next day. I agreed to this plan. I was eager to find the source that very day. Who knew what tomorrow might bring?

Oingerel, Amardavaa, and I leave camp at 3:00 P.M. A light drizzle is falling and great banks of ragged gray clouds billow and surge over the mountains ahead. From their midst comes the low grumble of thunder. I think back to my journey to the source of the Yenisei-Biy Khem river system in Tuva. My two Russian companions and I had climbed through boulder-choked ravines most of the day to reach the high pass leading to the headwaters of the Biy Khem. A solid dome of cobalt blue arched overhead until we reached a small lake just on the other side of the pass. Suddenly black clouds poured over the ridge above us. Many-forked bolts of lightning flashed among the peaks and deafening claps of thunder rolled down the valley. By time we hurried down a quarter of a mile to the source of the Biy Khem the first big raindrops were falling, and soon we were deluged. Then a great gust of wind swept over us, followed by a downpour of grape-sized hail which, within a minute, piled up an inch deep. I had then the feeling that the gods who guard the sources of rivers were not happy that someone had dared to penetrate their innermost sanctuary. I have this same feeling as we ride up the Ider.

We quickly trot to the fork in the river. Since the still aching Shandas has stayed in camp I have no translator, but from what I can gather Amardavaa insists that the long yellow alluvial fan which we thought was the source of the river is at the head of the right fork, which cuts sharply to the south. The ten-foot-wide left fork heading to the northeast is clearly the larger, however, and thus the main trunk of the river. This fork we follow upstream into increasingly thick banks of clouds and fog. The stream itself soon leads into a deep impassable gorge which we bypass by following the rocky slope to the left. After half a mile, a hundred-foot-high waterfall marks the beginning of the gorge. Above here we follow a grassy, relatively smooth bench along the left flank of the valley. The fog banks dissipate somewhat and soon a huge cirque appears off to the right where the valley apparently dead ends. Dropping off the bench we follow the creek, which I assume flows out the cirque. But as we approach the cirque the creek suddenly veers to the left toward some comparatively low ridges. The streambed coming out of the cirque apparently only accommodates snow melt and is now completely dry.

Continuing along the right side of the creek we soon pass into alpine tundra–patches of dwarf birch and reindeer moss interspersed with loose, platy rock and boulder fields. The horses, creatures of the grasslands, do not like this terrain. They plod forth hesitantly, and soon we have to continually lash at their hindquarters with our lead ropes to keep them moving forward. Finally the creek branches yet again. I can see the end of the left fork just below a pass about half a mile away. The right fork, the larger of the two, swings up a ravine to the right and disappears behind a ridge.

By now it is six o'clock. Assuming it takes the same amount of time to return we will not get back to nine even if we turn around right here. The rain clouds keep hovering lower and lower, threatening to deluge us, and a chilly, moaning wind blows off the ridges into our faces. Retracing our steps in a downpour is not a pleasant prospect, and the thought of getting caught in a thunderstorm in this high, exposed country is truly frightening. Still, I can't turn around. "*Dalshe, chut, chut* (a little farther)," I implore. We round another corner only to have our view up the ravine blocked by another ridge. Just ahead is a particularly nasty boulder field which looks impassable by horse. Oingerel and Amardavaa are not happy. Denizens of the steppe, they don't like this high, cold, barren mountainous country. Both are as close to surliness as I have seen them. I can't ask them to continue on foot. Rest here with the horses, I indicate, and then go on alone across the boulder field. Topping a small rise I was surprised to see, not three hundred feet away, the pass at the head of the ravine. Pointing ahead I shout to Oingerel and Amardavaa: *istok!* Then I scramble on upward about two hundred feet to a tiny waterfall. Numerous runnels seeping out of the rocks below the pass tumble down the boulder-strewn ravine and combine just above the waterfall to form a foot-wide stream. Here, at an elevation of 9,880 feet, is the source of Yenisei-Angara-Selenge-Ider river system. Amardavaa scrambles up–Oingerel stays with the horses–and we take a ceremonial drink from the waterfall.

From here at its source the Ider flows north and then east 283 miles, finally combining with the Delger Mörön to form the Selenge. The Selenge flows northeast 368 miles to the Russian border, then another 267 miles before entering Lake Baikal, contributing almost half the yearly input of water into this immense lake. By the time the waters from here at the source have reached Lake Baikal they have dropped 8,389 feet. They descend to the vast depths of the lake and circulate for hundreds of years before flowing out via Baikal's outlet, the Angara River. Pouring out of Baikal at the rate of over sixty cubic kilometers of water a year, the Angara falls 1,246 feet in a distance of 1,003 miles. Most of the great rapids of the Angara have now been flooded by the three hydroelectric dams which now check its flow: the Irkutsk Dam; the Bratsk Dam, which creates the second largest man-made body of water on earth; and the Ilimsk Dam. After clearing these obstacles the Angara continues on to its confluence with the Yenisei River, the source of which I had been to the summer before. Below the confluence the Yenisei slows down, dropping only 249 feet in 1,762 miles before emptying into the Kara Sea at the rate of 19,800 cubic meters of water a second. The waters tumbling over the tiny waterfall where we stand will thus drop 9,880 feet and travel 3,683 miles on their journey to the sea. Only four other of the earth's river systems–the Nile, Amazon, Yangtse-Kiang, and Mississippi-Missouri–are longer.

Moments after taking out my camera to record this spot, the long threatening rain suddenly deluges us. I struggle into a rain jacket, but Amardavaa, who is wearing only his deel and has no rain gear, is drenched within moments. Ignoring the rain, he erects a small cairn next to the waterfall and I place inside of it a small coffee can containing a note which identifies this spot as the source of the Yenisei-Angara-Selenge-Ider. Then we scramble back down over the rain-slicked boulders to the horses.

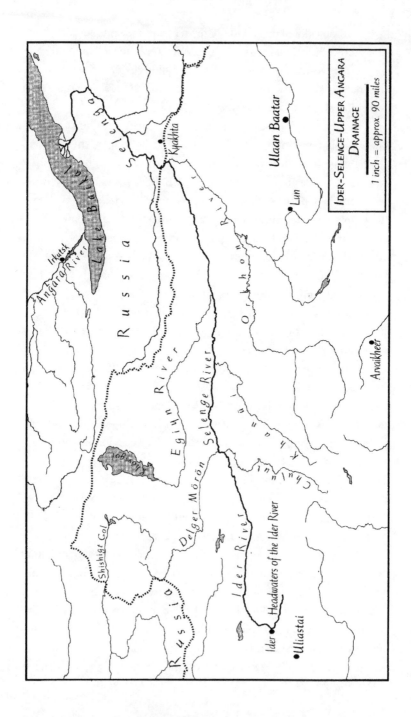

IDER-SELENGE-UPPER ANGARA
DRAINAGE
1 inch = approx 90 miles

Ulaan Baatar

Lun

Arvaikheer

Kyakhta

Irkutsk

Angara River

Lake Baikal

Russia

Selenga

Eg iyn River

Delger Mörön

Selenge River

Orkhon River

Khangai

Chuluut

Shishgit Gol

Ider River

Headwaters of the Ider River

Ider

Ulliastai

The Mongolians act like they can hear the dinner bell ringing back in camp. Our horses too need no prodding to get out of here. Quickly dropping down the ravine, we cross to the other side and climb to the high grassy bench that continues on down the right side of the valley. Trotting our horses the whole way we are back down to the big waterfall at the head of the gorge in forty minutes. Here the Mongolians decide to play tourist for a bit, climbing out on a precipice above the falls and insisting that I take their photograph. In another forty minutes, we are back to where the river breaks into two forks. From here all three of us gallop nonstop for about two miles. I think my horse is going flat out until we get within a mile of camp and it suddenly kicks into overdrive in an effort to catch up with the other horses. We three all pound into camp together. Purevbazar and Shandas see to the horses while the rest of us collapse around the fire with bowls of hot tea. Before I finish even the first bowl the rain clouds and fog suddenly blow over, leaving a solid dome of blue sky from horizon to horizon. At the very head of the valley can be seen the ridge just above the source of the Ider. It is now brightly illuminated and backed by azure sky. I feel like the gods who guard the sources of rivers are taunting me.

Sometime during the night the cloud cover reappeared. I awoke at just after dawn to the steady drumming of rain on my tent. A quick peek outside revealed that the horses, a hundred feet away, were just barely visible in the fog. Several times during the morning I checked for signs of life from the other two tents but no one was stirring. Rain continued until noon when the skies cleared just as suddenly as they had the evening before. Amardavaa got a fire going and we gathered for tea. Oingerel asked if we had heard the wolves. I hadn't. He had gotten up in the middle of the night to check the horses and had heard both the howling of a pack a mile or so down the valley and the yip-yapping of a bunch of pups on the hillside across the river from our camp. I mentioned that I was surprised by the number of wolves here in the upper Ider, where, apart from a few marmots, there seemed so little to sustain them. Wolves, explained Oingerel, usually don't live around their main food sources. These wolves here in the upper Ider raided the lower valley, killing sheep and other livestock, then quickly returned to their haunts here at the headwaters, where few people would be tempted to chase them.

By two o'clock we were moving back down the valley. We camped that night near the pass to Tsagaan Nuur and the next night at the gers of Oingerel's brother at Two Trees Ford. The following morning we continued on and arrived at Oingerel's encampment at noon. Oingerel went to the village and soon came back with a case of Chinese beer to celebrate our return. The neighbors got wind of this and soon a dozen or more people were gathered in Oingerel's ger. Another case of beer was sent for. Then Oingerel's mother-in-law came in and presented me with a new deel she had made for me in our absence. No store-bought deel would ever fit my outlandishly long frame, but she had apparently sized me up well because this one fit perfectly. "When you wear this deel in the future you must always remember us and your visit to the Ider Valley," she said, a tear sliding down her cheek. "I hope your trip has been a success," she added, dabbing at her face with the back of her hand. I assured her that it had been a complete success.

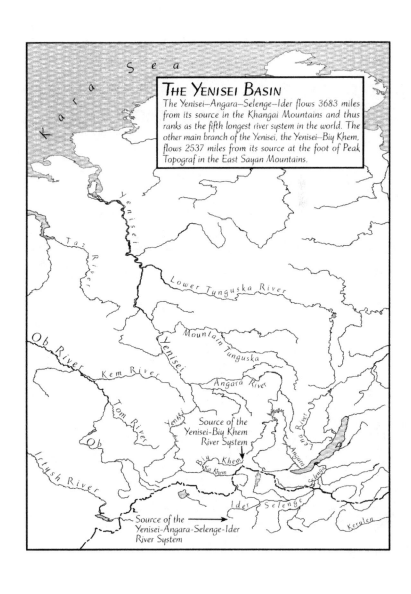

The Yenisei Basin

The Yenisei–Angara–Selenge–Ider flows 3683 miles from its source in the Khangai Mountains and thus ranks as the fifth longest river system in the world. The other main branch of the Yenisei, the Yenisei–Biy Khem, flows 2537 miles from its source at the foot of Peak Topograf in the East Sayan Mountains.

Kara Sea

Yenisei

Taz River

Lower Tunguska River

Ob River

Mountain Tunguska

Kem River

Yenisei

Angara River

Tom River

Lena River

Yenisei

Source of the
Yenisei-Biy Khem
River System

Biy Khem

Ka Khem

Ob

Angara

Selenge

Irtysh River

Ider

Selenge

Kerulen

Source of the
Yenisei-Angara-Selenge-Ider
River System

PART II

In Search of Zanabazar

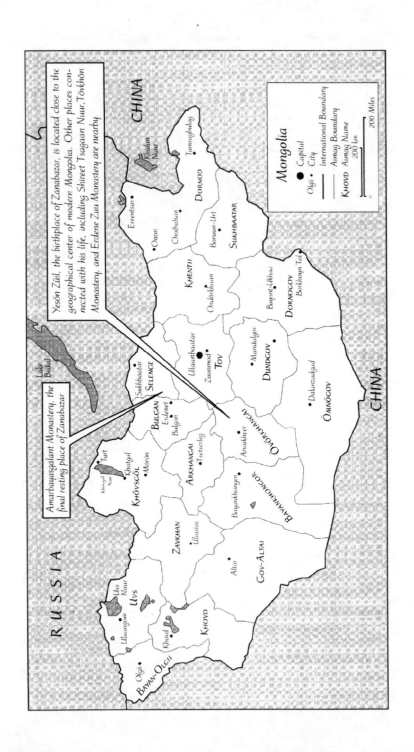

Yesön Züil, the birthplace of Zanabazar, is located close to the geographical center of modern Mongolia. Other places connected with his life, including Shireet Tsagaan Nuur, Tövkhön Monastery, and Erdene Zuu Monastery are nearby

Amarbayasgalant Monastery, the final resting place of Zanabazar

RUSSIA

CHINA

CHINA

Lake Baikal

Khatan Nuur

Tamsagbulag

Ereentsav

Onon

Choibalsan

DORNOD

Baruun-Urt

SUKHBAATAR

KHENTII

Öndörkhaan

Buyant-Ukhaa

DORNOGOV

Borkhoyn Tal

Sükhbaatar

SELENGE

Ulaanbaatar

Zuunmod

TOV

Mandalgov

DUNDGOV

BULGAN

Erdenet

Bulgan

Turt

Khövsgöl Nuur

Khatgal

Mörön

KHÖVSGÖL

Tsetserleg

ARKHANGAI

Arvaikheer

ÖVÖRKHANGAI

Dalanzadgad

ÖMNÖGOV

Bayankhongor

BAYANKHONGOR

ZAVKHAN

Uliastai

Uvs Nuur

Ulaangom

UVS

Khovd

KHOVD

Altai

GOV-ALTAI

Olgii

BAYAN-OLGII

Mongolia

- ● Capital
- Olgii • City
- — International Boundary
- — Aimag Boundary
- KHOVD Aimag Name

200 km

200 Miles

Ulaan Baatar to Amarbayasgalant

DURING MY FIRST visit to Ulaan Baatar I wandered quite by accident into the Zanabazar Fine Arts Museum on Khudaldaany Street a few blocks west of Sükhbaatar Square. There were very few visitors and the lights were turned out in most of the exhibit halls. At the top of the broad carpeted staircase to the second floor sat an elderly woman, and as I entered the exhibit hall directly ahead she flicked on a light switch. Along the right wall of the room were suddenly illuminated five bronze statues of figures sitting cross-legged in the lotus position. Elevated on narrow wooden columns, the statues, themselves about thirty inches high, seemed to exude their own radiance. Although by no means a connoisseur of Buddhist art I was instantly aware that these were remarkable works. A placard revealed that they were created by Zanabazar (1635-1723), the museum's namesake.

Zanabazar, I knew, was the first of the eight Bogd Gegens—reincarnated religious leaders similar to the more familiar Dalai Lamas of Tibet—who reigned in Mongolia from 1639 to 1924. I remembered reading that he was also an artist, and now here in front of me were the stunning examples of his work. The figure on the far right seemed vaguely familiar. The placard stated that this was the Sita Tara, or White Tara, a well-known figure in the Lamaist pantheon—although of course little known to Westerners—around which an elaborate cult of adulation has evolved. Originally she was esteemed as the celibate consort of the bodhisattva Avalokiteshvara, from whom the Dalai Lamas of Tibet are supposedly reincarnated. According to legend Zanabazar modeled his White Tara on his own consort as an adolescent girl. This young woman, whose name we don't know, apparently died at the age of eighteen under mysterious circumstances. Zanabazar, it is said, created his White Tara in her memory. I realize now that I have seen this statue depicted in several books, as well as on art prints, postcards, calendars, and other ephemera for sale in tourist shops and by street vendors around Ulaan Baatar. The White Tara and the Green Tara, the latter depicting his consort as a fully developed young woman, are probably Zanabazar's best known works.

To the left of the White Tara are statues depicting four of the five so-called "transcendent buddhas": Aksoba, Vairocana, Amitabha, and Amogasidi (the fifth, Ratnasanbhawa, is kept at the Choijin Lama Museum). At first glance all the statues appear alike, but each one differs in the position of the hands, the cast of the eyes, and the clothing and ornamentation. Along the other walls are more statues by Zanabazar; a painting which may be self-portrait, although some experts have questioned this; a painting of his mother, provenance also in doubt; a statue of Zanabazar; and several cases of works "by the school of Zanabazar" which are all too clearly not by the master himself.

In one corner of the room is a chart showing the so-called Soyombo script. Also a linguist of some renown, Zanabazar invented this script to more accurately and efficiently translate Sanskrit and Tibetan into Mongolian. The "crown symbol" which stands for the entire script was Zanabazar's personal seal. It looks familiar, as well it should. It was the emblem of the independent Mongolian State created in 1911, with the eighth Bogd Gegen—like Zanabazar a reincarnation of Javzandamba—at its head; of the Mongolian People's Republic, created in 1924; and of the present-day state of Mongolia. The symbol now appears on the Mongolian flag and also on several denominations of Mongolian money. And if you look south toward Bogd Khan Mountain from almost any part of Ulaan Baatar you can see on the hillside above the Tuul River a huge depiction of the crown symbol fashioned out of white stones.

I soon began stumbling upon other examples of Zanabazar's legacy throughout Ulaan Baatar. The city itself grew up around a temple which had been created for Zanabazar in 1639, when he was four years old. For the next 139 years this wandering temple-monastery changed locations about forty times before settling permanently here at the confluence of the Tuul and the Selbi rivers in 1778 and assuming the name Ikh Khüree Khot (Great Monastery Town). All of the subsequent Bogd Gegens, reincarnations of Javzandamba, lived here. A town soon grew up along side the monastery, and in 1911 the settlement became the capital of the country. The new communist regime which took power in 1924 likewise made the town their capital, giving it the name Ulaan Baatar (Red Hero).

Then one morning I climbed the hill to the west of downtown and found myself at Gandan, probably the country's leading monastery and one of the few that remained open during most of the communist era. Following the crowds which seemed to be aligning themselves like iron filings in the direction of one particular temple I was soon standing, along with dozens of others, in front of the monastery's most important relic, Zanabazar's statue of the Vajradhara, the embodiment of the contemplative buddhas of Tantrism. At the Choijin Lama Museum in downtown Ulaan Baatar, which was the former monastery of the brother of the eighth and last Bogd Gegen–I found several more of his statues, and the small gift shop on the grounds was selling newly minted silver commemorative coins with a portrait of Zanabazar on one side. At the eighth Bogd Gegen's own residence–now the Winter Palace Museum– I saw the immense fur robe made of dozens of fox skins and edged with pearls which had been worn by Zanabazar and also the remarkable chair of black ebony given to him by the Manchu Emperor Kang Hsi. With a seat that's at least four feet wide, high armrests, and a five-foot-high back, it is more of a throne than a chair. All the surfaces are covered with vividly colored and detailed Chinese scenes and inlaid with stones.

It was his relationship with Kang Hsi and the Manchus which cast a shadow on Zanabazar's otherwise unsullied reputation as religious leader, statesman, artist, and polymath. In 1691, after a bloody conflict between the Khalkha (Eastern) Mongols and the Jungarian (Western) Mongols, the first Bogd Gegen Zanabazar and other high-ranking Khalkha Mongols met with Kang Hsi at Dolonnor in Inner Mongolia.

Here he brokered a deal whereby the Khalkha Mongols would accept the suzerainty of the Ch'ing Dynasty, as the Manchus styled themselves, in exchange for protection against the Jungarian confederation. It was the end of Khalkha Mongolia as an independent political entity. Later, when the Jungars were crushed by the Ch'ing, the entire country of Mongolia became in effect a province of China, and over the next three hundred years the people of Mongolia were subjected to ever-increasing oppression at the hands of occupying Manchus and Chinese. Not until 1911 when the Ch'ing Dynasty finally crumbled would an independent Mongolia again emerge, with the eighth Bogd Gegen as its head. Even today there is a feeling among many ordinary Mongolians that Zanabazar had somehow "sold out" Mongolia to China. While discussing Zanabazar numerous people expressed just this view to me. But while opinions about him varied it eventually became apparent to me that next to Chingis Khan himself Zanabazar was probably the most remarkable personage in the history of Mongolia.

I was determined to find out more about this preternaturally talented but ultimately enigmatic personage. I managed to dig up some sketchy biographies of him, and now, on my third trip to Mongolia, I hoped to locate and visit various locations connected with his life. My first stop was to be a place called Yesön Züil, in Övörkhangai province, where Zanabazar was born in 1635. Due to a curious concatenation of circumstances I was unable to arrange either a vehicle or a translator for the trip to Yesön Züil and ended up stranded in Ulaan Baatar for almost two weeks.

In the interim Zanabazar had suddenly become front page news. On the night of July 12, when most people were in the midst of celebrating Naadam, the big summer festival in Mongolia, thieves broke into the Erdene Zuu Monastery, about 180 miles west of Ulaan Baatar, and stole twenty-two gold and silver gilded deities. Several of them were works of Zanabazar which a police spokesman opined were "priceless." It was not the first theft of Zanabazar statues. The previous August two of Zanabazar's lesser works, valued at $160,000 each, were stolen from the Winter Palace Museum. The thieves later apparently got cold feet and threw them in the Dund River near Ulaan Baatar, where they were eventually found by passersby. In the wake of the most recent thefts the authorities were stepping up customs inspections at the airport and at border crossings.

Then one day, as I was walking by the Bayangol Hotel in downtown Ulaan Baatar, who should come bolting out of the hotel's beer tavern but Shandas, the translator who had earlier accompanied me to the source of the Ider River. He had seen me passing by from the window and now invited me in for a beer. He was sitting with two school chums who had since gone on to college in the United States, one in Chicago and the other in Denver. They were now home for the summer vacation. Over mugs of Khan Bräu–the draft beer brewed locally by a Mongolian-German joint venture–Shandas related that he had just returned from Ulan Ude in Buryatia (part of Russia) just east of Lake Baikal. He, his brothers, and several friends had gone there and bought seven cars which they drove back to Ulaan Baatar in a convoy to protect themselves from Russian bandits. They hoped to sell all these cars but in the meantime Shandas had the use of one and was feeling rather expansive.

During our Ider River trip Shandas told me that he had been born and raised in the copper mining city of Erdenet, in Bulgan province, which I knew was in the same general area as Amarbayasgalant Monastery, where the remains of Zanabazar had been placed after his death. Shandas allowed that he knew where this monastery was located but had never been there himself. But if I ever wanted to go there, he went on, we could go together by train to Erdenet, where his mother still lived, and from there charter a jeep to Amarbayasgalant. Indeed, I intended go to this monastery, but I hoped to keep my researches into Zanabazar's life as much as possible in chronological order and thus visit his final resting place last. I had told Shandas that I would contact him when I was ready to make the trip. Now, however, he suggested that we go to Amarbayasgalant immediately. We could take the train to Erdenet tomorrow evening, arrive there early the next morning, visit his mother, and then charter a jeep to Amarbayasgalant. I realized that the peripatetic Shandas might not be available at some later date and anyhow I was anxious to get out of Ulaan Baatar, so I agreed.

The train to Erdenet leaves at 7:20 P.M. We arranged to meet at my hotel at 5:00 and then go to the train station and buy tickets. Shandas showed up at 6:00 after spending most of the afternoon enjoying more Khan Bräu. We flagged a cab and raced to the train station. After fifteen minutes he emerged from the ticket office. "We are very, very lucky," he told me, "we got the last two 'soft seat' tickets on the whole train." The train was indeed packed. We fought our way on board one of the "soft seat" cars and found our compartment. Shandas had informed me earlier that he never rode in the "hard seat" cars, which consist of one big compartment tightly packed with fifty or sixty people, and having ridden in similar cars on the Trans-Siberian, I didn't want to either. We had a four-bunk compartment measuring six and a half feet by six feet which we shared with an elderly country woman in a deel, her twenty-five-year-old daughter, and the daughter's six-month-old son. The train left right on time at 7:20, and after emerging from the suburbs of Ulaan Baatar we rolled north on the main line of the Mongolian railroad. First we have to go 145 miles to Darkhan, Mongolia's second largest city, where we will lay over for an hour or so. Then we will retrace our route back south about twelve miles to the station of Sakhit, and from there take the 101 mile-long branch line that turns off to Erdenet.

For the first two weeks of July Ulaan Baatar had sweltered under relentlessly clear skies and almost every afternoon temperatures reached the nineties. The much-awaited rains of summer had failed to materialize and the parched and sere hills around the city were still colored the buckskin tan of late spring. On July 11, the first day of Naadam, the big annual three-day wingding featuring horse races, wrestling, and archery contests, the temperature reached 99.5°F, the hottest ever opening day of Naadam and the second hottest day on record for Ulaan Baatar (hottest was 101.5°F on July 16 in the terrible year of 1937). Mongolians say that Naadam marks, if not the end of summer, the beginning of the end. Now many were saying that there had been no summer—summer being almost synonymous with the rainy season which refreshes and renews the great grasslands of Mongolia.

Then a few days after the end of Naadam the skies began to cloud over in the afternoons. Thunder rumbled on the Bogd Khan Uul to the south of town and a few light spritzes fell on the city. Then surprising cool winds blew in from the north, bringing with them heavy moisture-laden clouds. In the afternoons increasingly heavy showers fell, and several nights I was wakened by the pounding of hard, soaking rains. Now in the last week of July the grasslands which stretched out for miles on either side of the railroad had turned emerald green.

For several hours we roll north through this now lush steppe. The entire right-of-way of the railroad is lined on either side with barbed wire fences to keep livestock off the track, and here in this protected area the new grass grew six or eight inches high. The steppe outside the fences, although brilliant green, is kept trimmed to an inch or two by the plentiful herds of livestock. Farther north ridges topped with stands of larch start creeping closer and closer to the railroad. Scattered among the larch are thick patches of scarlet fireweed in full bloom, an unfailing sign that summer is peaking. By ten-thirty it's almost dark. The young woman in our compartment holds up her little diaperless baby boy and gently taps his testicles with her index finger until he dutifully pees on the floor. Her mother wipes up the floor with a rag and goes to the restroom at the end of the car to wash it out. Not being a parent, I don't know why they just didn't take the little baby to the restroom. We all climb into our bunks and someone turns out the light. I fall asleep immediately and don't wake up until the train has stopped and peddlers outside the window are crying *süü! süü!* (Milk! Milk!). This was the city of Darkhan, where we lay over for an hour. I drift off to sleep again and don't wake up till daybreak when we are crossing the Orkhon River bridge on the branch line to Erdenet.

We arrive at the train station about six miles outside of Erdenet at 8:20, exactly thirteen hours after leaving Ulaan Baatar. On the cab ride into town we can see off to the left the big mountain of almost solid copper ore which is the city's reason for existence. The immense open pit mine, which is slowly hollowing out the mountain, reportedly produces over twenty million tons of ore a year and ranks as one of the world's biggest producers of copper. The pit itself is not visible from the road, but I had once seen it from the air when I flew from Irkutsk to Ulaan Baatar. From the road can be seen only the millions of tons of spoil which have been dumped down the sides of the mountain. Near the base of the mountain is the gargantuan milling plant which processes the copper ore. Started in 1973, the mining complex was originally a

Mongolian-Soviet enterprise with overall Soviet control, but since 1992 it has been a Mongolian-Russian joint venture with 51 percent Mongolian ownership and a Mongolian director-general. The Mongolian share of the mine is still state owned and the sale of the copper and molybdenum concentrates it produces reportedly provide one-fourth of the Mongolian government's annual budget. Built from scratch in 1976 to accommodate workers for the mine, the city of Erdenet, with its one broad "boulevard" lined with ramshackle multistory apartment blocks, is indistinguishable from ready-made Soviet cities in Siberia like Bratsk and Angarsk, except that it is on a smaller scale and surrounded by steppe instead of taiga. Erdenet now hosts about fifty thousand people, making it the third largest city in Mongolia.

Shandas's mother lives with her sixteen-year-old son on the fifth floor of a five-story apartment just off the main drag, which was originally named, predictably, Lenin Street and is now named, also predictably, Sükhbaatar Street, after the most famous hero of the Mongolian revolution. As soon as we arrive she treats us to a breakfast of cheese and salami, cabbage salad, and bread slathered with thick cream. She speaks some Russian, so I can talk to her. A petite woman in her fifties, she's separated from Shandas's father, who now lives in Ulaan Baatar, and works as a teacher of Mongolian literature in a local high school. By coincidence she has just been reading a novelistic treatment of Zanabazar's life published in a Mongolian magazine. She asks if she can come along to Amarbayasgalant and of course I agree.

She suggests I rest in her son's room while she and Shandas go and round up a jeep and driver. This room turns out to be a veritable shrine to Michael Jackson. Every square foot of the walls, the back of the door, and part of the ceiling is covered with posters depicting each stage in the career of the King of Pop. By a big boom box is a collection of Michael Jackson tapes, and on a desk are stacks of Korean and Japanese pop magazines and Mongolian newspapers with stories about the Gloved One. Wandering into the living room I find a big new Sony TV and VCR along with a dozen tapes of Michael Jackson concerts and video clips. Indeed, when I turn on the TV I find it turned to Asian MTV and within minutes a Michael Jackson video appears. Only the bathroom offers a respite from rampant Jacko-mania. On the inside of the door is a big poster of Pamela Anderson displaying her mountainous mammaries.

I had been expecting delays in getting off to Amarbayasgalant; in fact, given Shandas's penchant for divagation I wouldn't have been surprised if we didn't get off until the next day. His mother must have provided a salutary influence, however, and not thirty minutes after leaving they reappear and announce that the jeep driver is outside and ready to go. This gentleman, thin and wiry and in his fifties, is named Batbayar. He has a brisk, competent air about him and the inside of his Russian jeep is spotlessly clean with nice carpets on the seats. He asks 60,000 tögrögs for the round-trip to Amarbayasgalant, but Shandas's mother, obviously not a person who throws money around recklessly, informs him that he will be happy with 35,000. Realizing he isn't going to get anywhere arguing, he just shrugs and said OK. After quick stops at a couple of markets for bread, sausage, smoked ham, tomatoes, cucumbers, and sodas we barrel out of town.

Just before the train station we cut off on the unpaved road which eventually goes to Darkhan, 112 miles to the east. To our left can be seen the breast of a huge dam which serves as a settling basin for the ore-concentrating plant. For several miles we drive along the Khangal River, which runs out of the man-made lake. The river water has an unhealthy, rusty-looking color and along the banks are piled up banks of reddish foam. Our driver allows that the river is highly charged with a toxic brew of pollutants from the refined copper ore but claims that animals–large herds of sheep and cows graze along the banks–drink the water. Humans get their water elsewhere. Further on we pass what our driver calls a dairy collective. Several cabins and a dozen or more gers are grouped around some big pens holding perhaps a hundred head of dairy cattle, and several hundred more are grazing nearby. In a big shed can be seen some milking machines run by electricity–the first I have ever seen in Mongolia. Batbayar isn't sure, but he assumes the dairy cows must drink out of the river.

We pass the town of Jargalant and approach a range of rounded mountains. These aren't high–the peak to our left is 5,327 feet in elevation and the one to our right is 4,722 feet (the city of Erdenet is at 3,384 feet)–but the road to the pass is very steep. At the top is a large ovoo where of course everyone stops. There is a convoy of eight cars leaving just as we pull in. When I ask Batbayar the name of the pass he says, "We never say the name of a pass near the pass itself." I have heard this taboo about saying the names of auspicious places within their "hearing distance" before. My map silently reveals that this is Khoshööt Pass, which marks the border between Bulgan and Selenge aimags. We dutifully walk around the ovoo and Batbayar adds a rock to the already sizable mound.

After switchbacking down the ridge we emerge in a broad basin. Although on either side of the road lush emerald-green grasslands stretch out for several miles they appear to be completely deserted, with nary a ger or a single head of livestock for as far as the eye can see. "No water," explains Batbayar. Indeed, the broad valley bottom we are driving through appears to have no creek or stream draining it, although recent rains have left puddles along the road. The road itself—the main highway between Mongolia's second and third largest cities, Darkhan and Erdenet—is in horrible condition. Large trucks have cut deep ruts through which our jeep can only just barely maneuver, and the sides of the road are too muddy for detours. Batbayar, while battling with the steering wheel and gear shift, claims that the Kuwaitis are providing money to upgrade and pave this road. Just why Kuwait is interested in this obscure corner of northern Mongolia is unclear. Soon a stream does come into view—the river Birgotoi—and we cross a rickety wooden bridge to the dusty little village of Baruun Buren, about forty-five miles from Erdenet. A mile beyond the Baruun Buren we turn off the main road and head north on the jeep track to Amarbayasgalant.

Again we find ourselves amidst lush grasslands—in some places the grass is over a foot high—but still there are no gers or livestock in sight. The steppe is broken up by huge fields which had once been turned by the plow but now grow nothing but rank weeds. By the edges of the fields sit the rusting hulks of combines and other abandoned farm machinery. Winter wheat was grown here during the hey-day of the communist era, when ambitious attempts were made to introduce modern agriculture into Mongolia, but now it's apparently cheaper to buy flour from China. The terrain finally turns hilly, the ridge lines mantled with larch and aspen and colored with huge patches of fireweed. Finally we come to a tiny creek, the first water we have seen since Baruun Buren. On the far side of the ford the jeep track branches off in several directions. Batbayar, who has never been to Amarbayasgalant before, is momentarily at a loss. Then a half mile to our right, coming down a steep ridge, we see someone riding a huge black animal. We ride over and find a hefty, sullen-looking teenage girl astride an ox. She tries to keep riding on without talking to us but in response to Batbayar's shouted queries about Amarbayasgalant she finally points back over her shoulder to the jeep trail behind her. We follow this track to a low pass marked by a small ovoo. A few miles beyond the pass we come around a hill and there, several miles away at the base of a high forested ridge, is a complex of buildings that can only be Amarbayasgalant. We soon join a well-traveled dirt road which emerges into the broad, green valley of the Iben River. Two dozen or more gers are scattered up and down the valley along with numerous herds of sheep, cattle, and horses. We cross the Iben and drive up to the parking lot in front of the monastery. The sixty-eight-mile trip from Erdenet has taken three and a half hours.

Amarbayasgalant Monastery

WHEN THE RUSSIAN ethnographer and linguist Aleksei M. Pozdneev visited here in 1892, Amarbayasgalant, with over two thousand lamas in residence, ranked as one of the largest and most important monasteries in Mongolia. Pilgrims from all over the Lamaist world came here to worship in its temples and pay homage to the sharil–the mummified remains–of Zanabazar, the first Bogd Gegen. I knew that the monastery had been closed and the various temples severely damaged by the communists during the 1930s, and that it had been reopened in the early 1990s and was once again the home of a small contingent of lamas. I had also heard that the monastery was undergoing extensive restorations financed by the UNESCO branch of the United Nations, which had declared it a "World Cultural Heritage Site", and by private donations, and that it was once again becoming a popular place for Mongolians on both religious pilgrimages and sightseeing excursions into the countryside. At the moment, however, the parking lot was deserted. Over to the right of the monastery huddled a small conclave of two or three dozen small cabins, shanties, and gers, but not a soul was in sight. Smoke rose from numerous chimneys: apparently everyone was inside having dinner.

Between the parking lot and the front of the monastery is the so-called *pailur*, or spirit shield, a freestanding brick wall about fifty feet long and eighteen feet high. According to traditional beliefs the *pailur* keeps evil spirits, which like to travel in straight lines, from entering the monastery gate; such walls are a common feature of Mongolian monasteries. The bottom pediment of the wall is covered with lustrous green tiles and on the middle of the wall on the side facing the monastery is a large circular bas-relief of green glazed plaster depicting two dragons entwined around the sun. Except for some chipped tiles and broken bricks, the wall appears much as Pozdneev described it in 1892.

Just to the left of the wall is a narrow column of brick decorated with the same motifs as the wall. In Pozdneev's day there was an identical column to the right of the wall—now only its base remains—and on the columns were wooden tablets with inscriptions in Mongolian that read, "The numerous wangs, dzasaks, and taiji [official ranks given to the Mongolians by the Manchus], and those of lower rank down to the commoner must dismount from their horses here."[1] Pozdneev was told that even the subsequent Bogd Gegens had to leave their horses here and walk the hundred feet or so to the monastery gate.

Above the entranceway is a large tablet with a blue background and gold frame. In gold letters are short inscriptions in Mongolian, Manchu, and Chinese. Pozdneev, who was fluent in each of these languages (in addition to Kalmuk), gives the translation: "The Monastery of Amarbayasgalant, Built at Imperial Command."

The command to build Amarbayasgalant was given by the Manchu emperor, Yung Cheng, the son of Kang Hsi. Kang Hsi was perhaps the most illustrious of the Manchu (Ch'ing Dynasty) emperors who ruled China from 1644 to 1912. Upon the death of his own father in 1661 the seven-year-old Kang Hsi was placed on the throne with his mother and four regents governing in his name. In 1667, when he was a mere thirteen or fourteen years old, Kang Hsi made his bid for personal control of the dynasty, and two years later he had the most powerful of the regents, Oboi, arrested and thrown in prison, where he died. For the next fifty-five years of his reign Kang Hsi faced innumerable challenges, including rebellions and revolts in the south of China and the Russian occupation of the Amur Valley on China's northeast border, but perhaps the most serious was the rise of the Jungarian Empire among the Oirat, or Western, Mongols who inhabited western Mongolia and the upper Irtysh-Lake Zaisan-Tarbagatai Mountains region west of the Altai.

I have mentioned in an earlier chapter how in the fifteenth century the Oirats gained temporary control of much of Mongolia following the dissolution of the Mongol Empire founded by Chingis Khan and his descendants, and how in the first part of the seventeenth century, under the leadership of Khara Khula, they again organized into a strong confederation known as the Jungarians. I have also mentioned the rise of the charismatic warlord Galdan Boshugt, Khara Khula's grandson, who entertained dreams of uniting once again all Mongols, including the Khalkhas, as they had been under Chingis Khan and ultimately displacing the Manchus as the rulers of China.

By the late seventeenth century the Khalka, or Eastern Mongols, were divided into three main groups—the Zasagt khanate in the western Khangai Mountains and the deserts to the south, the Setsen khanate in the Onon and Kherlen valleys, and the Tüsheet khanate in the Orkhon and Tuul valleys. The Tüsheet Khan was Zanabazar's brother, Chakhundorj, who, like the others in his line, claimed to be a descendant of Chingis Khan himself. The Khalka khans, at least in their own view, were the legitimate rulers of Mongolia, while the Jungarians were mere upstarts who had no right to the throne once held by Chingis. When the Khalkhas refused to submit to the Jungarians Galdan resolved to add them to his empire by force.

Early in 1688 his armies advanced eastward along the northern side of the Khangai Mountains. In April they sacked the great monastery of Erdene Zuu, built on the site of Kharkhorum, the old Chingis Khanite capital of Mongolia, by Abudai, the great-grandfather of the Tüsheet Khan Chakhundorj and Zanabazar. The Tüsheet Khan, Zanabazar, the Zasagt Khan, and thousands of their followers fled eastward. Galdan and his army chased them up the valley of the Tuul and into the drainage of the Kherlen, seizing immense herds of livestock and other property that had been left behind and razing numerous monasteries. The Khalkhas hoped to regroup in the domains of the Setsen Khan, in the valley of the Kherlen, but Galdan's armies routed them even here. The Khalkhas made one last stand at Olgoi Lake, but on August 28 and 29, 1688, they were overwhelmed by the Jungarians. The Khalkha khans and nobles and tens of thousands of their followers joined a mass exodus into the Manchu-controlled borderlands of China where they sought the protection of the emperor, Kang Hsi. The refugees eventually may have numbered upwards to 140,000. Galdan now controlled all of Mongolia and he stood poised to attack the Manchus themselves.

In September of 1688 the Bogd Gegen made his first appeal to Kang Hsi. In a letter he asked for protection from Galdan, pasture lands where the Khalkhas could settle, and the eventual restoration of his monasteries in Mongolia. Kang Hsi said he would consider these requests on condition that the Khalkhas renounce their autonomy and become Manchu subjects. In 1690, as a show of good faith, Kang Hsi sent a large army equipped with cannons into eastern Mongolia and defeated one of Galdan's armies at Ulanbudang. Galdan was far from beaten, but he was put on the defensive.

Then in April of 1691 Kang Hsi convoked a great meeting at Dolonnor, in what is now Inner Mongolia. In attendance were the three Khalkha khans, the Bogd Gegen, and some 550 Mongolian nobles. On May 29, Kang Hsi himself arrived at Dolonnor. He had come to officially accept the Khalka people as subjects of the Manchu empire. The Bogd Gegen, who, as a religious leader, enjoyed immense influence among most of the Khalka khans and nobles, became the spokesman for the Mongols. He had concluded earlier that in their struggle with the Jungarians the Khalkhas had only two choices—submit and seek aid from either the Manchus or from the Russians who by now occupied all of Siberia, north of Mongolia. He chose the Manchus, he said, because they were sympathetic to Buddhism, while the Russians were Christians, and because the culture, language, and dress of the Manchus were similar to that of the Mongolians. In return for their subjugation Kang Hsi promised to rout Galdan from Mongolia and allow the Khalkhas to return to their homeland.

Galdan's fortunes soon faded. He was faced with a rebellion in his own ranks by his nephew Tsevang Rabdan and by a series of offensives by the Manchus. Kang Hsi personally led a three-pronged attack into Mongolia in 1696. One of his generals finally caught up with Galdan's army and inflicted massive casualties. Galdan himself escaped with a small band of followers to the Altai Mountains. The following year news came of his suicide. The Western Mongols would continue to harry the Manchus until 1757, but their dream of a pan-Mongolian empire was dead. By 1700 the Khalkhas began moving back into Mongolia, but as Manchu subjects. They would remain so until 1911.

The great Dolonnor convention of 1691 at which the Khalkha khans accepted the suzerainty of the Manchus was a turning point in the life of Zanabazar, the Bogd Gegen. In appreciation for his role in bringing the Khalkha Mongols under the suzerainty of the Ch'ing Dynasty, Kang Hsi officially recognized the Bogd Gegen as the highest religious authority in Mongolia and also as the highest ranking of all Mongolian dignitaries, including the khans and other nobles. Thus Zanabazar became the de facto head of the country, while remaining, of course, under the authority of Kang Hsi, the Ch'ing emperor. Despite–or perhaps because of–his leadership role Zanabazar did not immediately return to Mongolia. From Dolonnor the Bogd Gegen went directly to Beijing and remained in China for the next eight years, until the spring of 1699. It is not clear from the record if Zanabazar went to China on his own accord, was invited by Kang Hsi, or was indeed ordered to the capital and held there where the Manchu ruler could keep a close eye on him.

Whatever the original relationship between the Bogd Gegen and the Emperor it took a new turn in 1693 when Kang Hsi fell seriously ill. After a prayer service by the Bogd Gegen Kang Hsi became visibly better and soon recovered completely. "This occurrence," says Pozdneev in his translation of the Bogd Gegen's life, "was proclaimed a miracle and served, it is said, as a basic motive for effecting a rapprochement between the Bogd Khan [Kang Hsi] and the hutukhtu [Bogd Gegen]. From that time on the Bogd Khan began constantly to invite the hutukhtu to visit him, brought him closer to the palace, and loved to converse with him about the most diverse subjects."[2]

In the winter the Bogd Gegen lived close by Kang Hsi in Beijing and in the summer he accompanied him to the emperor's summer palace in Jehol. They went on many tours of the countryside together and in 1697 the Bogd Gegen went out to meet Kang Hsi on his return from his successful campaign against Galdan and accompanied him back to Beijing. They frequented Buddhist temples together (at one they caused a stir by sitting side-by-side on a carpet; theoretically, no one was supposed to sit at the same level as the emperor) and in the summer of 1698 made a pilgrimage to the sacred mountain of Wu-t'ai-shan in Shansi province, believed to be the place where the boddhisattva Manjushri–whom the Bogd Gegen venerated–expounded the teachings of Buddha. Kang prepared a memorial stating that he "had not met a higher spiritual personage" than the Bogd Gegen, who eventually became revered throughout China for his holiness and supposedly miraculous powers.[3]

Even Kang Hsi's senior wife, Huang-t'ai-hou, was not immune to the Bogd Gegen's allure. Seeing him from the window of her apartment she told her husband, "Your hutukhtu is as beautiful as a bright moon on a night of a full moon; can't I invite him to my half [of the palace] and hear the sacred teaching from him?"[4] The Bogd Gegen gave a sermon to Huang-t'ai-hou and her retinue and in return they gave him a garland and a mantle embroidered with pearls. Of course there were dissenters. Courtiers in the emperor's court who were jealous of the Bogd Gegen's close relationship with Kang Hsi referred to him as a "stinking Mongol."

In early 1699 the Bogd Gegen went back to Mongolia to perform the funeral services for his older brother but was back in Jehol by the summer of the same year; and that winter he moved on to Beijing. In 1701 he went back again to oversee the restoration of Erdene Zuu monastery, which had been razed by the Jungarians, but soon returned again to China. Some time later, in exactly what year it is not clear, but prior to 1706, the Bogd Gegen went back to Mongolia to stay. His accompanying caravan was so long he had to ask for the emperor's assistance in getting it out of Beijing. All other traffic through the An-ting-men Gate was stopped and for three days and three nights camels laden with gifts he had received from Kang Hsi and other admirers passed through in single file.

At their first stop outside the Great Wall the Bogd Gegen and his entourage went to make offerings at the hill of Öndür-tologoi. According to legend, out of the north suddenly appeared five majestic-looking men riding on wild deer. They were dressed in panther-skin robes and boots and carried bows and arrows. Prostrating themselves at the feet of the Bogd Gegen they declared that they had come to welcome him back to Mongolia. Asked by his retainers who these mysterious personages were, the Bogd Gegen replied that they were the Spirit Rulers of the Northern Lands, and particularly of the Altai, Khangai, Khentii, and other mountains of Mongolia.

Upon arriving back in Mongolia the Bogd Gegen set out on an ambitious campaign of restoring damaged monasteries and building new ones, developing new styles of temple architecture, instituting new religious ceremonies, and even designing new attire for lamas. By 1710 the Jungarians under Tsevang Rabdan were again rampaging, and in the following years the Bogd Gegen was involved in diplomatic efforts to halt their raids on Tibet and the Khalkha Mongols. And so went the years.

Then in 1722 the great Kang Hsi died. The Bogd Gegen, who was then almost ninety, immediately set out for Beijing to pay his respects to the remains of the Manchu emperor. What happened after he arrived is somewhat of a mystery. We do know from his biography that on the fourteenth day of the first moon of 1723 he died at the Shar Temple in the capital. His biography gives no reason for his death (he was of course a very old man and had just made an extremely strenuous journey), but to this day a belief exists among many Mongolians that he was murdered by the Manchus. At least half a dozen Mongolians, when discussing Zanabazar with me, expressed just this opinion. This accusation was also aired in print as late as 1995 in the book *Undur Geghen Zanabazar* by Zh. Choinkhor, which was published under the auspices of UNESCO. According to Choinkhor, Kang Hsi's son and successor, Yung Cheng, had Zanabazar assassinated because he wanted to eliminate anyone who had been close to his father and thus might question his own power. Regardless of how he died, Zanabazar's emanations were soon reported in Mongolia. "They relate that, on the day of his death, there was a five-colored rainbow stretching above his palace in Urga, and on the hutukhtu's throne a clear light shone for a long time," says Pozdneev.[5]

The body was embalmed and put on display for several months. Yung Cheng, whatever his motives might have been, bestowed on the deceased Bogd Gegen the title of "Enlightener of the Faith" and awarded him posthumously a gold seal. Yung Cheng also stated, "The hutukhtu enjoyed the excellent love of my deceased regal father and extraordinary honors . . . The hutukhtu was an extraordinary man, and I am setting forth personally, for the sake of expressing respect to him, in order to present a *khadak* [prayer scarf] at his grave and to perform libations with tea."[6] Later that year the Bogd Gegen's body was taken back to Mongolia in a large caravan accompanied by an escort of honor sent by Yung Cheng. According to one account Kang Hsi had decreed before his death that 100,000 taels of silver be used to build a monastery which would serve as a repository for the Bogd Gegen's remains. It's unclear whether Yung Cheng's attentions to the deceased Bogd Gegen were guided by true devotion, a guilty conscience, or utter cynicism, but we do know that in 1728 Yung Cheng allotted this money from the state treasury for the building of Amarbayasgalant Monastery.

When we bang on the monastery door it opens slightly, and we allow ourselves into a grassy courtyard. Directly ahead is a small temple, which is now locked. On each side of the temple are two tall posts resembling telephone poles. According to tradition Amar and Bayasgalant, the two Mongolians after whom the monastery is named, are buried beneath these poles. Pozdneev relates that the Manchu emperor, Yung Cheng, sent a team of geomancers to Mongolia to search out a propitious location for the monastery to house the remains of the first Bogd Gegen. They searched far and wide but were finally drawn to the foot of Mount Bürün-Khaan. Here they found a little boy and girl playing together. When asked their names the boy said, "Amar" (*amar*= happiness, peacefulness) and the girl, "Bayasgalant" (*bayasgalant* = joy, pleasure, happiness). This was deemed auspicious, and it was decided to build the monastery on this spot and call it Amarbayasgalant. When Amar and Bayasgalant eventually died they were buried here in this courtyard, at least according to legend.

On either side of the poles are two wooden pavilions. One, according to Pozdneev, housed a "beater" used to call the lamas to their services. The beater is now missing. The pavilion to the right housed a bell presented to the monastery by the Emperor Yung Cheng. An elaborately embossed bell, almost three feet high, now rusted, cracked, and with two big holes in one side, leans against a nearby stone pillar. Presumably this is the same bell.

The main gateway to the second courtyard is actually a temple devoted to the Four Maharajas, a standard feature in Lamaist monasteries. This is locked, but off to the left is a small door through the wall separating the courtyards. In the next courtyard a short staircase leads to a square in the middle of the courtyard occupied by the big main temple of the monastery. It occurs to me that both in layout and architectural design this monastery resembles a smaller version of the Yonghegong (Lama) Monastery in Beijing which I had once visited. Perhaps this is not surprising, since the Yonghegong Monastery was originally the home of Yung Cheng before he became emperor in 1723. Also, the system of courtyards and elevated squares connected by stone steps found in the Forbidden Palace in Beijing, where both Yung Cheng and his father, Kang Hsi, lived, is replicated here, although of course on an infinitesimally smaller scale.

In front of the main temple, which is now locked, stand two more wooden pavilions. In each are large slabs of stone inscribed with old-style Mongolian writing in vertical columns. These obelisks, presented to the monastery by Ch'ien Lung, Yung Cheng's son, in 1737, the year the construction was completed, record a short account of the monastery's founding. (Very similar pavilions and inscribed stones are also found at the Yonghegong Monastery in Beijing.) Batbayar and Shandas's mother examine the engraved writing closely but claim they can't make out a thing. I pull out a xeroxed copy of the translation made by Pozdneev and read it to them. Batbayar is flabbergasted that over a century ago there was a Russian man who could translate Old Mongolian into the Russian language, that this Russian version would later be translated into English, and that now we are standing here listening to Shandas translate this English version back into Mongolian. The inscription reads, in part, "In the first year of the rule of Ch'ien Lung, the monastery was completed and I, [Ch'ien Lung], decreeing the name of Amurbayasqulangtu for the monastery, bestowed upon it an inscription from my own hand, calling it the 'foundation of the virtue of the worlds which are as many as the grains of sand in the Ganges.' Assenting later to the requests of the officials in charge of the business of construction, I commanded that an obelisk be erected and that it be engraved with an inscription setting forth all the circumstances attending this work." The message from Ch'ien Lung continues:

> As I will think, all men born by heaven possess one eternal and true quality. This true quality does not know rich or poor, does not make distinction by external appearance and surfaces . . . The Yellow Faith [Lamaism, in particular the Gelugpa sect to which Zanabazar belonged] is widespread in the northern countries . . . and there is no one who would not want to confess it with true devotion. The essence of its teachings are the principles by which evil vices are to be corrected and beneficial virtues are followed . . . My royal forefathers graciously showered the foreign aimaks with their favors and gave prosperity to all lands. Hence vast multitudes of peoples have been entirely happy, and works of every sort are in plenty and abundance. The superiors of the temple must exhort and guide all living creatures, bring them tidings of the true virtues, and urge them to strive unanimously for illumination and decorum, in order that all separate individuals and families may enjoy peace and tranquillity. Only then will they duly appreciate the lofty purposes with which my royal parent gave his favors and benefits . . ."[7]

Behind the main temple are three doors leading to the third courtyard, which contains five temples. In the middle is the temple of Dzu, which in Pozdneev's day contained a large statue of the Buddha Shakyamuni. It is unlocked and now contains nothing but boards and other building materials. To its left is a small wooden temple which once contained the remains of the fourth Bogd Gegen, and to the left of this is the temple of Manla, both now locked. To the right of the middle temple is the temple which Pozdneev says contains the sharil of the Zanabazar, the first Bogd Gegen, and to the right of this is the temple of Ayusha. Both these are locked also. Were the remains of the first and fourth Bogd Gegens still here at Amarbayasgalant? No one in Ulaan

Baatar could tell me for sure–I got various conflicting answers–and to find out is one of the main reasons I have come here. I try to peek through the wooden latticework covering the window of the Zanabazar temple but can see nothing.

The others are content to rest while I go to look at the fourth and last courtyard. Here are also five buildings. The one in the middle had a unique white tile roof, according to Pozdneev, and it was here that the Bogd Gegens stayed when they visited Amarbayasgalant. The tiles are gone and the roof is now nondescript wood, although there appears to be some restoration work going on. The temples on either side of the middle building are locked. When I return to the third courtyard my companions are talking to a red-robed young lama who was perhaps in his middle twenties. To my relief he doesn't seem to object to us being here when there is no one else around. I ask him through Shandas if the sharils of the two Bogd Gegens are still in the temples here in this courtyard. He ponders this question with pursed lips for a while, then says he's not sure about the remains of the fourth Bogd Gegen, but he thinks, is pretty sure, that the sharil of the first Bogd Gegen is still here. "There's a man in the small settlement that knows everything about the monastery. We should talk to him," the lama says. In response to our inquiries he also tells us that there is a woman in the settlement who rents out small cabins to pilgrims and other visitors to Amarbayasgalant. He suggests we stay in one of them and he'll send the knowledgeable man to see us.

We take the jeep over to the village and find the woman. One of her cabins is in use–two foreigners, a man and a woman she says–but the other one is available. It's very cozy with ger-style furniture, a wood stove, and curtains made from the same red material the lamas use for their robes. There's even electricity, but no running water. There's no outhouse either, but there's a big pasture right behind the cabin. I had planned to stay in my tent but now it's clear we can stay in this cabin. The price is eight dollars a night, which isn't cheap–I could get a decent hotel room in Ulaan Baatar for the same price–and the woman insists on being paid in dollars. I don't have any dollars, only tögrögs. The woman is surprisingly adamant and says, "Sorry, no dollars no cabin." This gets Shandas's mother riled. After a five-minute argument the woman stalks off clutching 6,400 tögrögs.

While we're tucking into our picnic dinner–sliced ham, sausage, bread, tomatoes, cucumbers, hot tea–the guests in the cabin next door appear, an Israeli couple in their late twenties. The man works for a mining company in Ulaan Baatar and he has borrowed one of their Russian jeeps for a weekend jaunt into the countryside. They arrived this morning and hope to leave at noon tomorrow, but at the moment they seem to be having mechanical trouble with their jeep. Our driver, with Shandas in tow as translator, goes to take a look at the problem. I walk back alone to the monastery for a last look before the sun sets.

The main part of Amarbayasgalant Monastery, consisting of the four interconnected courtyards and surrounding brick wall, was built by command of the Manchu emperor. In the 1890s there were also numerous temples outside of the monastery which were built with donations from the Mongols themselves. One of them contained a huge statue of Maitreya, the coming Buddha, which Pozdneev claimed was "sixty armspans" in height (the usually pedantically precise Pozdneev is a bit vague here about what constitutes an "armspan"). All these temples and whatever they contained, including the enormous Maitreya, are gone now, destroyed by the communists in the 1930s. Around the main monastery and its adjacent complexes of temples were six residential precincts which housed lamas belonging to each of the monastery's six aimags, or sections. In the 1890s there were a total of over 500 log cabins and gers in these suburbs, most in courtyards enclosed by log palisades. Now there is only the small huddle of cabins, shacks, and gers where we are encamped.

In addition to the main gate to the monastery, which as in all monasteries in Mongolia opens to the south, there are two small doors in the east and west walls opening into the second courtyard. I enter the door in the west wall. The grounds are again deserted except for big flocks of pigeons. These are obviously a nuisance. The temples are whitewashed with their droppings, and chicken wire has been draped over the elaborately carved wooden decorations under the eaves of the temple roofs to keep them from nesting there. I head back to the third courtyard for a closer look at the temple which supposedly houses Zanabazar's remains. Pozdneev reports that in the 1890s services were held over the remains of the first and the fourth Bogd Gegens each day at five in the morning and again between eight and nine in the evening. "To officiate at these services," he adds, "five distinguished and most honored lamas are appointed in turn, whereas all the other more humble inhabitants of the monastery do not even have the right to approach these holy objects and must confine themselves to worshipping before the door of the temple in which they are."[8] It is now 8:30 P.M., so a hundred years ago one of these services would have been in progress right now. At the moment there is only a preternatural silence. Even the pigeons have ceasing cooing. Amarbayasgalant was believed to have two guardian spirits: one, Lha-ma, protected the monastery itself; and the other, Jamsaran, safeguarded the first Bogd Gegen. Are they still hovering in the silence, or have they, like the crowds that once assembled here, long since departed?

Next to the Ikh Khüree (Great Monastery) in what is now Ulaan Baatar, Amarbayasgalant was once probably the greatest pilgrimage site in Mongolia. Pozdneev relates that in 1892, "There were Mongols here from every Khalkha aimag without exception."[9] Most of the subsequent Bogd Gegens also made pilgrimages here. In 1797 the fourth Bogd Gegen—known as the "Terrible Fourth" because of his ferocious devotion to his duties and his rages of temper at the less vigilant among his followers—visited here and was immediately disgruntled by the small number of sacred books he found. He ordered the lamas to start copying out new facsimiles at once. He also had the tomb of the first Bogd Gegen opened and ordered that the finest available painter make a portrait from the mummified remains. Whether or not the so-called self-portrait of Zanabazar now found in the Zanabazar Fine Arts Museum is in fact this painting continues to perplex art historians. In 1798 the fourth Bogd Gegen also ordered up statues of Zanabazar using the portrait as a model. It's also unclear if any of these are the three or more statues of Zanabazar now found in Ulaan Baatar museums. In 1813 the fourth Bogd Gegen, aged thirty-eight, died of pneumonia while on a pilgrimage to Wu-t'ai-shan in China, the same mountain which Zanabazar and Kang Hsi had visited. In 1816 his remains were transferred here to Amarbayasgalant, where they still resided in Pozdneev's day. And now, according to the young lama we had talked to the day before, they are probably gone.

Not all of the subsequent Bogd Gegens lived up to the high standards set by Zanabazar and the Terrible Fourth. The notoriously profligate seventh Bogd Gegen, known for his drinking bouts and frolics with prostitutes, both male and female, visited the monastery in 1867. He stayed for two months, apparently using this opportunity to engage in bacchanalian revelries far from the eyes of monastic and civil authorities in Ikh Khüree. The eighth and last Bogd Gegen came to the monastery in 1889 on an official trip sanctioned by the Manchu Emperor. Apart from performing his religious duties, he too apparently found time for indulging his legendarily catholic appetites. He had such an enjoyable interlude that he returned twice the following year, in 1890, both times without the permission of the Manchu government, which was strictly against the rules. According to Pozdneev, who visited two years later and picked up the story from scandalized locals, "[the Bogd Gegen] was surrounded by six or seven young lamas who . . . were distinguished only by their inclination and ability to carouse."[10]

There would be little carousing tonight. It was dark when I let myself out of the side door of the empty, silent monastery. Back at the shack Shandas's mother was already sacked out. Shandas was in his bunk reading month-old newspapers someone had left behind. Only our driver had gone out to see what diversions might be available in the nearby gers and cabins. I went straight to bed.

Next morning the sun rises over the ridges to the left of Amarbayasgalant at exactly 6:53. I had sneaked out of our quarters at the first hint of light and climbed to a conspicuous ovoo on the top of a high barren hill behind the monastery. To the southeast stretches the wide verdant valley of the Iben River. Directly below, in front of the rectangular monastery complex, the Iben river doglegs to the north-northwest before disappearing among encroaching ridges decked with larch. Directly behind me looms Mount Bürün-Khaan, forested nearly to its top. Yung Cheng's geomancers had picked well; it's a vista which seems to inspire meditations. I sit for an hour, until the last shadows fade from the valley, then slowly walk back down to my quarters. Shandas and his mother have tea ready—our driver is still asleep in the back seat of his jeep—and while we're breakfasting a young man appears and informs us that man who supposedly knows everything about the monastery has agreed to meet us at 10:00.

This man does appear at ten sharp. Over six feet tall, lean, with finely chiseled facial features and close-cropped hair showing a hint of gray, he has a look and bearing which can only be described as aristocratic. He listens to Shandas intently and answers in what even I can tell are carefully chosen, well-modulated words. He would have come to see us last night, he says, but he had glued some leather together for a new saddle and couldn't leave until the glue had set. He says that he himself had once been a lama but had since rejoined the secular world. Given his age he would have had to have been a lama during the communist era, but when I try to question him about this he merely shrugs and suggests we go look at the monastery.

There were from two thousand to three thousand lamas here at Amarbayasgalant during its peak years, he relates as we walk over to the main gate, and perhaps forty temples in all, counting the ones outside the main compound which were later destroyed. That was just the main monastery. In the Iben Valley downstream from here, there were over two hundred additional temples representing all four provinces of old Mongolia—the aimags of the Tüsheet, Zasagt, Setsen, and Sain-Noyon khans—and served by perhaps eight thousand or more lamas. Why, I wondered, did this relatively remote corner of Mongolia become such an important religious center? What differentiated it from any number of other propitious sites around the country? Choijiljav says that of course the remains of the first Bogd Gegen were kept here, but I interrupt and ask why then did the Manchus pick this spot to keep his remains? Why not somewhere closer to China, instead of here, less than a hundred miles from the Russian border? With pursed lips Choijiljav considers this question for a while. "We only know that in the 1720s this was thought to be an auspicious location. Why it was thought to be so we can't say today," he finally allows.

He does know what happened in 1937 however. One day seventeen large army trucks manned by both Mongolian and Soviet Russian troops pulled up in front of the monastery. The soldiers ransacked the temples and hauled away seventeen truckloads of rare books and scriptures, thangkas, statues, and other artwork. They were taken behind the mountains to the right of the monastery and burnt in a huge bonfire. For days huge plumes of black smoke roiled from the fire. Some lamas and local people had been expecting the arrival of the troops and had hidden away some of the more valuable books and statues but the vast majority were lost. In the settlement there is an old lama, now eighty-two years old, who witnessed the destruction of the monastery, reports Choijiljav. Normally it would have been possible to talk to this man, but he has been very sick for the last ten days and it's uncertain when, or indeed if, he will get better.

Either during the first attack on the monastery or sometime shortly thereafter, says Choijiljav, the remains of the first and fourth Bogd Gegens were taken away and presumably burnt. Wait a minute, I say, a lama we talked to yesterday said that he thought the remains of Zanabazar were still in his temple. "Oh, that guy," says Choijiljav, "he is Zanabazar's grandson and he doesn't . . ." Interrupting Shandas's translation I blurt out, "Zanabazar's grandson?! I didn't know Zanabazar had children, and if he did how could this be his grandson? Zanabazar died in 1723!" Choijiljav and Shandas have a lengthy side-bar. "Well, you know," says Shandas finally, "not just grandson, but, how do you say, great, many greats, grandson?" Is Choijiljav saying that the young lama is an actual descendant of Zanabazar? I pressed. Choijiljav is indeed saying this. Also, this young man's father lives in Ulaan Baatar and works at the Ulaan Baatar Hotel. It's fairly common knowledge that he is a descendant of Zanabazar. I had never read anything about Zanabazar having children, although of course this is something which the largely hagiographic accounts of his life would have chosen to omit. Theoretically, the Bogd Gegen was not supposed to be married, let alone siring children. So, I wondered further, was his consort, the one who reputedly died as a young woman, the mother of Zanabazar's child? "We know very little about this person, not even her name," says Choijiljav, "she is known only as the Girl Prince. One story is that the

Manchus did not approve of her relationship with the first Bogd Gegen and had her killed, but we don't know for sure. But we think Zanabazar's White and Green Taras, which you might have seen, are modeled after her. When she died she was cremated and her ashes were mixed in ink used to make sacred books. These books were once kept here at Amarbayasgalant, but it's not clear what happened to them. Perhaps they were destroyed, perhaps not."

At the main monastery gate we stop for a moment beneath the plaque which announces "The Monastery of Amarbayasgalant, Built at Imperial Command." I say that I am bit surprised that this rather obvious symbol of Mongolia's subjugation by an "imperial" power survived the wrath of the communists. It didn't, according to Choijiljav. It is a finely executed replica based on old photos. That raises the question of why any of Amarbayasgalant survived. Hundreds of monasteries had been razed to the ground with hardly a stone remaining–for instance, the Ilagukan Monastery in the Ider Valley, whose barely discernible traces I had stumbled across earlier. "We're not sure why," says Choijiljav. "As you know, a few places like the Choijin Lama Monastery and the Winter Palace and its temples in Ulaan Baatar were not destroyed. Perhaps they were considered historical or architectural monuments. It's hard to know what was going in people's minds in the 1930s. They were strange times."

Restoration of the monastery began in 1990. In addition to funds from the United Nations a wealthy Tibetan now living in the United States has reportedly made large contributions. At least the exteriors of all the temples described by Pozdneev in 1892 have been refurbished. A workshop has been set up to make roofing tiles from the local clay which had been used originally, but no one has succeeded in duplicating the glazing process employed by the Chinese workmen who were brought here back in the 1720s and '30s. Choijiljav finds a chunk of one of the original tiles and holds it up for our inspection. For once he is less than totally lucid–or perhaps Shandas's translation is not up to the task–but from what I gather these are the so-called two-color tiles which were a unique feature of Amarbayasgalant. Up close they appear a lustrous olive green, but if held at a certain angle, an underglaze of bright yellow can be seen. Thus the roofs of the monastery buildings usually appeared green but at certain times during the day they glowed a brilliant yellow so incandescent that it frightened horses. People approaching the monastery at these times had to blindfold their mounts and walk them up the last mile or so. Choijiljav then holds up one of the new replica tiles and turns it in his hands. It is a dull green with no hint of yellow, clearly a product of a more prosaic age.

We continue on to the main temple, where a service is now in progress. At present there are only about twenty-five lamas at the monastery. A large contingent of those usually in residence is currently making a lengthy pilgrimage in Switzerland, which has apparently become a redoubt of Tibetan Buddhism. The lama we had met the day before, the reputed descendant of Zanabazar, is sitting in a row of chanting lamas. In truth, he looks rather undistinguished. As if reading my mind Choijiljav says, "The lamas had big hopes for him, but unfortunately he is not so . . . ah, clever. It will do you no good to talk to him further."

We pay one last visit to Zanabazar's now empty temple. I have not found his body as expected, but strangely enough I seem to have found one of his earthly descendants, perhaps the fruit of his relationship with the mysterious Girl Prince who became enshrined forever as the White Tara.

Choijiljav says he is sorry, but he must get back to work on his saddle. He walks back with us to the shack where Batbayar is champing at the bit. He wants to get back to Erdenet by early evening. The jeep is loaded up and ready to go. Choijiljav waves to us as we drive away. Shandas's mother says, "So, now I have finally met the famous Choijiljav. You know, he is a well-known artist. For a long time he worked as a pattern designer at the carpet factory in Erdenet. His designs have won several national awards. It's true he was once a lama, but I hear that now he is married. They say he even has children. He's quite a guy."

Shireet Tsagaan Nuur

UPON RETURNING FROM Amarbayasgalant, the final resting place of Zanabazar, I was even more determined to visit his birthplace at Yesön Züil and other places connected with his life. Yesön Züil, I was told, was a fairly well-known place in Övörkhangai aimag. I simply had to take the road from Ulaan Baatar to Arvaikheer, the capital of Övörkhangai aimag, and near Sangiyn Dalai Nuur turn east to the village of Ölziit, then head north to the village of Züil. Locals could then direct me to the small monastery which marks the spot where Zanabazar was born. Nothing could be easier. I also wanted to visit a place called Shireet Tsagaan Nuur, a small lake where, at the age of four, Zanabazar was enthroned as the first Bogd Gegen of Mongolia. Shireet Tsagaan Nuur, I soon discovered, was one of those places, not uncommon in Mongolia, which everyone has heard of but whose actual location nobody seems to know. A standard reference book to Mongolia says it is located in Lün sum of Arkhangai aimag. The Mongolian head of a well-known tourism company assured me it was only a stone's throw from the famous Orkhon waterfall in the upper Orkhon Valley, in Övörkhangai aimag, but when I tried to hire a jeep to go there I was politely but with some celerity shooed out of his office. Still another Mongolian man, one usually quite knowledgeable about landmarks and historical sights, opined that it was "not far" from the well-known tourist attraction of Kharkhorum in Övörkhangai aimag. I should go to Kharkhorum and ask directions from there.

I finally decide to hire a translator and a driver with a Russian jeep and simply head in the general direction of Yesön Züil. Somewhere along the way, I hope, someone can direct us to Shireet Tsagaan Nuur. We leave my hotel at nine in the morning and head west on the road to Arvaikheer, the capital of Övörkhangai. The jeep driver, a heavyset man in his thirties named Tumur, came recommended as very capable at finding his way around the countryside. If anyone could find Shireet Tsagaan Nuur it was Tumur, I was told. My translator, Badmaa, a thin, short-haired pixieish woman in her late twenties, has made a few inquiries on her own and she seems to think Shireet Tsagaan Nuur is somewhere near the so-called Mongol Els (*els* = sand dunes) which we will pass through not long after leaving Töv aimag. This information jars something loose in Tumur's thickly thatched head. "Now I know where Shireet Tsagaan Nuur is," he announces. "It's near some old monastery ruins I once visited at Khögnö Khan Mountain, near the Mongol Els. We'll find it. No problem."

We careen westward through steppes dotted with dozens of togoruu (demoiselle cranes) and after an hour and a half or so cross the Tuul River at Lün. Cutting off on a road to the southwest we drive for another hour and a half to Erdenesat, a tiny town backed by dog-toothed ridges where we refuel our jeep. Beyond Erdenesat stark ridges rise to the north, and soon the steppe is pierced by numerous fang-like granite tors, some a hundred feet or more in height. Farther on an immense massif of granite looms to the north. According to Tumur this is Khögnö Khan Uul, and just to the west of this mountain begins the Mongol Els. A man on horseback says he has no idea where Shireet Tsagaan Nuur is but advises us to go to a ger camp a couple a miles north of the main road, on the edge of the Mongol Els, and ask directions. The Mongol Els, which soon appears directly in front of us, is a two-to-five-mile wide belt of sand dunes running north-south for about fifty miles. We turn off on a dirt road north to the ger camp, which is run by a Mongolian-owned tourist company in Ulaan Baatar. Business is slow. There's one van in the parking lot but the huddle of guest gers and the building which serves as a dining hall seem deserted. Finally a slovenly looking, slightly drunk man appears out of a ger. He's the ger camp manager, and he doesn't know anything about Shireet Tsagaan Nuur. A man who lives nearby, apparently attracted by our arrival, rides up on horseback. His deel is little more than an assemblage of loosely connected rags, but he has an American filter cigarette screwed into the corner of his mouth. Tumur asks him about the monastery ruins in the Khögnö Khan Uul and whether they are close to Shireet Tsagaan Nuur. He knows about the monastery. He says it was razed by Galdan and the Jungarian Mongols a long time ago.

I have related earlier how in the spring of 1688 Galdan's armies invaded Khalkha Mongolia, advancing eastward along the northern side of the Khangai Mountains. In April they trashed the monastery of Erdene Zuu at Kharkhorum, then proceeded to the valley of the Tuul, apparently looting this monastery on their way. But the monastery ruins are in the Khögnö Khan Uul to the north of here, says this man, and Shireet Tsagaan Nuur is about thirty or so miles to the south. He asks for my pen and proceeds to carefully draw out a sketch map on the back of my Mongolian aimag map. "You have to find Ikh Mongol Uul first," he repeats a couple of times, "Shireet Tsagaan Nuur is not far away." Ikh Mongol Uul is a well-known mountain, he says, and people along the way can give us further directions. We ask the manager if there is any chance of us getting lunch here. There isn't. He tells us to go to the Bayan Gobi ger camp, also on the edge of the Mongol Els, a few miles south of the main road.

The Bayan Gobi ger camp, thirty or more sleeping gers circled around a huge ger which serves as a dining and assembly hall, is located on the edge of the steppe right next to some big sand dunes. A Mongolian man tells us that a large tour group from Japan is currently in residence but that we are welcome to buy lunch in the dining room. Various forms of amusement are in progress in front of the camp. Frail crotchety oldsters and giggling girls alike are hoisted onto horses which are then led by Mongolian boys to a tree a hundred yards away and back. Another group of people snap photos of each other with wolf and fox skins draped over their shoulders. A metal "Mongolian warrior's helmet" surmounted with cow horns is modeled by several people. Other small groups stand around looking faintly bewildered. We duck into the huge dining ger where techno-pop is booming over the intercom system. Bread, mutton soup, cabbage salad, and stewed beef and noodles cost an outrageous six dollars a head—much more than such a meal would have cost in the capital.

Badmaa says this ger camp—Bayan Gobi (Rich Gobi)—is fairly well known. The big selling point here is that just a few hours drive from Ulaan Baatar by tour bus one can experience four different types of terrain—sand dunes, steppe, mountains, and forest (the mountains to the south have thick stands of birch and larch)—all within a few miles of the ger camp. The sand dunes really aren't the Gobi, of course, but as Badmaa points out they look more like what most people think the Gobi looks like than most of the Gobi itself, and if you have a picture of yourself standing among them who's to say you actually haven't been to the Gobi?

Back outside Tumur chats up some of the local guys loitering around the gate of the ger camp. "There is Ikh Mongol Uul," one says, pointing to the pyramid-shaped mountain about ten miles away to the south. "Shireet Tsagaan Nuur is just on the other side of it." According to our first set of directions, however, the mountain should still be over twenty-five miles away. Anyhow, the guy tells us to take a trail from here across the dunes instead of going back to the main road. Then just follow the edge of the dunes south. We'll soon find Shireet Tsagaan Nuur, no problem.

The dune belt here is about four miles wide and some of the dunes are thirty to forty feet high. We follow a faint trail which threads among the ridges of sand and soon get bogged down. Tumur puts the lugs in the front wheels and we go on in four-wheel drive. Emerging abruptly back on the hard grassy steppe we pick up a faint jeep trail and head south. Soon we pull up even with the big pyramid-shaped mountain. If the man at the second ger camp was correct we should be near Shireet Tsagaan Nuur. Five men on horseback approach and we ask directions. One laughs when we ask if the pyramid-shaped mountain is Ikh Mongol Uul. No, no, he says, that mountain is Bat Khaan Uul. Ikh Mongol Uul is farther south. Bat Khaan Uul is actually on my Mongolian map.

Centered around it is the eighty-five square-mile Bat Khaan Uul Natural Reserve, created to safeguard the four differing habitats–steppe, desert, mountains, and forests–found here so close together. Half a dozen more times we pull up to gers or stop passing horsemen and ask about Ikh Mongol Uul. Some point to the east, most to the south. We head south on a faint jeep trail, twice fording the Tarnayn River, which runs north-south parallel to the Mongol Els, and finally come to a sizable river flowing out of the east. This is apparently the Jargalant River, a tributary of the Tarnayn. The Mongol Els and a row of mountains which we believe includes Ikh Mongol Uul are on the other side. The river flows between four to five-foot-high banks and we have to drive several miles along its banks before finding a ford where we can safely cross.

About a mile away we can see four gers and we head straight for these. We're greeted by three huge black baying dogs. A man comes out and calling them off invites us in. His wife is inside and half a dozen people from the neighboring gers soon appear. The mare milking season is in full swing and we must drink some *airag*–mare's milk. Unfortunately a trader from Ulaan Baatar has come through just before us and bought thirty liters of his best stuff, so there's only a little left in a big leather bag by the door. He fills up a wooden bowl and hands it to Tumur, who after politely blowing a dead fly or two floating on the surface to the far side of the bowl takes a big sip. The bowl is handed back, filled up and given back to Tumur. This time he drains it. The same procedure is followed with Badmaa and me. The man asks if I have ever drunk airag before. I say that I had some already this year in Zavkhan aimag. This elicits a snort of derision. The grass in Zavkhan is poor and the mares there produce thin milk, he says; furthermore, the people in Zavkhan are lazy and they don't beat the airag enough, so it's usually of poor quality. The airag of Övörkhangai is the best in Mongolia, he claims. Finally we go outside and the man points to a mountain about five miles away. That is Ikh Mongol Uul, he says. Shireet Tsagaan Nuur is just at its southern foot. There's a jeep trail across the sand dunes to the site, which is marked by a large white stupa, but it is hard to find. He would take us there himself but he has business to attend to. The river flowing close by his ger, he says in response to my question, is the Dongod, not the Jargalant, although my map shows no other rivers in this area besides the Tarnayn and the Jargalant.

Driving on, we soon find ourselves separated from the mountain by a mile-and-a-half-wide belt of sand dunes. We continue along of the edge of the sandy ridges for a mile or so but fail to see any track through them. Hoping to get a better view I get out and hike a quarter of a mile to a high hillock. All I can see to the north and south are barren dunes and hummocks covered with patchy sod and low brush. The dunes appear to swing around to the south of Ikh Mongol Uul but even with my binoculars I can see no trace of a small lake or a white stupa. Tumur is convinced the track through the dunes is farther south. We drive four or five miles in that direction until Ikh Mongol Uul begins to recede in the distance. The track can't be this way, I insist; we have to turn around and go back. Soon we're back where we started and we still haven't seen a trace of any track across the dunes. I insist on continuing north and Tumur reluctantly drives on, while maintaining that according to the instructions given by the man at the ger the track has to be to the south. Badmaa is translating our argument back and forth when suddenly she stops and pointing to the right says, "There is a jeep track going toward Ikh Mongol Uul." Indeed, a faint track which may have been made by only a single vehicle heads off to the west and disappears around a brush-covered hillock. But someone has gone this way, so more to stop our argument than anything else Tumur turns off and follows the path. After going over a sandy ridge where we almost bog down, the trail drops into a sod-covered crease which seems to run westward through the dunes. Here there is a definite jeep track. Continuing on for fifteen minutes we top a small ridge and there, about a mile away, on a grassy slope below the southern flank of Ikh Mongol Uul, we see a white stupa. Dropping down a steep sandy bank we find ourselves in a steppe-covered basin perhaps a half-mile in diameter and surrounded on three sides by hills covered with dunes and grassy hummocks. In the bottom of the basin is Shireet Tsagaan Nuur, or what is left of it. Once this lake covered several acres—its old shoreline can clearly be seen and the old lake bottom is covered with grass much greener than the surrounding steppe—but now it is little more than two puddles each about fifty feet in diameter. To the north of the old lake bottom a long steppe-covered slope rises to the rocky flanks of Ikh Mongol Uul. Halfway up this slope is the white stupa that marks the spot where in 1639 Zanabazar was proclaimed the first Bogd Gegen of Mongolia.

Zanabazar was born about fifty miles southwest of here at Yesön Züil, which of course I hoped was going to be my next stop. He was the middle son of Gombodorj, the Tüsheet khan, who claimed to be a descendant of Chingis Khan, and Khandu-jamstso, also known as Queen Khandjav. According to his biographers Zanabazar impressed people from the moment of his birth, which itself was announced by various auspicious portents and omens. When the little boy was little more than a year old his parents were visited by the Gegen-Setsen Khan, one of the other two khans who ruled Khalkha Mongolia. The Khan was dandling the boy on his knee when, according to Zanabazar's biography, three spiritual beings known as *acarya* suddenly appeared before them in the ger. Little Zanabazar stretched out his arms toward these beings and seemed to be trying to talk to them. It was decided that these were spiritual entities from India that he had known in a previous lifetime. The Gegen-Setsen Khan, awed by this incident, then decided to give the baby his own honorific of Gegen (illuminated one) and henceforth went by the name of Setsen Khan only. When he returned home he sent an expert on portents to further examine Zanabazar. This individual reported that "the new born son [of Tüsheet Khan] is in truth a darling child; the oblong quality of the corners of his eyes and the unusual regularity in the texture of the pupil and white of his eyes attest to the fact that he is able to contemplate all the ten lands of the earth; as for his body, there are combined in it all the signs of the Buddhas, and that is why one may consider beyond any doubt that he is a real Buddha."[11]

When Zanabazar began to talk supposedly the first words he spoke were the Tibetan versions of Lamaist prayers. He eschewed the company of similar-aged playmates and spent his time performing services, making offerings, and fashioning pictures of lamas and burkhans (Buddhist idols)—a foretaste of his future accomplishments as an artist. His father concluded that the boy was obviously destined for a religious life, and in 1638, when he was three, Zanabazar took his first monastic vows from the lama Jambaling and received his first monastic name–Jnanavajra. The next year it was decided to establish a monastery for him at a place called Tsagaan Nuur, which was renamed Shireet Tsagaan Nuur.

Khans and princes from all over Khalka Mongolia assembled here with their followers and recognized Zanabazar as the head of the Sakhya sect of Buddhism for all of Mongolia. With this position came another name, Lobsang Dambi Jantsen–meaning roughly, "religious flag of good omen"–and a title, *sumati-sakya-dodza*–"one who holds the sakhya banner of the great mind." The khans in attendance presented the little Bogd Gegen with a ger temple which, because it was encircled with yellow cloth, became known as the Shar Bösiyn Ord, or "yellow cotton place." It was supposedly located on this flat spot on the hillside where the stupa now stands. This ger temple was the beginning of the traveling monastery which would change locations for the next 139 years before settling down permanently in 1778 at the confluence of the Tuul and Selbi rivers, the future site of Ulaan Baatar.

Tumur and Badmaa drive down to the old edge of lake where there is some brush and small trees. Here they make a fire for tea. I sit in front of the stupa and contemplate the scene. Why, of all the possible places in Mongolia, I wonder, did the khans decide to meet in this out-of-the-way spot to proclaim Zanabazar the first Bogd Gegen of Mongolia? It's true Shireet Tsagaan Nuur was known as the khüis–"navel"–of Mongolia and was thought to be very near the geographic center of the domains of the Khalkha Mongols; indeed, the geographical center of the current country of Mongolia is just twenty-five miles southwest of here. It's also true that the lake, larger than now, would have been a handy source of water for a large gathering and its level shores a convenient place to set up gers, and that the hills on three sides of the basin would have created a dramatic amphitheater-like setting for the Bogd Gegen's ger temple, with the massif of Ikh Mongol Uul as an imposing backdrop. But surely these criteria could have been met elsewhere, somewhere nearer what were then the already established centers of Lamaism such as the monastery of Erdene Zuu, and not here at this place which to this very day remains an out-of-the-way, hard-to-find cranny of the country. Not for the first time this summer, I wonder if these places imbued with a special significance—Tsagaan Lake near the source of the Ider is another example—were a part of a spiritual rather than physical geography and were chosen for reasons that are simply not apparent to the five senses of the casual viewer. Was there some vortex of energy, usually imperceptible to most people, that not only drew people here to this spot to consecrate Zanabazar but perhaps even in some way empowered the young Bogd Gegen?

The beeping of the jeep horn interrupts these ruminations. Tumur says it's best we leave if we want to get out of here before dark. I suggest we camp here for the night. I would like to visit the stupa again at sunrise. Tumur and Badmaa don't seem thrilled by this idea, but we're going to have to camp somewhere so it might as well be here. There's one problem: we unwisely started across the dunes with only two quarts of drinking water. While there may have been a sizable lake here in Zanabazar's day the water in the two small puddles which now constitute Shireet Tsagaan Nuur is muddy and reeking of rotting vegetation. Also, there is a serious infestation of gnats which appears as the winds die down toward dusk. Tumur builds a smudge fire of cow dung upwind of our camp fire to drive off the bugs and we settle down to a picnic dinner of sausage, cheese, bread, cucumbers and tomatoes, and rationed tea. Later, during the night, I awaken in my tent to the hard drumming of rain which continues for over two hours. I can't help thinking about the steep sandy hills we dropped down to get into this basin. Will the jeep be able to get back up the now wet trail, or will we be spending more time at Shireet Tsagaan Nuur than we planned?

The rains have ceased but a thick fog is hunkered down in the basin when I awaken the next morning. Ikh Mongol Uul is completely enshrouded and the stupa part way up the slope can just barely be seen. I walk up to the shrine anyhow and circumambulate it three times, then sit down here where the little four-year-old Zanabazar himself once sat in his ger temple, surrounded by the khans of Mongolia who had just named him the Bogd Gegen.

Not everyone agrees with the version of Zanabazar's elevation to Bogd Gegen which is given in his biography. ". . . It is quite obvious that these miraculous happenings," says one well-known historian of Mongolia of the events surrounding Zanabazar's early life, "are only clichés, adduced retrospectively to enhance the splendor of the saintly infant and to account for his recognition."[12] Of course it is quite easy today to dismiss the portents and omens which accompanied Zanabazar's birth, the appearance of spiritual entities from India, the soothsayer's prognostications that the little boy possessed the signs of a Buddha, etcetera, as just so much mumble-jumble and folderol, and present instead what might be termed a secular history of the Bogd Gegen dealing only with the political realities of seventeenth-century Mongolia as interpreted by late-twentieth-century historians. According to this viewpoint Zanabazar's father, the Tüsheet Khan Gombodorj, alarmed at the state of disarray into which the Mongol people had fallen and convinced that no one khan could unite them on a secular level, hoped to create a figure similar to the Dalai Lama of Tibet who could rise above mere political partisanship and on the elevated plane of religion become a leader around whom all could rally. If this figure was a Mongolian he would also provide a useful counterweight to the power of the Dalai Lama himself, who may have been conniving with the Manchus to create a pan-Asiatic lamaist theocracy in which Mongolia would play a subordinate rule. Was this really fair, since it was the Mongolian Altan Khan who had given the Tibetan religious leader his exalted title of Dalai Lama in the first place? Taking all this into consideration, Gombodorj may have decided to engender such a figure himself, and who better to fill the role than his own son? There is little doubt that such considerations went into the creation of the first Bogd Gegen. There's something lacking in this interpretation, however. Given the fallibility of human clay, the chances were great that the son whom Gombodorj chose for this office would turn out to possess merely average capabilities and would have had to have been tucked away in a monastery somewhere to serve as a figurehead while regents or advisors to the powers-that-be actually ruled in his stead. This is not what happened. Zanabazar is a name which resonates down to the present day, and to account for this we have to admit the possibility of the miraculous. Could Gombodorj himself had imagined, when his little son was sitting on this spot, that the boy would later became the most influential personage in the Mongol world?

Finally Tumur, who like most jeep drivers prefers to sleep in his vehicle, appears and struggles with wet wood to get a fire going. When he finally has tea ready I walk back down the hill for breakfast. The fog shows no sign of lifting and the sodden skies seem poised to unleash another deluge at any moment. After a skimpy repast and a cup of tea each we decide to decamp. With our front wheels engaged we head up the steep sandy hills out of the basin, slipping and sliding for a while, but finally finding purchase on the wet sand, which having been pounded down by the rain actually seems more stable than when dry. We barrel through the sand dunes and fifteen minutes later emerge out on the hard steppe of the river bottom. Stopping again at the same ger which we visited on the way in, we drink more airag and ask directions to Yesön Züil, the birthplace of Zanabazar.

Yesön Züil

THE FOG AND clouds of early morning have dissipated completely by the time we recross the Dongod, or the Jargalant, or whatever river it is, and under a vault of immaculate blue sky we follow a faint track which according to our informants leads to the sum center of Bürd about twenty miles to the southwest. We soon find ourselves in a broad basin with a maze of jeep tracks going in all directions. Several of the more well-traveled paths which we follow soon head off in the wrong direction and we end up bearing southwest across the trackless steppe. For ten or fifteen miles we don't see any gers where we can ask directions, even though the grass here is quite plentiful and we cross several tiny streams which could provide water for people and livestock. Finally we happen upon a good dirt road which takes us into the tiny village of Bürd.

According to the man at the gas station in Bürd the geographical center of Mongolia is about eight miles to the south of here. In the early 1990s local people built a big stupa on the site and now Mongolians on countryside excursions and the odd van of tourists show up here looking for it. They reach Bürd from the main road between Ulaan Baatar and Arvaikheer, however, and not the way we have come. Tumur assumes of course that I will have to visit this place and starts asking directions. I tell him to forget it. I am not interested in contemporary monuments and don't want to get sidetracked on my way to Yesön Züil. The gas guy points out the road to the sum center of Züil and advises us to ask for further direction to Yesön Züil from there.

Again we head off to the southwest. After crossing some ridges outside of Bürd we enter a vast tableland. It's perhaps fitting that here, near the geographical center of the country, the countryside resembles what I, and I suppose many other people, have in mind when we think of the great steppes of Mongolia, an impression which in my case was garnered from descriptions and photographs in books consumed when I was a school boy. There are no mountains or ridges on the horizon. The gently undulating hills, mantled with short but verdant grass, roll on for miles in all directions before dropping off beyond the curvature of the earth. White gers sprout up like mushrooms, flocks of sheep flow over the wavy hills like a single living creature, and herds of chestnut, ginger, gray, white, and black horses speckle the green sward. By the gers along our track are tied strings of twenty or more mares being milked by women in brightly colored deels. Tumur allows that this is prime airag country, and we stop half a dozen times at gers where we are always welcomed in and given as much airag to drink as we like for free. This hospitality is the unalterable rule of the countryside. Badmaa, who gives me a lengthy–for her–dissertation on the health benefits of airag, polishes off at least a pint at every stop, as does Tumur, but I am a bit more constrained. Airag has unpredictable consequences on the digestive tracts of many visitors to Mongolia and I don't want to overindulge. (As it turned out, I never had any ill effects from airag.)

Eventually some ridges do appear to the southwest. Nestled among them is a small huddle of cabins, shacks and gers. This is the sum center of Züil. In front of the largest building, which appears to be a sort of community center, are half a dozen men and women making felts. Beside them are big piles of crude wool which they are pounding into a thin felt stretched out on the ground. When the felt is thick enough it will be used to line gers. We ask for directions to Yesön Züil but the guy who seems to be in charge, apparently welcoming a diversion, has to slowly load and light his pipe and ask all the standard questions–where are we coming from; how many days have we been traveling; where did we spend last night; how do we find the airag; where is the foreigner from and what is he doing here? etc.–before proffering that to get to Yesön Züil, which is about thirty miles away; we should take the only road out of town to the south but that this road forks many times and we'd best stop and ask for more directions every chance we get.

For the first three or four miles this is a perfectly good dirt road. Then, as the man had noted, it starts branching off until finally there is no track at all and again we are driving cross-country. We also seem to be climbing ever-higher into some fairly lofty mountains. After wending our way among boulders up one particularly steep slope we find ourselves on a high pass with spectacular views for thirty or more miles in all directions. Off to the west is a high peak, which if I am reading my Mongolian map correctly–by no means a certain assumption–is 7,874-foot Züün Khairkhan Uul, the highest summit in this small range of mountains. Dropping down from this pass we find ourselves amid barren, desiccated desert-like ridges. There is not a trace of a trail or any gers or livestock in sight. Tumur is becoming more and more perplexed. It would be very easy to spend a day, or even a couple of days, in this country futilely driving up dead-end valleys. We skid and spin up over loose, slaty rock to a high summit in an attempt to see a way out of this jumble of ridges, but even from this vantage point we appear hemmed in on all sides.

Finally topping yet another ridge we espy two lone gers by the base of some high cliffs. There are no horses by the gers and no livestock visible anywhere nearby, but as we approach an immense black dog, bigger than the average St. Bernard and with a head the size of a beer keg, bounds out to meet us. This beast actually tries to bite the front tires of our truck, then jumps up at the front window and with long streams of saliva dripping from its jaws, barks ferociously at Tumur. Presently, two men, perhaps in their sixties, with shaved heads and dressed in tattered deels, come out of one of the gers and yell at the dog. Five kids tumble out of the other ger and grabbing the dog by the collar pull it aside and force it to lie down. Then all of them actually sit on the dog's front quarters, holding it down on the ground. From the safety of the jeep Tumur yells that we need directions to Yesön Züil. One of the men motions to us to get out and we hesitantly make our way to the ger. The dog barks venomously and tries to get up on its front legs but the kids pull it back down. In the ger an elderly woman and two young girls sit on the bed to the right and stare at us wide-eyed. I get the impression they don't see a lot of visitors here in this isolated nook. There's a big leather bag of airag by the doorway and the taller of the old men offers us some in a wooden bowl. It is cool and creamy, sour and sweet at the same time–to my taste the best we've had yet. All the horses, one of the men explains, are out at pasture and the young men of the encampment are looking after them.

Of course they wonder what has brought us here. By now Badmaa has her story down pat. I am an American who is interested in the life of Zanabazar. Earlier I had been to Amarbayasgalant Monastery, where the body of Zanabazar had been kept, and just last night we had camped at Shireet Tsagaan Nuur, where Zanabazar was named the first Bogd Gegen. Now we are looking for the place where Zanabazar was born but seem to have strayed off the beaten path. If any of these people think it odd that an American–I am obviously the first one any of them has met–should suddenly appear on their doorstep looking for traces of Zanabazar, none of them reveal it by word or gesture. Both of the men have been to Shireet Tsagaan Nuur and Yesön Züil themselves– though not Amarbayasgalant–and think it only natural that a foreigner, a visitor to their country, should also want to visit these places connected with the life of the great Zanabazar. Do all Americans know about Zanabazar? they wonder. No, not many, but maybe in the future more will, I reply. Both nod solemnly, as if this is a foregone conclusion. Then the shorter one roots under the bed in the back of the ger and produces a bottle of clear *arkhi*, milk vodka. The two men and Tumur and I each drink a bowl full. Soon it's time to go.

Outside the kids hold the dog down while one of the men gives directions. Head through that gap in the hills, he says, pointing to the southwest, and soon you'll come to a jeep trail which leads to a broad valley. Yesön Züil is not far down the valley. Then he wonders if we have any razors with us. Both men had just recently shaved their scalps, as they do every summer to "let their heads breathe," but their razor was dull and didn't do a good job. Indeed their bare heads are covered with nicks and scrapes. Tumur pulls out a first aid kit from under the seat and gives them a disposable razor. As an afterthought he hands the two young girls a string of safety pins. Surely even in this remote spot people must have seen safety pins before, but these two girls hold them up and examine them as if they are artifacts which have just dropped out of a passing UFO. Now it's difficult to say exactly what impression these people have gotten during our short stay, but the men must have gathered that I am some sort of pilgrim, because as we pull away in the jeep both of them put their hands together in front of their chests and bow deeply to me.

We pass through a narrow defile which soon opens into a small valley flanked by grass-covered ridges. On the slopes of these ridges are a large flock of sheep and several herds of horses which apparently belong to the people at the ger we just visited. Suddenly the hills and ridges disappear altogether and we enter a valley bottom ten or more miles wide. We pick up a good jeep track but this soon peters out to nothing and again we're driving cross-country. Off to our right, to the southwest, we see smoke and thinking that it is coming from a ger we go to ask directions. Instead we discover three men lying around a campfire of cow dung drinking tea. Nearby are three camels with saddles and seven more camels loaded with heavy packs. They tell us they are from Bayankhongor province. They had gone to Ulaan Baatar to sell wool and other commodities and then used the money to buy these camels and various supplies. Now they are on their way back to their homes in the Gobi Desert of southern Bayankhongor. They have already been traveling for ten days, covering about 200 miles, and they have another 300 miles to go. They say they aren't in any great hurry and are taking their time. They want the camels to arrive in good shape. Of course they aren't from this area but they know that Yesön Züil is not far away, maybe about ten miles to the south. Leaving them to their tea we drive on. Twenty minutes later we spot a small white building on a slight elevation to the right of the valley bottom.

This turns out to be a temple built in the early 1990s on the site of the Övgön Monastery, which was destroyed during the antireligious campaigns of the 1930s. Now all that remains of the old monastery are some jagged sections of stone wall and heaps of rubble. It was here, I had been told earlier, that Zanabazar was born in 1635. Nearby is a ger with smoke coming out of the chimney. Badmaa goes to see who is in the ger while Tumur and I rustle up some tea on a camp stove and lay out a picnic lunch. Upon returning Badmaa says that there is a very old sickly woman in the ger who was married to a lama who served here at the old Övgön Monastery. (What is with these lamas, Badmaa interjects, so many of them seem to have been married!) The woman remembers when the monastery was destroyed. She would like to talk to the foreigner and tell him about it but she doesn't feel well enough. Her granddaughter will be returning shortly and she can open up the new temple for us. And no, Zanabazar wasn't born right here at the location of this monastery. He was born nearby and her granddaughter can show us where.

The granddaughter appears while we are lunching. To welcome us she has brought a teapot full of clear arkhi. She opens up the temple but admits there isn't much to see. Inside is a plain altar with some small bronzes and a couple of *thangkas* of the kind that can be bought in tourist shops. About half a dozen lamas come here occasionally to hold services but there is no one in residence. Maybe later a real monastery will be built here, but now who knows? Outside she points to a barely visible ovoo along the creek bottom about a mile away. "That is where Zanabazar was born. You can drive there. Now I must go. I hope you find what you are looking for."

Just as we arrive at the ovoo an elderly man in a purple deel and carrying an uurga rides on up horseback. He says that there was another monastery on this spot but it too was destroyed in the 1930s. It was called the Eight Stupas Monastery because it was surrounded by eight stupas. The stone bases of at least three of the stupas can still be seen in the ground, along with the foundation stones of the main temple. People have since heaped up the broken bricks and building stones of the demolished temple into a big ovoo. Nearby are nine mineral springs which never freeze over in winter, and it is these which give the place its name (*yesön* = nine; *züil* = types, or kinds).

It was Zanabazar's great-grandfather Abudai Khan who in 1585 declared that the Tibetan form of Buddhism known as Lamaism would henceforth be the ruling religion of Khalkha Mongolia. A year later he founded the great monastery of Erdene Zuu on the site of the old Mongolian capital of Kharkhorum in the Orkhon Valley. Soon thereafter Abudai made the lengthy journey to Tibet to meet Sönam Gyatso, the third Dalai Lama. ". . . I wish to invite a good lama," Abudai told the Dalai Lama, "who will be of advantage to the faith which is revered for ever, and to install the most blessed shrines."[13] The Dalai Lama told him, "Look among all the lamas for one and invite him yourself." Attracted one day to a lama sitting by himself, Abudai Khan asked him to come to Mongolia. "At the present time I am not able to, but later I will come," replied the lama.[14] This lama was named Taranatha. A teacher who was also known as a great humorist, Taranatha had once made a joke to his students about where he would be reborn. A young Mongolian studying under him cried out, "Oh, please come to Mongolia next time!"[15] This request was fulfilled: Zanabazar was believed to be a reincarnation of Taranatha.

Abudai also wanted the Dalai Lama to come to Erdene Zuu in Mongolia. "There is a temple which I have erected on our lands," he told the Dalai Lama, "I should like to invite you and have the full inauguration performed there."[16] The Dalai Lama, however, told Abudai that he could not go back to Mongolia with him to perform the inauguration of Erdene Zuu: "Though I cannot go now, later I will meet you in your own place," he said. [17]

Abudai returned to Mongolia. A few years later, while out hunting with his retinue, he saw smoke from a campfire out on the steppe and sent his servants to investigate. Returning, they reported that they had found a strange, poor-looking man sitting by his campfire eating some thin gruel. He was dressed in a dark blue gown and seemed to be a layman but nevertheless had his hair shorn like a lama. Abudai went to meet this man and much to the astonishment of his servants bowed down in front of him. "How blessed is this khan, having offered a bow at a time when all others do not think to bow," said the strange man, and added, "This place of our meeting will be remarkable in the highest degree; put some sort of sign on it!"[18] After sharing some of his gruel with Abudai the man suddenly disappeared. Abudai came to believe that the stranger was the Dalai Lama, who as promised had come to meet him in Mongolia. Abudai ordered that an ovoo be constructed on the spot, and he named the place Yesön Züil.

Another story recounts that some fifty years later the Tüsheet Khan Gombodorj, Zanabazar's future father, was riding by this ovoo when he spotted a lama sitting nearby. Asked what he was doing there, the lama replied that he was honoring the spot with sacrifices. Then the lama suddenly disappeared and a rainbow appeared in the sky. Gombodorj considered this a good omen and indeed not long after his wife Khandu-jamstso became pregnant.

When the Gegen-Setsen Khan, like the Tüsheet Khan, one of the three rulers of Khalkha Mongolia, heard that Khandu-jamstso was with child he wrote a letter to the Gombodorj: ". . . the thought continually comes to me that through the power of the former good prayers of the kings, princes and dignitaries of the Khalkhas there will be born to you a fine boy of the golden family of Chinggis Khan, who has the majesty of heaven, and that this boy will be our leader . . ."[19]

Wishing to acclaim this happy occurrence, the Gegen-Setsen Khan came with his retinue to the camp of the Tüsheet Khan and for several days they celebrated with games, contests, and fetes. Eventually the Gegen-Setsen Khan went home. There followed, in the words of Zanabazar's biography:

> . . . a splendid time, a time when there were no periods of great heat, no droughts, no epidemics, and no sickness; there were rain and water in abundance, the forests and steppes were luxuriant with flowers, and great numbers of birds sang merrily new and beautiful songs; everyone had dreams of good omen, particularly the khan and khansha [Gombodorj and his wife], now and then dreaming of burkhans, hearing the words of the sacred writings, and a rainbow descended above them so low that it seemed as though one could grasp it in one's hand.[20]

When the time came for Gombodorj to move his family to their winter camp he again passed by the ovoo set up by his grandfather Abudai. A white dog had recently given birth to pups nearby and he considered this another auspicious sign. Deciding to establish a winter camp here he ordered that a ger be set up. As soon as it was erected a white flower sprang up in the middle of the ger, even though it was already the ninth month of the year and there was snow on the ground.

The morning of the twenty-fifth day of the month came and Khandu-jamstso suddenly felt birth pangs. A little while later a baby boy was born. He was given the name Zanabazar, a combination of the word *zana*, which is derived from a Sanskrit word meaning "knowledge" or "wisdom," and the word *bazar*, meaning "thunderbolt." Thus in English his name might be rendered "thunderbolt of wisdom."

According to the old man who has come to meet us the ovoo built from the rubble of the Eight Stupas Monastery marks the spot where Abudai built his ovoo after meeting the mysterious stranger whom he believed was the Dalai Lama. The ger in which Zanabazar was born was located, if not exactly here, then close by. I am satisfied that I have found the birthplace of Zanabazar. The little boy born here in 1635 on the steppe of this broad valley bottom would later be named the Bogd Gegen at Shireet Tsagaan Nuur; he would travel to Tibet and study with the Dalai Lama and the Panchen Lama; he would become the most revered leader in all of Khalkha Mongolia, founding many monasteries and creating great works of art; he would spend over a decade of his life in the Chinese capital of Beijing as a guest of the great Kang Hsi, emperor of the Ch'ing Dynasty, and his fame as a miracle worker would spread throughout China; he would eventually die in Beijing and the magnificent monastery of Amarbayasgalant would be built in his honor and serve as the final resting place of his remains; and in 1937 those remains would be destroyed in a bonfire by Mongolian and Soviet soldiers under the orders of a communist government goaded on by Joseph Stalin.

The story has a beginning and end, but there is a lot missing in between. In order to fill in some of the blank spaces I want to visit next the Tövkhön Monastery in the Orkhon Valley, which was Zanabazar's personal retreat and workplace where he reportedly created his famous statues, and then the great monastery of Erdene Zuu, created by Zanabazar's great-grandfather, Abudai Khan. With this in mind, Tumur announces that we should try to reach the spa resort of Khujirt on the edge of the Orkhon Valley by evening. The spring on one of the back wheels of his jeep–Badmaa insists on calling it a "bridge," as a spring is called in Russian–is going out and he thinks he can get it repaired there. There's a ger camp there where we can stay—it has hot water and showers, adds Badmaa—and we can visit the famous Khujirt hot springs. So we ask the old man on horseback for directions back to main road, which is supposedly about forty miles to the northwest. The trail is patchy out of Yesön Züil but soon we find a fairly decent dirt road and make good time to Olziit, a no-account village of perhaps a thousand. From here an even better dirt road leads to the highway between Ulaan Baatar and Arvaikheer which we had left the day before. Just before the junction with the main road, off to the left, is a small lake named Sangiyn Dalai Nuur. Badmaa relates that long ago a man tried to take a caravan of camels carrying salt across this lake in the winter time. The ice broke and the man and all the camels drowned. The salt all belonged to the government, which had a monopoly on salt at the time, and thus the lake became known as Sangiyn (state) Dalai (ocean) Nuur.

Back on the hard-topped highway we stop at a *guanz*—a tiny roadside restaurant located in a ger—and ask direction for the shortcut to Khujirt. Six miles south on the main road we cut off to the right on a jeep track we are told goes to Khujirt, about thirty miles to the northwest. This track soon turns into a passable dirt road through hard, level steppe and we cruise along at thirty or forty miles an hour. The sky, which had been perfectly clear since morning, now clouds over and we drive on through heavy showers. Suddenly the skies clear again and rainbows arc across the sky in all directions. At one point I count eight at once, most of them with both ends touching the green steppe. We drive on through the cool evening air, scoured clean by the rain and scented with the fresh smell of sage, and soon pull into the resort town of Khujirt.

Tövkhön Monastery

THE TOWN OF Khujirt, occupying a large bowl in the valley of Khujirtyn Creek, a tributary of the Orkhon River, is famous for its medicinal hot springs and attendant resort. Many Mongolians come here to take cures under the supervision of the resort's therapists or simply to relax in the hot springs with their fellow countrymen. Since the town is located on the road from the now must-see attraction of Erdene Zuu at Kharkhorin and the equally renowned Orkhon Waterfall in the upper Orkhon valley, it also attracts a lot of foreign tourists, many of whom overnight here, and so there's a fairly decent hotel and a sizable ger camp in addition to quarters at the resort itself. We check into the ger camp where indeed Tumur is already known. He has brought tourists here to the hot springs before. The gers each have four or five beds inside, electric lights, and a wood stove. Badmaa and I share a ger, and Tumur will again sleep in his jeep. The dining room, in a permanent building off to the side, is full of German tourists who have just returned from the Orkhon Waterfall. The road is very muddy from recent rains, they say, and their four vans only just made it out.

In Ulaan Baatar I had been told that the Tövkhön Monastery, the next stop on my itinerary, was "within hiking distance of the Orkhon Waterfall." It was unclear if it was possible to drive there and what actually remained of the monastery, since it was reportedly damaged during the anti-religion campaigns of the 1930s. Tumur, who had gone to see about getting his jeep fixed and ask directions, soon joins Badmaa and me over dinner and reports that the monastery is on the other side of the Orkhon River about twenty miles downstream from the waterfall and a good distance back up in the mountains. We should proceed to the bridge over the Orkhon and ask directions from there, he was told. There is a road to the monastery but no one here can say for sure if it is passable after the recent rains. Thus is it not necessary to go the whole way up the Orkhon Valley to the waterfall as I had originally thought, but having come this far, it seems positively churlish not to visit this landmark which has been memorialized on countless calendars, postcards, tourist brochures, and other ephemera to the point where it has became virtually a symbol of Mongolia. I tell Tumur we'll check out the waterfall—the road permitting—then backtrack and try to find Tövkhön Monastery.

It's raining hard the next morning, which Tumur says does not bode well for the road to the waterfall. He suggests we wait till noon to see what the weather does and in the meantime he'll try to get a new spring for his jeep. Badmaa and I stroll through the resort complex, where several hundred Mongolians of all ages are milling about. Water is fed to the bathhouses via pipes from the hot springs in a marshy area some distance away. Near the springs is a statue of a female deer and two fawns. An old man puffing away on a pipe on a nearby bench tells us that long ago a hunter named Shunkhlai shot a female deer in the leg and began to follow it, but then a big male deer ran across his path and he decided to follow it instead. The stag climbed to the top of a nearby mountain and waited for the hunter. The old man pointed to a rocky knob overlooking the town: "That is Shunkhlai Mountain, named after the hunter, and there on top is the stag." Indeed, on the summit is a statue of a male deer which I had noticed the evening before when we arrived in Khujirt. The hunter, Shunkhlai, climbed the mountain, the old man goes on, but when he got to the top the stag suddenly disappeared. Then he looked back and saw that the doe had lain down in the mud along the valley bottom. Shunkhlai decided to go after the doe, but when he approached it jumped up and ran off, the wound in its leg apparently healed. Shunkhlai noticed that the deer had been lying in the mud next to some hot springs and concluded that it was the mud and the water which had cured the wound. This was how the hot springs and their medicinal properties were discovered. The statues of the doe and the fawns by the hot springs and the stag on nearby Shunkhlai Mountain commemorate this event.

An interesting story, but having heard almost an identical tale when visiting the celebrated Shumak hot springs, on the Shumak River in the East Sayan Mountains in Siberia just north of the Mongolian border, I assume it is simply a legend commonly associated with medicinal springs. Not so, counters our informant. Shunkhlai was a real man and lived in historical times. It was he who discovered the medicinal properties of the Khujirt springs and not, as some people like to claim, Zanabazar. Hold on, I say, Zanabazar visited these springs? In fact, I had read that Zanabazar was very interested in the therapeutic properties of hot springs and had done considerable research on the subject, but I was unaware he had any connection with Khujirt. Zanabazar may have visited these springs, the old man allows, but he adamantly maintains it was Shunkhlai who discovered their medicinal properties.

The rain clouds dissipate during the morning and by noon when we leave Khujirt the stag on Shunkhlai Mountain is outlined against a deep cobalt blue sky. The road to the Orkhon Waterfall goes over some ridges due west of Khujirt and after about ten miles drops into the Orkhon Valley. The Orkhon River, the longest river totally within Mongolia, begins in the Khangai Mountains, about fifty miles west of here and flows 697 miles before conjoining with the Selenge River just south of the Mongolian border with Siberia. Here in its upper reaches the Orkhon Valley is several miles wide and flanked by wooded spurs of the Khangai Mountains. The road skirts around huge basalt flows which in places blankets the valley bottom for miles. About thirty miles from Khujirt we come to a wooden bridge across the Orkhon, here about 150 feet wide. By the bridge a man and a woman repairing a motorcycle tell us that the Tövkhön Monastery is about ten miles away, across the river and back up in the mountains. We continue on up the left side of the river. The road has apparently dried out quickly in the hot afternoon sun and there is little mud. The road does go through some nasty lava flows. Bouncing and careening over these–Tumur had been unable to get a new spring in Khujirt–we finally reach the waterfall, which in fact is thirteen miles upstream from the bridge.

In a parking lot just about the falls are about fifteen vehicles–though no tourist buses–and a half dozen tents are set up on the riverbank nearby. About a hundred yards downstream the river suddenly drops about eighty feet into a cliff-lined bowl 200 feet across and then continues on through a narrow canyon another hundred yards before joining a larger river. I assume that the stream with the falls is a side channel of the Orkhon, since all the tourist brochures and guides I have read say the falls is on the Orkhon River, but some local people lounging on the grass above the bowl say no, the river that goes over the falls is in fact the Ulaan River, a tributary of the Orkhon. The waterfall's name in Mongolian, Ulaan Tsutgalangiyn (*ulaan* = red; *tsutgalan* = waterfall), reflects this fact. Badmaa and I clamber down a steep path into the canyon bottom and hike back up into the bowl for a close-up look at the bottom of the falls, then return to the parking area where we find Tumur having dinner with a Mongolian family. A quick tour of the campground along the river reveals parties from Germany, France, and Slovakia, in addition to a half dozen groups of Mongols. I decide we too might as well spend the night here, which pleases Tumur. He has soon moved on to dinner with another group, and appetizing smells are drifting from the campfires of still others.

Tumur did indeed seem to make a lot of friends. The next morning at breakfast about a dozen Mongolians gather around our campfire to chat and drink tea. Badmaa doesn't bother to translate most of their palaver, which she assures me is merely local gossip. Not until nine o'clock do we finally head back down the valley. We cross the wooden bridge on the Orkhon and stop at the first ger we come to. The Tövkhön Monastery is about eight miles over the mountains to the north, but you can't get there from here, at least not in a straight line, the man tells us. We have to go down the Orkhon Valley maybe ten miles, then go up a side valley another six or eight miles. The last part of the trail is very steep and we may not be able to make it by jeep. The monastery has been partially rebuilt, he adds, and there should be several people staying there, including two lamas. Heading down the north side of the Orkhon our transmission begins to make dire noises. By the time we head up the narrow side valley we're down to only one gear, third.

Near the head of the valley the road veers to the left and heads up a steep wooded hillside. Soon it's obvious we can't make it up this grade in third gear. Tumur gets out a tool box and begins what looks like ominously complicated repairs. Figuring the monastery can't be far I suggest to Badmaa that we continue on by foot while Tumur fiddles with the transmission. She agrees without a great deal of enthusiasm. The jeep track inclines sharply upward through a thick larch forest. The temperature has risen into the low eighties and we're soon soaked with sweat, but when we stop to rest we're besieged by mosquitoes. We slog upwards for forty-five minutes before emerging into a clearing. At the base of a high cliff is a ger and log cabin, and at the top of these cliffs are several small temples. Directly behind the temples more cliffs soar up another hundred feet or more to the summit of a mountain. This is Tövkhön Monastery, the personal retreat and workshop of Zanabazar.

From the ger at the base of the cliffs a stout, elderly woman appears and invites us in for milk tea and chunks of rock-hard curds. From her cheery demeanor it almost seems as if she is expecting us. Then a middle-aged man enters and says, "So, you are here for the consecration of the new god." It turns out that in four days a delegation of lamas from Ulaan Baatar is bringing a new statue of the deity Gombo Makhgal which will be placed in one of the refurbished temples and consecrated. The monastery was actually reopened on October 27, 1993, says this man, who works for a cultural organization in Ulaan Baatar and is here to help organize the upcoming events, but the presentation of this deity will mark, as I understand his words through Badmaa's translation, its official reconsecration. Many local people are expected to come and in addition to the religious ceremonies there will be horse races—these will be held in the valley through which we came—and other games and festivities. He apparently thinks that I am the first of a wave of foreign tourists who will be arriving for this event. To his disappointment I tell him that I had no idea this reconsecration was taking place, and as much as I would like witness it I don't think my jeep driver and translator would be willing to hang around that long.

Well, no matter, he says, let's take a look at the monastery. To the right of the ger a wide ramp of carefully fitted field stones leads to a cleft in the cliffs. More stone steps wind up through this cleft to a shelf at most sixty feet wide and a hundred feet long behind which sheer cliffs rise another hundred feet. Here in this aerie are the several small temples which constitute the monastery. At the moment there's a lot of activity. In front of one temple two men are painting long tables–altars apparently–a brilliant red, and at least a half dozen more are sawing and hammering away at last-minute repairs on the temples. We stop for a moment to examine a deep narrow well near the top of the staircase. This well, according to our guide, has clear water in it, while maybe twenty feet away is another well with slightly brackish water. No one has been able to explain why one is brackish and the other not, or for that matter, how there can be wells at all here in the solid rock very close to the summit of a mountain, where ordinarily there would not be any underground water courses. This, allows our friend, is just one of the many oddities of this place.

While we're pondering this curiosity a red-robed lama, perhaps in his early thirties, comes over to greet us. This is Shagdarsuren, one of the two lamas now in residence here, and he offers to show us the main temple, which is not much larger than the average living room. This temple was ransacked but not totally destroyed by the communists during the 1930s, he says. Part of the roof was torn off, but the beams were thrown nearby and some of them were used in the reconstruction. Inside, on the altar of the temple, are statues of three gods: on the left Bandanlkham Burkhan, in the center, Bogd Lkham Chorsum–the main god of the temple–and on the right, Gombo, although of course the names mean nothing to me. On a shelf above Bogd Lkham Chorsum rests a small statue of Zanabazar. Below the gods is a large chunk of rock in which can be seen an impression that, with a little bit of imagination, resembles a human hand. This, claims Shagdarsuren, is the hand print of Zanabazar himself. I ask if this is simply a natural phenomena which resembles a hand–any hand, but perhaps Zanabazar's, who knows?–or does he really believe that Zanabazar somehow imprinted his hand in this rock? He and Badmaa have a long discussion about this, and according to her brief paraphrase it's all a matter of what you want to believe.

In fall of 1649, when Zanabazar was fourteen years old, he traveled to Tibet where he hoped to further his religious training. His caravan overwintered at the great monastery of Kumbum, and the next spring he met with the Panchen Lama, like the Dalai Lama, one of the great reincarnated religious leaders of Tibet. After receiving religious instruction and additional ordinations from the Panchen Lama he proceeded to Lhasa, the capital of Tibet, to meet the fifth Dalai Lama, by name, Losang Gyatso. Here he spent at least six months receiving still more religious training, some apparently from the Dalai Lama himself, and most significantly, the Dalai Lama, after due consideration, also announced that Zanabazar was in fact the sixteenth appearance of a khuvigaan (*khuvigaan* = reincarnation) known as Javzandamba.

The various biographies are unclear or contradictory on this matter, but from most we get the impression that up until then Zanabazar was considered an extremely gifted young man obviously destined for a religious life, but that he had not been known to possess what might be termed a spiritual lineage. It was the Dalai Lama who declared that Zanabazar was, as I alluded to earlier, a reincarnation of Taranatha, who was the earthly vehicle of Javzandamba before Zanabazar. Javzandamba had first appeared, according to the spiritual genealogy which eventually became attached to Zanabazar, as Lodoi-shindu-namdak, who lived during the lifetime of Buddha Shakyamuni, the founder of Buddhism, and who served as one of the Buddha's five hundred original disciples. The next three reincarnations also appeared in India; the fifth through the eleventh in Tibet. The eleventh was known as Jamyang Choje and established the famous Drepung Monastery outside Lhasa. The twelfth reincarnation was born in Ceylon, the thirteenth in Tibet, and the fourteenth in India as the son of an Indian king. The last reincarnation before Zanabazar was the fore-mentioned Taranatha. As a symbol of his elevation into the ranks of these esteemed reincarnations the Dalai Lama presented Zanabazar with a yellow silk parasol which reportedly can be found to this day in the Bogd Khan Museum in Ulaan Baatar, although it is usually not out on public display.

Since there were only fifteen incarnations of Javzandamba between the time of Buddha, generally recognized as about 2,500 years ago, and the birth of Zanabazar, the first Bogd Gegen, in 1635, and given the average life span of human beings, there would appear to be long periods of time when there was no living representative of the line, and that it was in effect dormant. This is not precisely the case, however. As learned lamas explained to Pozdneev in the 1890s:

> . . . during the rest of the time he [the Bogd Gegen] was reborn in diverse parts of the universe with the purpose of benefit not only to people but to beings of other worlds; these reincarnations of him are unknown to anyone beside the Gegen himself, and that is why there are no legends about them whatsoever.[21]

Empowered by his newfound spiritual lineage Zanabazar then made a tour of monasteries in Tibet which previous incarnations of Javzandamba had founded or where they had lived. In addition to making offerings at these places, he also managed to collect numerous statues and other artwork, books, and various valuable relics which he took back to Mongolia with him and placed in his own monasteries. Among these was a religious text written in gold on leaves of sandalwood. This document can be found today in the State Central Library in Ulaan Baatar.

The Dalai Lama also contrived to convert Zanabazar to the Gelugpa sect of Lamaism to which he himself belonged and which by then had become dominant in Tibet. It will be remembered that at Shireet Tsagaan Nuur Zanabazar had been ordained as a member of the Sakhya sect, and most of the monasteries of Mongolia, including the main one of Erdene Zuu, still followed the Sakhya teachings. (The precise nature of these teachings and how they differed from the doctrines of the Gelugpa sect is, I am afraid, outside the scope of this brief travelogue.) Zanabazar became such a firm proponent of the new Gelugpa sect that when he returned to Mongolia in 1651 he brought with him, according to one account—and the accounts do vary—six hundred Tibetan lamas of the Gelugpa sect (plus assorted artists, craftsmen, and other useful individuals) to help him spread the new doctrine. He also apparently refused to live in any monastery which followed the old Sakhya faith.

His followers, therefore, established for him several new monasteries. One of these eventually settled at the confluence of the Tuul and Selbi rivers, at the current site of Ulaan Baatar. In addition, in 1653 Zanabazar asked of his followers that a small retreat be built for him where, presumably, he could escape the time-consuming demands of the larger monasteries. This was done, and the place became known as Tövkhön Monastery.

From the main temple our lama guide leads us to a narrow, precarious path that winds up through the cliffs to the left of the monastery. Part way up the cliff is a broad sloping shelf of rock where the lama stops and points out three more impressions pressed into the native rock. These, he announces, are the "footprints of the gods." Crouching down and carefully outlining these indentations, he explains that one represents a Mongolian-style boot, the second the foot of a small baby, and the third the hoof of a horse. Badmaa and Shagdarsuren engage in a lengthy discussion about these prints and from what I can gather from her brief paraphrases it would appear that the first two represent Zanabazar as a small child and as an adult, while the third represents his horse. Despite repeated inquires however I still cannot determine if the lama believes these impressions were made by Zanabazar, either by conventional or supernatural means, or if they are simply natural phenomenon which resemble footprints, but from the way the lama lovingly strokes the outlines of these depressions it's clear that he considers them imbued with a special significance and that they are yet another indication of the sacred nature of the environs.

From this shelf of rock we climb still higher up the cliff face until we come to the mouth of a cave. This, explains the lama, was a kind of retreat within the retreat of Tövkhön Monastery, a place where Zanabazar came alone to meditate and "talk to the gods," as Badmaa translates it. The cave is perhaps eight feet high, ten feet wide, and fifteen feet deep. Daylight just barely penetrates to the back wall, where there is a small wooden bench. Apparently this bench is where Zanabazar sat when he meditated. I ask if I can sit down here and the lama motions me to go ahead. Perhaps it was when sitting at this very spot that Zanabazar got the idea for his second trip to Tibet.

According to his biography Zanabazar spent the summer and early fall of 1655 engrossed in religious exercises here at Tövkhön. Suddenly, in the midst of his meditations, Zanabazar decided to return to Tibet. This trip, while it apparently did occur, presents a number of historiographical problems for the current-day student of Zanabazar's life. First of all, Zanabazar and his six companions allegedly traveled to the monastery of the Panchen Lama in Tibet, a sojourn which normally took months, in seven days. This nature of this speedy journey becomes perhaps more evident when we realize that "of those who were honored by witnessing it, it seemed to some that there were seven mounted men riding and to others that there were seven turpans [large ducks] flying."[22] The host of miraculous events that occurred to the travelers on their way to Tibet, either on horses or flying as birds, need not be detailed here. Anyhow, despite their haste the party arrived at the monastery of the Panchen Lama too late; he had died three days before. "'O, how unhappy I am,'" cried out Zanabazar. "Knowing my teacher . . . to be of great age, I purposely made great haste that I might bow to him and acquire the rest of the precepts which I was not able to get before from his spiritual treasure house.'" The spirit of the Panchen Lama, hearing this lament, suddenly reanimated his body. "'I should not have returned,'" announced the now alive Panchen Lama, "'but once it became known to me that thou didst come from a far land and art wasting away in such sorrow, I resolved to come back.'"[23] He thereupon commenced to instruct the young Bogd Gegen in new and varied teachings, precepts, and doctrines.

Back on firmer ground, Zanabazar's biography states that he returned to Mongolia in the late autumn of 1656. Thus he had been gone at least a year, enough time to travel to Tibet by more conventional means and in the usual time frame, receive religious instruction, and return back home. Whether he received these instructions from the reanimated Panchen Lama or from some other exalted personage is open to speculation; however, we do know that Zanabazar returned from Tibet further empowered and that from this point on his star began to rise. Pozdneev, commenting on the miraculous stories surrounding Zanabazar's sojourn, says, "There is no doubt that the lamas' tales of such a nature had in their time an enormous influence on the minds of the superstitious Mongols and thus we are inclined to trust the biography of the Öndur-gegen, which states that the Khalkhas, on hearing of the circumstances of this trip made by their hutukhtu to Tibet, began to venerate the hutukhtu and pray to him far more than they had before."[24]

The following year, in the spring of 1657, the princes of Khalka Mongolia held a huge convocation in honor of Zanabazar during which he performed the rites he had supposedly learned from the Panchen Lama, thus greatly increasing his standing among both the nobles and the common people. In 1559 another great convention was held and by this time Zanabazar, then twenty-four years old, was deemed powerful enough to bestow titles on both the Mongolian aristocracy and leaders of the Lamaist religion. It was from this time that he began to play a political as well as religious role in the life of the Khalka Mongols. Thus he soon became the most influential Mongol of his day.

Leading us back down to the main temple our lama tells us that he must continue work on the preparations for the consecration of the new god, but that we should continue on the path to the right of the monastery which leads to the summit of the mountain. There are two little boys lurking nearby and he tells them to show us the way and to point out Zanabazar's secret tunnel. Also, he warns Badmaa that while she can go up the mountain, she cannot proceed the whole way to the top; women are forbidden to stand on the summit. Following the two dandiprats we climb to a knife-edged spine that leads upward to the summit. Part way up an inconspicuous trail edges back along the face of the cliff. Following this we soon come to the opening of a cave which is hidden from view from below by overhanging rocks. Proceeding through this cave about fifty feet we find ourselves overlooking the steep wooded backside of the mountain. According to the boys, who have apparently acted as guides before, this was Zanabazar's secret escape route. If anyone attacked the monastery from the front side he and his followers could climb up and take the hidden path to the cave. Those who followed them would continue on to the summit of the mountain where they would be confronted by impassable cliffs which prevented access to the back side of the mountain. This is how Zanabazar escaped from the forces of Galdan during the invasion of the Jungarians back in the 1680s, according to the boys.

We retrace our path back to the spine and continue on to the summit. There are actually two domes on the top of the mountain, the first a little lower than the other. Here on the first dome, the boys indicate, Badmaa must stop. The two domes are connected by a narrow neck of rock, perhaps originally impassable, over which a passageway has been laboriously built up with field stones. The higher dome appears to have been originally rounded, but tall walls of carefully fitted field stone had been built up around its sides, creating a sort of crown, and then this area was filled in with dirt, resulting in a fairly level area perhaps sixty feet in diameter. In the middle is the requisite ovoo. Someone went to an enormous amount of work creating this mountaintop aerie. The stones for the passageway connecting the two domes and retaining walls on the higher dome, many tons of them, and the dirt to fill in the top of the dome must have been laboriously carried up here by hand. And to what purpose? Simply to provide a scenic view, or were some kind of ceremonies held up here on this altarlike platform? The boys just shrug when asked.

The view from this platform certainly is impressive. According to my altimeter the altitude is 7,110 feet. Just to the south is another mountain, thickly forested almost to its top, which appears to be slightly higher, and to the northwest not far away is another peak of about equal height, but in all other directions the horizon appears fifty or more miles away. And looking straight down from the edge of the retaining walls can be seen the temples on a narrow shelf of rock, and then more cliffs dropping down into a clearing in the forest. If an artist had to picture an appropriate setting for a monastery he could have hardly come up with anything more appropriate or dramatic. The boys insist I take their photos by the ovoo and then leave me alone to my own thoughts. I sit down on the edge of the cliffs and try to imagine Zanabazar coming here for a brief respite from his artistic labors.

It was at his workshop here at Tövkhön that Zanabazar created the great statues which to this day grace the temples and museums of

Mongolia. These include at least twenty-one Taras, including his masterpieces, the White Tara and the Green Tara; his five magnificent dhyani-Buddhas; at least two Vajradaras, one residing in the main temple at Gandan Monastery in Ulaan Baatar and the other, which has a huge emerald embedded in its forehead, at Erdene Zuu (this was one of the Zanabazars reportedly stolen, as I alluded to earlier); figures of Amitayus and Manjushri (the latter is in the Fine Arts Museum); a thirty-inch-high bronze stupa (likewise in the Fine Arts Museum); and at least eight silver stupas. These are the works we know about; there may have been many more about which no contemporary record was made and which have subsequently been lost or destroyed. Most, if not all, of these works were reportedly created in the 1680s, although certainly before 1688 when Zanabazar was forced to flee this area because of the invasion of Galdan and the Jungarians. Zanabazar would have been forty-five in 1680 when this creative period in his life began. How do we explain that this man who had spent his entire life engaged in religious activities was also able to develop into an artist whose works are now considered world-class masterpieces?

As I mentioned earlier, even as a little boy Zanabazar had occupied his time fashioning small burkhans and drawing pictures, but from his biography we get no further indications of artistic leanings in his early life. We do know that at the age of fourteen he was in the Tibetan capital of Lhasa when the Dalai Lama's great palace the Potala was being constructed and here he would have come in contact with a wide variety of artists and craftsmen, including sculptors from Nepal, some with whom he may have studied. Art historians, at least, have pointed out traces of Nepalese influence in his work. When he returned from Tibet, as I noted earlier, he brought, in addition to lamas, a number of artists, some of whom may have been able to instruct him on the complicated procedure of casting bronzes. During his studies he would have certainly been exposed to the vast corpus of aesthetic theory which had grown up around Buddhist art. On this subject I'll simply repeat without comment the observation of Mongolian art historian N. Tsultem: "Zanabazar's work reflects a sound knowledge of the teaching contained in the Tanjur [commentaries on the teachings of Buddhism] on the canons of the classical proportions of the human body and, in particular, a knowledge of the ancient shastras Pratimalakshana, Chitralakshana and Sambarudaiya, whilst observing the Dashatala–10 palm linear measurement."[25]

Then there's a legend that Zanabazar's consort, the Girl Prince–it should be repeated here that there is no mention of her whatsoever in his biography–not only served as a model for the White and Green Taras but also may have instructed Zanabazar in a unique way on casting bronzes. According to this tale a group of Mongolian nobles visited Zanabazar one day and chastised him for living with a woman, apparently in violation of his religious vows. The Girl Prince then appeared out of Zanabazar's ger with a lump of molten bronze in her hands, which she proceeded to knead into a beautiful statue as if it were dough. So awed were the nobles by this performance that they went away without another word. In the end, however, none of these influences seem enough to explain Zanabazar's art, and we must simply accept the fact of his creative genius. "During his lifetime he was the greatest Buddhist sculptor in Asia," flatly states one current-day art historian, and in contrast to all the insubstantial legends and myths which swirl around Zanabazar the results of his artistry are very real physical evidence of his extraordinary life.[26]

My mountaintop reverie is interrupted by the distant whine of an engine. Soon a large gray van emerges out of the woods into the clearing below. Then right behind the van appears our jeep with the trusty Tumur at the helm. Badmaa, who has been lost in her own cerebrations on the dome below, shouts that we should go down and check in with Tumur. It develops that he was able to get the jeep into first gear and thus drive up here to the monastery, but the transmission still isn't working. He is going rip out the whole gear box and do some major readjustments. It sounds to me as if we might be here for the consecration of the new god after all.

The gray van contains six people from France, plus a translator and driver. The Mongolian man from Ulaan Baatar is disheartened to learn that they also have not come for the upcoming consecration and celebration. Instead, they had just been to the Orkhon Waterfall where someone had informed them about this monastery, and they had decided to make a quick detour here. Apparently their translator had told them that no other foreigners ever came here, and thus thinking they were in for a unique treat, they seem a bit petulant to find me, an American, already present. Or perhaps they are just being irascibly French; anyhow, their translator seems to have her hands full.

Ignoring all this, I spread out our remaining scraps for a picnic lunch. The two boys we had met earlier, reappearing at our side in anticipation of a free meal, offer to take us to a nearby spring for water—the two wells at the monastery are not used for mundane purposes—and on the way they show us what they claim is Zanabazar's hitching post. He had apparently found two saplings growing close by each other and had tied the tops together in a knot. Over the centuries the two saplings had grown together so that now there is a U-shaped tree with both ends rooted in the ground—very handy for tying horses. Zanabazar, it seems, thought of everything.

After taking a rueful look at our transmission, which now consists of about two dozen parts laid out on a piece of canvas, I drag the long-suffering Badmaa back up the steep stone steps to the monastery. I am very curious about this story about Zanabazar escaping from here when Galdan and the Jungarians attacked. The lama, however, just laughs. This is just a story the local people tell, he says; actually Zanabazar was staying somewhere near Kharkhorum when he was forced to flee the invaders. But the tunnel did serve as a secret escape route in case someone did come here with evil intentions. After all, Zanabazar was the most important religious and political figure in Mongolia and there were those who might have wanted to eliminate or kidnap him. And yes, the hitching post we had seen was indeed made by Zanabazar, of this I can rest assured.

I go back to the summit of the mountain while Badmaa returns to the jeep to take a nap. I sit quietly for over an hour, simply trying to soak up any vibrations which might be emanating from this spot. Soon a car appears—one of those tank-like Russian models which go anywhere—and a half dozen Mongolians emerge, including two in lama dress. Then half an hour later Badmaa shouts and motions to me to come down. On the way down the rocky spine to the monastery I encounter the Mongolians who had arrived a bit earlier. This group includes two ancient lamas from Ulaan Baatar who are making a pilgrimage here. Although they can barely walk, the two old men insist on going to the summit of the mountain. I have to stop and help hoist the old-timers up over a couple of steep spots on the trail. Offering my arm to the one old man he grips it with a viselike lock of someone truly afraid of losing his balance and falling.

Back at the jeep Badmaa informs me that the transmission is just about fixed and that Tumur says he will soon be ready to go. I find this hard to believe, but indeed the gearbox is reassembled and Tumur is pounding out new gaskets from a cardboard cigarette carton he got from the driver of the gray van. When we do pull out of the clearing a half an hour later I look back and see the two ancient lamas standing on the very top of the mountain behind the monastery.

Erdene Zuu

ERDENE ZUU MONASTERY is seated on the east bank of the Orkhon River about thirty miles northeast of Tövkhön as the crow flies. To get there by the regular road from Tövkhön, however, it's necessary to backtrack twenty miles to the bridge over the Orkhon, then return almost thirty miles to Khujirt and from there take the road which goes another thirty miles to the town of Kharkhorin, where the monastery is located. (*Kharkhorin* is the correct transliteration of the name of the modern-day Mongolian town; *Kharkhorum* is the name of the ancient Mongol capital nearby.) As we exit the side valley into the valley of the Orkhon Tumur proposes that instead of backtracking to the bridge we go downstream and find a place to ford the river, then pick up the road to Khujirt. So we take a faint track along the north bank of the river and head northeast. The river where we come in sight of it is at least a hundred and fifty feet wide and fast–not rapids, but a strong, surging flow.

Finally we come to a place where it looks like vehicles have crossed before. Stripping to his underwear Tumur wades out sixty or seventy feet into the river and finds that the water comes up to mid-thigh. He seems to think the river can be crossed. He pulls out a big wide roll of cellophane tape and wraps up all the wires coming from the distributor cap to keep out moisture. Then he unloosens the fan belt so the fan won't spin and blow water up over the engine. Plunging into the river we make good progress until about halfway across where the river suddenly becomes deeper. We loose traction and soon bog down sickeningly. Tumur attempts to back up but simply spins his wheels. The river surges all around us and within moments six inches of water is running over the floor of the jeep. Our situation doesn't look good.

There is however a ger visible on the far bank about a half mile away and there appears to be a vehicle parked nearby. Tumur says he will try to wade to shore and get help. Opening his door on the downstream side he struggles out into the now almost waist-deep river. Several times he is nearly bowled off his feet by the current but he finally does reach the far bank. Badmaa and I sit with our feet up on the seats. If she has any feelings about our predicament she does not reveal them. I can't help but notice that just outside my window an impressive mayfly hatch is in progress—light cahills if I am not mistaken—and some rather large fish are feeding off the surface. Had I some fishing gear, I could have put this unfortunate little contretemps to good use.

After a half hour a jeep appears with Tumur on board. With coiled-up tow cable in hand he wades out to our jeep. After fastening this cable to the cable wound around the front bumper of our truck he heads back to shore. The two cables together still come up fifteen feet short of the bank. After some discussion the other driver agrees to pull into the river, which quickly rises above the hubs on his vehicle. The cables are fastened on and the driver attempts to back up but can find no traction on the slick river cobbles. (Why he didn't back in to begin with, I don't know; I am not a jeep driver.) He seems to be spinning himself holes in the river bottom, and when Tumur eventually unhooks the cable he can go neither forward nor backward. So now we have two vehicles stuck in the river.

For a half hour Tumur and the other driver sit on the bank presumably cogitating on further action. I begin to detect on Badmaa's usually unfurrowed visage a slight hint of disapproval at these carryings-on. Finally she allows that her own father was a jeep driver—he drove the same jeep for fourteen years, doing all the repairs himself—and he would have never gotten in a fix like this. Well, if necessary she'll sleep here in the river. She is not going to attempt wading ashore. Indeed, she appears to be building herself a nest on the front seats. Then I look up and see coming over a nearby rise a huge Soviet army troop transport truck known by the acronym, GAZ. Many of these are now in civilian hands and are used to haul freight and whatnot. They have huge tires and four-wheel drive and are famous for going anywhere. The driver throws his cable out to the first jeep, which the big GAZ easily extracts. Then he drives out into the river to our cable–the water barely reaches the hubs of the GAZ–and unceremoniously jerks us ashore like a child's toy. With a wave he continues across the river as if it isn't there.

After a brief stop at the ger of the man with the jeep where we refresh ourselves with airag we proceed on to Khujirt. (The man demands 1,500 tögrögs for the aborted tow job; the airag is free.) I had suspected that Tumur and Badmaa would want to stay in the town but both are noncommittal. We continue on the road to Kharkhorin until after sunset and finally find a camping spot on a level bench near a small rivulet. Perhaps 300 feet away a white ger can just be made out in the darkness. As we are setting up our tents by the headlights of the jeep a group of people from the ger approach us. A man and woman dressed in tattered deels and four scruffy children line up in a row and silently watch. Finally the man says something to Tumur. It occurs to me that he might be objecting to us camping here in what is basically his front yard, but no, it seems he would like us all to come and join him and his family in their ger for dinner. Tumur, who has probably never turned down a free meal in his life, readily agrees, but Badmaa demurs and so do I. For the last hour or so I have had a headache and feverish feeling. All I want to do is stretch out in my sleeping bag. The air here seems curiously damp and a sickly gibbous moon hangs just over the hills on the horizon. Even in my usually warm bag I have the shivers. I toss back and forth for an hour or more, my physical discomfort exacerbated by a feeling of ungratefulness for having declined the hospitality of the people in the ger. Finally I fall into an uneasy sleep.

The next morning I still have an odd, discombobulated feeling. Tumur announces that the people in the ger have told him that some friends of his are staying in gers nearby. We'll go and have breakfast with them. We finally track down these people at the end of a long draw about ten miles away. There are three gers and perhaps a dozen people at this isolated spot. First we have milk tea, yogurt and homemade cheese, and then an old man announces that we must stay long enough for his granddaughter, who lives in the neighboring ger, to cook us up some mutton and homemade noodles. This young woman, perhaps in her mid-twenties and wearing a trim robin's egg blue deel, soon appears carrying a large basin of cut-up mutton. I simply gape at her. With a long oval face, straight black hair parted in the middle and hanging to her shoulders, and full pink lips she has an uncanny resemblance to someone I once knew in Alaska. For the briefest of moments the notion flashes across my brain pan that the woman in Alaska, through some fantastic concatenation of circumstances, is actually here in Mongolia, dressed in a deel and standing in this ger. The likeness is in fact so startling and disconcerting that my heart starts pounding painfully against my rib cage. I quickly recover but I can't help staring at the young woman who could easily be an identical twin of my acquaintance in Alaska.

I lethargically plow through a big plate of mutton and noodles which comes to rest in my stomach like a lump of lead. A young girl in the ger offers to get some drinking water for us at a nearby spring and I go with her, thinking that some fresh air might clear my head. It doesn't. By the time we get back to the gers I have another ponderous headache. Thankfully, Tumur is ready to go. As we pull away from the gers the young woman in the blue silk deel raises her arm to her shoulder and gives a fluttering little wave of her hand, just as the woman in Alaska would have done. I start shivering, even though there is a faultless expanse of robin's egg blue sky overhead and the temperature is already in the seventies.

Located about halfway between Khujirt and Kharkhorin is the Shankh Monastery, founded by Zanabazar in 1647 when he was twelve years old. Originally known as the monastery of Braibun-gaji-gandan-shat-dublin, or more commonly as the Baruun Khüree (West Monastery), it was essentially a collection of ger temples which changed location several times before permanently settling at its present location. The monastery then became known as the Baruun Khüree of Shankh, or in common parlance the Shankh Monastery. Although several large stone and brick temples of Tibetan design were eventually constructed on the site the monastery retained its roots as a traveling tent camp at least up until the late nineteenth century. When Pozdneev visited here in 1892 he found five huge gers each holding from 150 to 200 people which were still being used as temples. These white felt gers were "decorated very beautifully on the outside," according to Pozdneev, but inside he found only the most commonplace accouterments; in fact, there were no "significant Buddhist religious objects of any kind to be found at Baruun Khüree."[27] Oddly, he did find that the contingent of lamas outnumbered those of the much bigger and more well-known Erdene Zuu monastery nearby.

The ger temples are of course long gone, and now only the main Tibetan-style temple and several smaller buildings remain. Shankh has however become a repository of relics connected with Zanabazar. Here can be found, reportedly, robes that Zanabazar wore as young man, several statues and a long ceremonial horn which he himself had fashioned, a statue which his great-grandfather Abudai had brought back from Tibet, and various other items. I had been told in Ulaan Baatar that most of these hallowed objects were not usually out on public display, but still I wanted to spend several hours at Shankh, which is once again an active monastery, while on my way to Erdene Zuu. I had a ferocious headache when we pulled into the parking lot but I was determined to tour the monastery.

Two rows of lamas facing each other are chanting the morning service as we enter the main temple. We work our way around clockwise to the back where there are several cases of small statues. Several of these looked like they might be Zanabazars, but as I stand peering at them I suddenly become faint and have to grab at one of the altar tables to steady myself. Deciding that I better get some fresh air I hurry out of the temple, noticing on the way that several lamas look up from their Tibetan scriptures and glance at me with questioning looks on their faces. Back in the parking lot the sun is broiling but at the same time I'm shaking with cold. Getting back in the jeep I tell Tumur to drive to Kharkhorin. All I want to do is get a hotel room and lie down.

A half hour later we pass by the huge compound of Erdene Zuu Monastery—it's now clear I won't be visiting it today—and continue a mile or so into the small town of Kharkhorin. After numerous inquiries we finally locate a dilapidated hotel near the city market. It takes another half hour to track down the hotel clerk and another twenty minutes for her to find some room keys. I collapse on my bed and start shivering uncontrollably even though it must be in the eighties inside the room. Finally I crawl into my sleeping bag with my clothes on and pile all the covers on top. My head feels like it is three-quarters full of half-molten metal which at the slightest movement threatens to slosh a hole in my cranium. Sometime in the afternoon I drift off into sleep. When I awake again it's dark and I am as drenched as if I had just taken a bath fully clothed. My head still throbs but if I lay perfectly still the pain is just bearable. I nap fitfully, finally falling into a deep sleep, and when I awake again the sun is shining through the windows. I feel lightheaded but my fever is gone. What's more, I'm hungry, which I interpret as a good sign: dying men are never hungry, I've heard. Badmaa says there's a canteen on the first floor of the hotel with fairly good food; she herself ate there last night. By the time I am halfway through a big plate of mutton and fried potatoes the last lingering pangs in my head subside. Perhaps noticing the avidity with which I attacked the first plate, the waitress—she's also the cook—asks if I want another plateful. Of course I do. I also sluice down five cups of instant coffee which seem to have a positively anodyne effect. By the time breakfast is done I feel completely refurbished. Tumur is waiting with the jeep and we drive straight to Erdene Zuu. The exact cause of my brief malady I never did determine.

At the end of the last century Erdene Zuu vied with Ikh Khüree (at the current site of Ulaan Baatar) and Amarbayasgalant as Mongolia's most important monastery. Ikh Khüree was of course the home of the Bogd Gegens and thus played a special role in the religious life of Mongolia, but Erdene Zuu was sanctified by greater age and by a larger collection of burkhans, relics, and other holy objects. Also, Erdene Zuu had a hallowed history, as Pozdneev noted in 1892:

> The burkhans of Erdene Dzuu were untiring witnesses of many of the truly most important historical events of Khalkha. Thus here almost every column and hill, every temple and every burkhan, calls to mind some individual or holds the tale of some event close to the heart of every

Khalkha. This is why the mention of Erdene Dzuu arouses
love for his native land in the heart of every Mongol, and
ultimately, moves him to fall on bended knee in trembling
delight before this holy place.[28]

The huge compound of Erdene Zuu monastery presents an imposing
sight on the steppe just outside of Kharkhorin. Its surrounding walls,
over ten feet high, create a perfect square 1,308 feet long on each side.
Evenly spaced along the walls are tall white stupas: twenty five on each
side and two additional ones at each corner for a total of 108 (although
several are currently damaged or missing). The parking lot in front of
the west gate of the monastery already contains a dozen or more cars
and jeeps and two tour buses on this broiling, faultlessly clear day. Just
inside the west gate is a large, three-room building that serves as a
ticket office and gift shop. Although part of Erdene Zuu is once again a
functioning monastery most of the complex is still a museum and a
ticket is needed to enter its temple-exhibit halls. The gift shop has a
refrigerator stocked with soft drinks and beer–the first cold drinks I
have seen on our trip–and being thoroughly dehydrated by the previous
night's bout of fever, I quickly chug down two icy Cokes.

Erdene Zuu was built on or near the site of the old Mongol capital
of Kharkhorum. In 1220 Chingis Khan himself decided to build a capital
for his empire here, although apparently little was done at the site by
the time he died in 1227. In choosing this location where the Orkhon
River emerged from flanking ridges into a vast flat-bottomed basin
Chingis was acting completely within tradition. Almost all the great
empires of the steppe were headquartered or had capitals here on
the upper Orkhon, including the Hsiung-nu from about the second
century B.C. to the second century A.D., the T'u-chüeh (Turks) from
552 to 734, the Uighurs from 745 to 840, and numerous lesser empires
and tribal confederations. It was from here, in the words of one historian,
that "successive peoples have constantly over the centuries appeared, as
if out of the blue, and spread over Asia and Europe in recurrent waves;
it was almost as if the womb of mankind was still conceiving and giving
birth every so many centuries."[29]

It was Chingis's son Ögödai who actually began the construction of Kharkhorum, and by 1235 it was recognized as the capital of the Mongol empire. The same year Ögödai held here a great khural (*khural* = assembly) where it was decided that the Mongols would attack the Sung Dynasty which ruled southern China. The splendor which eventually made Kharkhorum legendary has been amply described in the well-known account of the French Franciscan monk William of Rubruck, who arrived in the capital on April 4, 1254, and thus need not be elaborated upon here. I will only mention in passing the famous tree of solid silver, fashioned by the French silversmith Guillame Boucher, one of the many foreign craftsmen and artists in residence at Kharkhorum, which spouted streams of rice wine, airag, mead, and beer from its branches and which now has been memorialized on the back of 5,000 and 10,000 tögrög bank notes.

The efflorescence of Kharkhorum was as brief as it was brilliant. After the death of Ögödai convoluted wrangling for control of the Mongol empire ensued between Chingis's grandsons. Ögödai's son, Güyüg, ruled for two years before he died and was replaced by his wife as a regent. Then Möngke, son of Tolui, the youngest of Chingis's sons, seized power. When he died in 1259 a vicious rivalry broke out between his brothers, Ariq-bögä and Khubilai. Ariq-bögä had assumed the governorship of Kharkhorum while Khubilai was in China leading an army against the Sung Dynasty. At Möngke's death Khubilai withdrew his army to near Dolonuur in what is now Inner Mongolia, and at a khural attended by his loyal officers and men he had himself declared khan of the Mongol empire on June 4, 1260.

Claiming that Khubilai's ascension was invalid because the khural at Dolonuur had not been attended by other claimants to the throne nor had it been held at one of the traditional Mongolian meeting places, Ariq-bögä then convened his own khural at Kharkhorum where his followers named him khan. A civil war ensued. In 1260 Khubilai's partisans drove Ariq-bögä out of Kharkhorum, forcing him to decamp far north to the Yenisei River region. Ariq-bögä reclaimed Kharkhorum briefly but by 1264 he finally surrendered to Khubilai. The nexus of power then shifted to China. Khubilai moved the Mongol capital to Beijing and founded the Yüan Dynasty. For the next 100 years Kharkhorum was little more than a provincial capital.

The Yüan Dynasty, led by a series of ever-less competent Mongol khans, lasted until 1368 when it was ousted from Beijing by native Chinese warlords and replaced by what became the Ming Dynasty. Shorn of their Chinese empire, the Mongols regrouped around their old capital of Kharkhorum. As I mentioned earlier, in 1372 a huge army mustered by the Ming crossed the Gobi and advanced on Kharkhorum. It was forced to retreat, but in 1380 the Ming launched another invasion and this time sacked and burned the once-magnificent Mongol capital. The Mongols again regrouped, but in 1388 another Ming army consisting of over 100,000 troops defeated them in a decisive battle south of the Kherlen River. It was the end of Chingis's empire in Mongolia and the beginning of anarchy among the Mongols.

For the next two hundred the ruins of Kharkhorum slowly sank into the steppe. Then in 1577 Zanabazar's great-grandfather Abudai, one of three khans who shared power among the fragmented Khalkha Mongols, traveled to Köke Khota, the city in what is now Inner Mongolia which had been founded by Altan Khan of the Tümed Mongols, an early convert to Lamaism. Here he met the religious leader of Tibet on whom the Altan Khan had bestowed the title of Dalai Lama, which of course is still in use today. At this time the Dalai Lama gave Abudai a supposed relic of the Buddha Shakyamuni and a burkhan which was impervious to fire and instructed him to build a temple to house these objects, adding, "There is in your territory an area with the name of Old and New Orqon [Orkhon]. You should select an auspicious site and build it [the temple] there."[30]

Not until eight years later did Abudai fulfill these instructions. In 1585 he sent to Köke Khota for a lama to help him build the monastery. This lama's name was Gumi Nansu, who belonged to the Sakhya sect. Thus the Sakhya sect of Lamaism became the accepted religion of Khalkha Mongolia. By the summer of 1586 the first temple had been constructed and a "minor dedication" performed by Gumi Nansu. As I mentioned earlier, Abudai then invited the Dalai Lama to perform the "major dedication" but he refused, perhaps because the monastery belonged to the Sakhya sect and not the Dalai Lama's own Gelugpa sect. He did send in his place the Sakhya lama, Lodoi Jambo, who performed a "major" or full dedication in 1587. According to legend, however, the Dalai Lama did send down a shower of flowers during the dedication to indicate his blessings on the monastery. "To this day," wrote Pozdneev in 1892, "a few dried forget-me-nots and some yellowish flowers are preserved . . . before the statue of the Great Dzuu, which the lamas say are the very flowers which fell from heaven during the dedication of the Great Dzuu temple."[31] And of course, as I related earlier, the Dalai Lama did later come to Mongolia and meet Abudai at Yesön Züil, or so Abudai believed.

This first small temple can now be seen near the middle of the vast Erdene Zuu compound some distance from the rest of the other temples and buildings. Reportedly it and other later temples were built in part with bricks, cut stones, and other building materials from the rubble of Kharkhorum. Unfortunately this temple does not now seem to be open to the public. In front of it and to the south is the stone foundation of Abudai's ger. At first Abudai apparently had a smaller version here, but for a big convention of Khalkha nobles held in 1658 his successors constructed an immense ger almost 150 feet in diameter and fifty feet high in the middle. This ger, which might well be the largest ever built in Mongolia, was supported by eight wooden posts almost two feet in diameter which were inserted into holes cut in huge slabs of rock mounted flush to the ground. Several of these sockets can still be seen, and Badmaa, examining them, asks the inevitable question: how did seventeenth-century Mongolians carve these holes into solid rock? Slowly, I would suspect. Just in front of this monumental ger was a small artificial pond, the outline of which can still be seen. In the seventeenth century water was apparently channeled or piped here from some nearby stream. Having a private pond just outside of your 150-foot-in-diameter ger must have seemed like the height of luxury in parched Mongolia. Obviously the Tüsheet khans were men of some means.

As one of the two or three most important monasteries in Mongolia and located as it was in the strategic Orkhon Valley, Erdene Zuu inevitably got caught up in the almost constant internecine battles which raged across Mongolia in the seventeenth and eighteenth centuries. As I related earlier the Jungarians under the leadership of Galdan ransacked Erdene

Zuu in 1688. A Manchu diplomat who was passing through the area at the time sent this report to Beijing:

> Galdan's army has thoroughly plundered all the people surrounding Erdene Juu [Zuu] and has reached the place called Black Orkhon. It is only one day's journey from where the Jetsundamba Khutukhtu [the Bogd Gegen] was. The Khutukhtu, with the [Tüsheet] khan's son wife, people, lamas and disciples, in all more than three hundred persons, fled away by night. The Khalkhas abandoned all their yurts, their vessels and tools, their horses, camels and sheep, and fled, night and day alike, in all directions. I do not know where the Tüsheet Khan is. Some say that Galdan himself is with the army, and that nearly ten thousand soldiers are advancing in various ways . . . It is quite true that they have killed Khalkhas, forced nobles to surrender, set fire to temples, and destroyed scriptures and images.[32]

From then until about 1700, after Galdan had been defeated and the Khalkhas Mongols had slowly began returning to their homeland, the monastery was apparently abandoned. In 1702, Zanabazar, returning from China where he had been the guest of the Manchu emperor Kang Hsi, had the temples refurbished and re-consecrated. Erdene Zuu was again attacked in 1732 by the revamped Jungarians under Galdan's nephew, Tsering. According to legend they were chased away from the monastery by idols in the temples which leaned toward them threateningly and also by the stone lions at the main gate which began to growl and roar. The terrified soldiers ran out and threw themselves into the Orkhon River where they were drowned. Although the animated idols and stone lions may be merely a legend, apparently some Jungarian soldiers did drown in the Orkhon, since it has been asserted on firmer ground that the Manchu emperor, in appreciation for the Orkhon's role in defeating the Jungarians, actually bestowed upon it a title, and declared that each summer, on a date set by astrologers, 300 Chinese ounces of silver were to be thrown into the river as a reward for its services.

Apparently no preternatural phenomenon intervened when troops sent by the communist government of Mongolia ransacked the monastery in 1937, although the details of what did take place remain vague. In the words of Charles Bawden, the renowned historian of modern Mongolia, "It is impossible to find recorded in any book how the great lamasery of Erdeni Juu came to be ruined, but an album of photographs, kept in the lamasery, showing how it looked originally, and how it looked immediately after the closure of 1937, with stupas overturned, walls breached and temple buildings shattered, suggests the use of high explosives."[33] We do know that of the sixty-two temples which were standing when the communists arrived, only about a dozen survived. These, and of course the surrounding wall, were designated cultural and historical landmarks in 1941. In 1965 what remained of the compound was turned into a museum which became one of the standard stops on the extremely limited itinerary open to foreign visitors through the state-run tourist agency. Of course then the communist government collapsed, and in 1992 a group of lamas reinstated religious services here. In June of 1997, after being claimed by the state for almost six decades, Erdene Zuu was given back to the Lamaist church, although apparently most of it will continue to function as a museum.

The lamas now hold services in the Lavran Temple, in the northeast corner of the compound. As Badmaa and I are examining Abudai's ger site two boys appear on a high platform built into the courtyard wall which surrounds the temple and blow on the long horns they use to announce the beginning of the morning services. We heed their call, along with perhaps fifty other sightseers who have been examining the nearby museum temples. As we approach I see several people taking pictures of the boys with the horns, who are eight or ten years old and dressed in red robes and enormous high-peaked yellow hats. Interrupting their blasts on the horns they agitatedly wave at the people, motioning for them not to take pictures.

The three-story whitewashed brick temple was apparently built in 1785, although it may have been a remodeling of an earlier building. A Tibetan influence can be seen in several monastery buildings in Mongolia—the temple at Shankh in which I had nearly passed out in earlier and the temple at Gandan in Ulaan Baatar which holds the immense statue of Janraisig are a few examples—but the Lavran Temple is said by the cognoscenti of such matters to be the country's finest example of Tibetan architecture.

On the gate in the courtyard wall is a sign saying that photography is not allowed inside the compound of the Lavran Temple—it is a functioning temple and not a museum—but nevertheless about half the crowd in the courtyard is clicking away furiously. A lama runs up and waves a hand in faces of several photographers who momentarily desist but then start again as soon as he turns his back. The crowd seems even more international than in thirteenth-century Kharkhorum where the Frenchman William of Rubruck was amazed to find not only several of his own countrymen but also Persian architects, a Greek doctor, a Ruthenian goldsmith, an Englishmen named Basil, and assorted other foreigners in attendance to the Mongol Khan. Indeed, about half of the current visitors seem to be speaking French. There're also Germans, Britons, various hues of Slavs, and of course a tightly bunched pack of Japanese. By the time I get to the door of the temple there's not even standing room behind the rows of chanting lamas.

Suddenly losing all desire to see the inside of the Lavran Temple I round up Badmaa and head for the so-called Three Zuu temples which now serve as the main part of the museum complex. On the way we pass the small temple built in 1675 by Zanabazar's brother, Chakhundorj, who ruled as the Tüsheet Khan, to commemorate his pilgrimage to Tibet and his meeting with the Dalai Lama the year before. Nearby, several large temples surrounded by stacks of bricks, tiles, and lumber and encased in scaffolding are undergoing extensive repairs. The masons, as is usually the case throughout Mongolia, are all women. Not for the first time this summer I marvel at the time, effort, and money going into the restoration of cultural monuments destroyed or damaged by the previous regime in Mongolia. Whether these efforts will survive the next wave of barbarians is at this time uncertain.

The three Zuu temples are in a separate courtyard surrounded by a brick wall. The first of them, the so-called Western Temple, was built under of the auspices of Abudai, the great-grandfather of Zanabazar; the other two, the Central and Eastern temples, apparently were constructed at a slightly later date. In the Western Temple are idols depicting Sanjaa, the buddha who appeared prior to the historical buddha Shakyamuni, Shakyamuni himself in his old age, and Maitreya, the coming buddha. In front of the temple is a small square building of plaster-covered brick which supposedly holds the remains of Abudai. Nearby is the foundation of a similar building which once housed the remains of Gombodorj, Zanabazar's father.[34] Almost completely demolished during the upheavals of the 1930s, it is now being reconstructed and is about half completed.

As I am examining this building a Mongolian woman who works as a guide for the museum and who has just finished shepherding a group of French tourists through the three Zuu temples comes up and politely asks if I have any questions. In fact I have just been wondering if Abudai's monument does in fact hold his physical remains, as is implied in most accounts, or whether it is simply a memorial to him. She doesn't know for sure; apparently the building has never been opened since it was originally built. If Gombodorj's remains were in his tomb they were obviously removed and presumably destroyed after it was razed in the 30s. Why the communists chose to destroy the one tomb and not the other is unclear.

Also, I can't help but wonder what happening to the art work, including some invaluable statues by Zanabazar, which had been stolen from the museum earlier in the summer. On this subject she has some news. Acting on a tip, police made a predawn raid on a ger in Töv aimag and recovered twenty-one of the twenty-two statues, including all the Zanabazars. A forty-one-year-old unemployed man and his son and nephew were arrested and reportedly confessed that they had driven to Kharkhorin and cased the monastery for forty-eight hours before breaking in at midnight and heisting the artwork. They had planned to smuggle the statues across the border to China and sell them there in the thriving black market for Buddhist art. The statues have been returned to the museum but are currently being examined for damage and are not yet out on public display. This is not the first theft here at the museum, the woman adds. In 1973 eight statues were stolen and in 1995 another fifteen, all of which were eventually recovered. Sensing what she perhaps considers an inordinate interest in this subject the guide asks, "You're not a buyer of Buddhist art are you?" I assure her I that I am merely a harmless tourist studying the life of Zanabazar and have no interest in acquiring Buddhist art, hot or otherwise.

Badmaa and I exit via the big gateway on the western side of the monastery and without thinking turn left, hoping to circumambulate the monastery's vast outer wall. A man who appears to be stationed here for this specific purpose halts us with an outstretched palm and informs us that if we wish to circle the wall we must turn around and do so clockwise. Thus chastised and redirected, we begin our circumambulation. The wall with its 108 stupas, which to many viewers may be the monastery's most singular feature–it certainly presents an imposing site rising out of the otherwise featureless steppe–is a relatively late phenomenon. Not until 1804, over two hundred years after the founding of the monastery, were the first fifty-six stupas built along the course of the present wall. By 1809 an additional thirty-six had been built, and all the stupas had been connected by walls of clay and unfired bricks. The stupas, noted Pozdneev, "as is evident from the inscriptions found on them, were erected by alms givers and worshippers of Buddha of the most diverse calling, from princes of the first class to the most ordinary Mongolian common people distinguished at the time by their having surplus means."[35] When Pozdneev first visited Erdene Zuu in 1877 the walls connected the stupas had crumbled to the point where they "did not even resemble walls, but formed so to speak, earthen banks around the whole monastery between which the suburgans [stupas] stood out like beacons of some kind."[36]

By the time Pozdneev returned in 1892 a new, much more substantial stone slab and clay wall had been built and parts of it had already been faced with brick. Lamas informed him that all of it would be brick-faced when sufficient funds were found. Presumably the wall was finished at some point in time. Then in 1937 it was, along with the monastery buildings, damaged by the communists. Now, twelve of the 108 stupas and portions of the wall are being repaired. UNESCO is reportedly kicking in $35,000 for restorations, along with about $20,000 from the current Mongolian government and an unspecified amount from the Japanese government. A half-dozen Mongolian women are up on scaffolding around one of the stupas as we walk by. Looking up from her troweling, one shouts, "Hey, you Richard Gere?" A couple of the others find this comparison so preposterous that they almost fall off the scaffolding from laughter.

Near the northeast corner of the monastery is one of the four immense turtles carved from solid stone which once stood at the four corners of the ancient Mongol capital of Kharkhorum. Two of the other turtles have been lost in the intervening centuries–perhaps stolen, although transporting these multiton monsters would have presented obvious logistical problems–but the fourth is said to be nearby, although no one can tell us precisely where. Around the turtle at the northeast corner has sprung up an open-air market where thirty or forty people are hawking the ubiquitous water color landscapes available everywhere in Mongolia; antique religious paraphernalia including brass bells, incense urns, and amulets; handmade silver rings, bracelets, and pendants; thangkas both antique and new; wood carvings, old coins and Soviet-era pin; fur hats and fox and wolf skins, cigarettes, sodas, tattered postcards, and assorted detritus.

Fending off the entreaties of this voracious throng I continue on to a white stupa a few hundred feet from the corner of the monastery wall. This is the tomb of Khandjav, the mother of Zanabazar and Chakhundorj, the Tüsheet Khan. The stupa was constructed in the 1670s, around the time Chakhundorj made his pilgrimage to Tibet. It was placed here because Khandjav, being a woman, could not be buried within the monastery itself. From the looks of the untrammeled grass around the tomb it appears that few, if any, of the many sightseers to the monastery ever come here. Khandjav, who at Yesön Züil gave birth to the little boy who became the first Bogd Gegen of Mongolia, rests here in silence. I sit down to contemplate the scene and ponder the legacy left behind by Khandjav's son.

For much of the twentieth century Zanabazar was castigated as a figurehead of religion in a country which officially espoused atheism, a representative of a feudal system which had supposedly oppressed the Mongolian "masses" (whoever they may be), and a quisling who colluded in the takeover of Mongolia by imperialist China. This viewpoint was expressed as late as 1989 by the art historian N. Tsultem, who opined that Zanabazar and feudal princes "provided the basis for the more than 500 [sic] years long Manchu control of the Mongols. Little justification can be found for Zanabazar during whose theocratic reign this sad page was added to Mongolia's history."[37] Author J. Choinkhor, writing in 1995, took a somewhat revisionist stance: "History writers of the communist period denied Zanabazar's contribution into Mongolian science, literature, philosophy and art, and led by socialistic principles, they regarded Zanabazar guilty in the conquest of Mongolia by Manchu empire without taking into account then prevailing situation in the country and the region."[38]

Among non-historians, however, Zanabazar's reputation remains tainted. Of perhaps two dozen people I questioned about Zanabazar the majority had a negative opinion of him. One highly educated man in his fifties, a skilled linguist who once translated for Y. Tsedenbal (Mongolian president, 1974-84) but who now is an outspoken democrat, told me, "I can't see why there is all this fuss about Zanabazar. Just the other day someone was telling me what a great man he was. He was a bad man! He betrayed this country to the Chinese!" A young man in his early twenties, the son of formerly high-ranking communist party members, very well educated, with a remarkable knowledge of Mongolian history, and who now works in a private bank, told me that Galdan, Zanabazar's nemesis, was "a real warrior, a fighter, a hero who stood up for Mongolia against the Manchus. Zanabazar sold out Mongolia to the enemy." Thus Zanabazar's legacy remains ambiguous.

Although there are numerous, indeed countless, other places in Mongolia connected with the life of Zanabazar, my own investigations, at least for the moment, must end here at his mother's grave. Late the following afternoon, after a short side trip to visit the famous stone stele commemorating the life of Kul Tegin (685-731), one of the rulers of the Turkish empire which controlled all of Mongolia from 683 to 734, and a further detour to the extensive ruins of the ancient city of Karabalgasun, the capital of the Uighur empire from 745 to 840 when it was sacked by marauding Kirghis from the upper Yenisei basin, we started back to Ulaan Baatar.

About fifteen miles outside of Kharkhorin we stopped at a roadside ger where people were selling airag. Tumur and Badmaa each filled ten-liter plastic jugs to take back to Ulaan Baatar. Tumur also bought a couple of kilos of cooked marmot, some of which we ate immediately. Then he proceeded to drink more airag and chatter with the people at the ger. This went on for about twenty minutes. We had a long drive in front of us and I chided Tumur about getting back on the road. One more bowl of airag, he kept repeating. Soon the real reason for his dilatoriness appeared in the form of eight jeeps which roared up and parked beside ours. Tumur effusively greeted the drivers of the jeeps who, it seemed, he had met while carousing in the town of Kharkhorin the night before. These jeep drivers had earlier delivered a large group of French tourists to Kharkhorin. The tourists were taking other transportation farther west and the drivers were returning the jeeps to Ulaan Baatar empty except for some translators and other hired hands. Tumur had agreed to meet up with them somewhere on the road outside of Kharkhorin and drive back to Ulaan Baatar together. So, in the words of the old country-western anthem, we had ourselves a convoy. Tumur was in his natural element here, leapfrogging among the string of jeeps, taking roadside breaks to chitchat with the other drivers, and stopping together at guanzes for tea and later dinner. The sun set just as we crossed the Tuul River at Lün.

Driving on in the dark, lost in my own mediations, it occurred to me that the story of Zanabazar was not complete without considering the fate of the subsequent Bogd Gegens. As I mentioned earlier, Zanabazar was thought to be the sixteenth incarnation of Javzandamba. He was also the first of the eight Bogd Gegens, all considered incarnations of Javzandamba, to appear in Mongolia. On May 17, 1924, the Eighth Bogd Gegen "changed his vestments"; i.e., he died. For the previous three years he had reigned as a powerless king, stripped of any secular authority by the revolutionary government, but still held in awe and revered by the Mongolian people. The Mongolian People's Revolutionary Party, which just that year had proclaimed the People's Republic of Mongolia, did not feel strong enough at that point to ban outright a search for his successor, although they must have realized it was an opportune time to end what they considered the feudal, reactionary institution of the Bogd Gegen and the Lamaist religion which he headed.

According to one account they attempted to delay the matter by announcing that any new reincarnation of Javzandamba would not be recognized until he turned eighteen. They probably did not want to see the rise of any Bogd Gegen who might serve as a rallying point for anticommunist movements in the future.

In 1926 high-ranking lamas made a formal petition to the government asking that they be allowed to search for a reincarnation. Later that year the Communist Party Congress made a curious announcement: ". . . as there is a tradition that after the Eighth Incarnation he will not be reincarnated again, but thereafter will be reborn as the General Hanamand in the realm of Shambala, there is no question of installing the subsequent, Ninth Incarnation."[39]

The Shambhala (as it is usually spelled) referred to here is, in the words of the noted Shambhalist Edwin Bernbaum:

> . . . a mystical kingdom hidden behind snow peaks somewhere north of Tibet. There a long line of enlightened kings is supposed to be guarding the most secret teachings of Buddhism for a time when all truth in the world outside is lost in war and the lust for power and wealth. Then, according to prophesy, a future King of Shambhala will come out with a great army to destroy the forces of evil and bring in a golden age. Under his enlightened rule, the world will become, at last, a place of peace and plenty, filled with the riches of wisdom and compassion.[40]

Now it is true that Taranatha, the incarnation of Javzandamba immediately preceding Zanabazar, was a leading proponent of the so-called Kalachakra, or "Wheel of Time" doctrine, which supposedly emanated from the mythical-spiritual kingdom of Shambhala, and during his later years in Tibet he performed Kalachakra initiations two or three times each year. Doubtless, Zanabazar himself was familiar with the Kalachakra teachings and the whole Shambhala myth, as were subsequent Bogd Gegens. In 1798, during the time of the Fourth Bogd Gegen, a Temple of Astrology which specialized in the Kalachakra teachings was established in Urga (Ulaan Baatar) and remained active at least into the

1920s (it's active again now). And it's true that the whole Shambhala myth, with its promise of a king to come who would defeat the forces of Evil and initiate a golden age of Buddhism, had enormous resonance among the populace of central Asia, including Mongolia, as is well documented by Nicholas Roerich, George Roerich, Edwin Bernbaum, and other Shambhalists. It is also true that many Mongolians believed, and continue to believe up to the present-day, that Javzandamba eventually will be reincarnated as a general in the army of Shambhala and serve under the 25th King of Shambhala of Tibet in the final battle against Evil. However, it seems odd that the communist party of Mongolia would have taken this tack of relegating Javzandamba to the Kingdom of Shambhala, since by the 1920s and thereafter the forces of Evil with which the legions of Shambhala would do battle had become specifically identified with the philosophy of materialism as promulgated by Marxist-Leninists.

Anyhow, it soon appeared that despite the imprecations of the communist party the next reincarnation of Javzandamba, the Ninth Bogd Gegen, had been born not in the ethereal realm of Shambhala but on the banks of the Yeröö River in northern Mongolia. In the early summer of 1928 two Mongolian lamas named Gombojitshin and Gendensodnom returned to Urga from a pilgrimage to Tibet and announced that while on the way to Lhasa they "had heard that near the Selenga, at a place called Yalban, a marvelously auspicious child was born . . ."[41] After further inquiries in Mongolia they became convinced that this child was indeed the reincarnation of Javzandamba, and they reported their findings to both the government and the Central Committee of the Communist Party. Russian author, linguist, ethnologist, and Shambhalist George Roerich, traveling through northern Mongolia in the late 1920s also heard rumors of this reincarnation:

> Here on the banks of the Iro [Yeröö], a boy was recently born who manifested strange faculties. Mysterious signs accompanied his birth. His mother, a shaman woman, heard mysterious voices, and the boy himself uttered amazing prophecies about the future glory of Buddhist Mongolia.

The news of the appearance of the strange child spread like lightning all over Mongolia. The lamas everywhere whispered about the coming of a new incarnation of Je-tsün tam-pa [Javzandamba] Hutukhtu. The government was obligated to send out a commission of inquiry and to post proclamations in Urga to calm the population. It is sometimes difficult to discount rumors by printed words and the news about the new Bogd Gegen continues to agitate the minds of the deeply religious Mongols.[42]

Finally a group of thirty or so influential lamas spearheaded by Gombojitshin and Gendensodnom called for the induction of the boy as the Ninth Bogd Gegen. This, the new government decided, was going too far. The Bogd Gegen phenomena had to be stamped out. The group was arrested and Gombojitshin and Gendensodnom received jail sentences. Further discussion of inducting a new Bogd Gegen was henceforth banned. I have been unable to discover, either from written sources or from Mongolians with whom I have spoken, what eventually happened to the Mongolian boy believed to be the ninth Bogd Gegen, but given the anti-Lamaist tenor of the government at the time and thereafter it may be assumed that his fate was not a happy one. Thus it would seem that the whole line of the Bogd Gegens of Mongolia of which Zanabazar had been the first had come to end.

If we accept the premise of reincarnation, however, we must allow that while it is possible for a secular government to declare the end of the Bogd Gegens as an institution within Mongolia it is hardly within its grasp to stop the process of rebirth altogether. Javzandamba would presumably be reborn, but when and where? With the dissolution of the communist regime in Mongolia and the reinstitution of religious freedom lamas and others in Mongolia began asking just this question. In 1991 delegations of Mongolian lamas visited the Dalai Lama at his headquarters in India and beseeched him for enlightenment on the fate of the ninth Bogd Gegen. They were not disappointed. In September of 1991 His Holiness the Dalai Lama of Tibet formally announced that the Ninth Bogd Gegen, the reincarnation of Javzandamba, was alive and well and residing in India.

It seems that Jampal Namdrol Chokye Gyaltsen, the Ninth Bogd Gegen's secular name, had been born decades before in Tibet. (His connection, if any, with the boy born on the banks of the Yeröö is unclear.) At the age of four he had been recognized as the reincarnation of Javzandamba by Reting Rinpoche, the Regent in Lhasa, and by other high-ranking lamas and state oracles, but his identity had been kept secret to protect him from possibly deleterious repercussions from the anti-Lamaism government in Mongolia. At the age of seven he entered the Drepung Monastery in Tibet where he studied with a teacher from Mongolia with the Tibetan name of Geshe Thupten Nyima. Like Zanabazar, who had studied with the Fifth Dalai Lama and the Fourth Panchen Lama, he also received instruction from the then-current Dalai Lama and Panchen Lama. At the age of twenty-one he left Drepung and spent the next four years in retreats and on pilgrimages around Tibet. At the age of twenty-five he moved to Ganden Phunstok Ling Monastery, which had been established by Taranatha, the incarnation of Javzandamba immediately prior to Zanabazar. He was twenty-nine when the Chinese invaded Tibet and along with tens of thousands of other Tibetans he fled to India. Living a quiet life as a lama serving the needs of exiled Tibetans, he resided in Darjeeling, Mysore, and Madhya Pradesh until 1991. Upon his public recognition as the Ninth Bogd Gegen he moved to Dharamsala, the headquarters of the Dalai Lama, with whom he had maintained a personal relationship since his early days in Tibet. He has since assumed a somewhat higher profile. In 1994 he toured the United States and Canada where he lectured and met with American followers of Tibetan Buddhism. He has still not returned to Mongolia. The Dalai Lama, however, has visited Mongolia several times in the 1990s, and on his August 1995 sojourn he performed an initiation into the Kalachakra teachings, which, as noted earlier, are believed to have emanated from Shambhala. Some Mongolians I have spoken with believe the Dalai Lama is paving the way for the return of the Ninth Bogd Gegen to Mongolia.

Influential lamas, including D. Choijamts, a top official at Gandan Monastery, have publicly invited the Bogd Gegen back, but the matter is a little stickier than it might appear at first glance. Will he come back merely to visit, as the Dalai Lama has done, or will he come back to stay? If he stays would Mongolian Lamaists again recognize him—a Tibetan after all (although in the past several Bogd Gegens have been Tibetans)—as their undisputed leader, and if not, exactly what place would he take in the Lamaist hierarchy? Given the proclivity for schism in any religious body there are probably influential lamas in Mongolia who are less than thrilled about the reinstitution of a Bogd Gegen who might usurp some of their own powers and perquisites. A tiff has already arisen between the Gandan Monastery in Ulaan Baatar and the Amarbayasgalant Monastery over which is the leader of Lamaism in Mongolia and a returning Bogd Gegen might just exacerbate such tensions.

Although a religious leader, a reinstated Bogd Gegen would inevitably be drawn into politics. Would the current political establishment in Mongolia really greet him with hosannas upon his return? The current president of Mongolia, N. Bagabandi, is after all a member of the Mongolian People's Revolutionary Party, the very same party which banned the Bogd Gegens in the first place and which carried out the horrific reprisals against Lamaism in the 1930s. Now he makes all the right noises about religious freedom—indeed, he showed up at Amarbayasgalant seeking the blessings of the lamas a few days after I was there—but many believe he is a watermelon (i.e., red on the inside) waiting for the resurgence of the communists in Russia, by whom he was educated and politically trained, to reveal his true colors. The rise of a powerful Bogd Gegen in Mongolia is something he and many other politicians could probably do without.

Then there is Mongolia's neighbor to the south which might be expected to bring its immense weight to bear on the issue. Chinese mandarins have had centuries of experience with reincarnated religious figures and know full well the power they can exert on their followers. The Chinese leadership's vicious feud with the current Dalai Lama is the stuff of front page news and need not be elaborated upon here. (Even as I write this comes word of an alleged scheme by Chinese security forces to assassinate the Dalai Lama.)

The situation with the current Panchen Lama is even more

convoluted. The Tenth Panchen Lama (1938-89) was enthroned in 1951, but after a 1964 speech supporting the exiled Dalai Lama he was arrested and held in Beijing under virtual house arrest for many years. He died in 1989 at the age of fifty-one of an apparent heart attack, but rumors persist to this day that he was murdered. On May 14, 1995, the exiled Dalai Lama recognized six-year-old Gendhun Choekyl Nyima of Tibet as the Eleventh Panchen Lama. Three days later this boy was arrested by Chinese authorities and whisked away. Often described as the world's youngest political prisoner, his current whereabouts are unknown. The lama–Chatrel Rinpoche–who had first found the boy was also arrested and is rumored to have died in prison. Shortly thereafter Chinese authorities produced their own six-year-old boy who they claimed was in fact the reincarnated Panchen Lama. On a nationally televised newscast in January of 1996 this boy was shown meeting President and Communist Party General Secretary Jiang Zemin and presenting him with a prayer scarf. Of course, followers of the Dalai Lama consider this boy an impostor, a puppet of the Chinese authorities.

The choice of the Panchen Lama is crucial because traditionally he has played a decisive role in the selection of the next Dalai Lama. The Fourteenth Dalai Lama is now in his sixties and presumably the current Panchen Lama would be instrumental in choosing his successor. If the Panchen Lama is merely their puppet Chinese authorities could use him to choose their own future Dalai Lama, or perhaps even have him announce that the Fourteen Dalai Lama is the last of the line, as was done with the Eighth Bogd Gegen. On another level, they might well wish to control the earthly coil of the reincarnation some believe will eventually be reborn as the King of Shambhala and lead the final battle against the forces of Materialism.

In light of its problems with these troublesome reincarnations the specter of a Bogd Gegen once again enthroned in Mongolia must give Chinese authorities pause. The reemergence of the Dalai Lama-Panchen Lama-Bogd Gegen triumvirate such as existed from the seventeenth to early-twentieth centuries, but now with the Bogd Gegen seated in an independent Mongolia serving as the linchpin of a Lamaist world stretching from the ramparts of the Himalayas north to the taiga of Buryatia in the Russian Republic, an area which would include Tibet,

Inner Mongolia, and much of western China, is not a scenario for which the current Chinese regime can be expected to exhibit a great deal of enthusiasm. And thus the future of the Ninth Bogd Gegen remains uncertain.

It was after midnight when we crossed the Tuul River just outside of Ulaan Baatar. We soon passed by the Winter Palace of the Eighth Bogd Gegen. A full moon shone its refulgent light on the white palace and the tops of the temples visible above the walls of the compound. Will the Ninth Bogd Gegen ever come here and reclaim his position as the religious leader of Mongolia, carrying on the tradition started by Zanabazar in 1639? Shortly after I returned from my search for Zanabazar I wrote to the Ninth Bogd Gegen at his headquarters in Dharamsala, asking what his future plans are, but as I write this I have received no reply.

PART III

The Birthplace of the Mongols

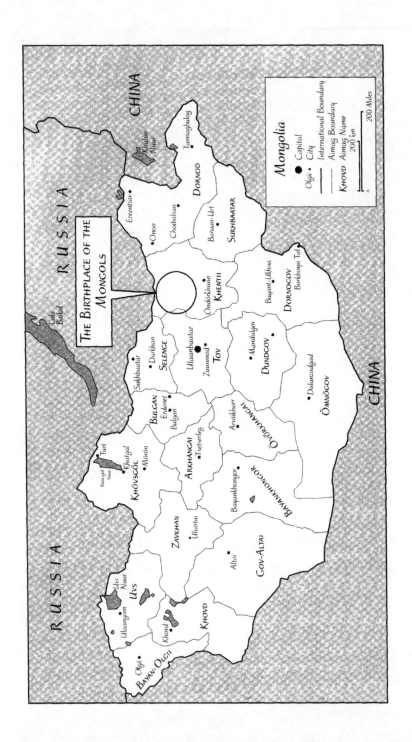

RUSSIA

CHINA

CHINA

RUSSIA

Mongolia

- ● Capital
- Olgii ● City
- International Boundary
- Aimag Boundary
- KHOVD Aimag Name

200 Miles
200 km

THE BIRTHPLACE OF THE MONGOLS

Khulun Nuur

TAMSAGBULAG

DORNOD

SUKHBAATAR

Ereentsav

Onon ●

Choibalsan

Baruun-Urt

KHENTII

Öndörkhaan

Bayan-Ulhaa

DORNOGOV

Borkhoyn Tal

Darkhan

SELENGE

Sukhbaatar

ULAANBAATAR

Zuunmod

TOV

MANDALGOV

DUNDGOV

Dalanzadgad

ÖMNÖGOV

BULGAN

Erdenet

Bulgan

ARKHANGAI

Tsetserleg

Arvaikheer

ÖVÖRKHANGAI

Lake Baikal

Turt

Khovsgol Nuur

Khatgal

Mörön

KHÖVSGÖL

BAYANKHONGOR

Bayankhongor

ZAVKHAN

Uliastai

GOV-ALTAI

Altai

Uvs Nuur

UVS

Ulaangom

Khovd

KHOVD

BAYAN-ÖLGII

Olgii

Ulaan Baatar to Möngönmort

ACCORDING TO THE thirteenth-century chronicle entitled the *Secret History of the Mongols* the people now known as Mongols first appeared at the headwaters of the Onon River just north of a mountain called Burkhan Khaldun in the latter half of the eighth century. These people, then still just one tribe among the many which inhabited what is now Mongolia, soon expanded into the valleys of the nearly Kherlen and Tuul rivers. The upper basins of these three rivers–the Onon, the Kherlen, and the Tuul–make up the so-called Three Rivers Region considered to be the traditional homeland of the Mongols. Also, the mountain known as Burkhan Khaldun, located between the headwaters of the Onon and Kherlen, figured in several episodes recounted in the *Secret History* and was the scene of a crucial event in the life of Chingis Khan himself. As a result he worshipped this mountain, and he gave specific instructions that it should be honored by his descendants' descendants forever. As I would learn, modern-day Mongolians have not forgotten this injunction.

Apart from historical considerations, the Onon is of geographical interest. It is the ultimate source of the great eastward-flowing Amur River, which eventually empties into the Pacific Basin across from Sakhalin Island, north of Japan. For much of its length this river forms the border between Russia and China. The Amur begins at the confluence of the Argun and Shilka rivers; the Shilka, in turn, begins at the confluence of the Ingoda and the Onon. The Onon is the larger of the two, and thus the beginning of the Onon is the source of the Amur-Shilka-Onon river system. According to the *National Geographic Atlas of the World* the Amur-Shilka-Onon measures 2,738 miles in length and thus ranks as the ninth longest river system in the world.

Naturally I was interested in visiting the Three Rivers Region and most particularly the headwaters of the Onon. The Onon begins in a remote part the Khentii Mountains in north central Mongolia, not far from the Mongolian-Russian border. Inquiries in Ulaan Baatar soon revealed that the only practical way to get to the upper Onon was to go by jeep to the small sum center of Möngönmort, in the Kherlen valley in Töv province, and from there travel by horse up the Kherlen. From the upper Kherlen a pass just west of Khentii Khan Uul, which I was told was another name for Burkhan Khaldun, leads to the headwaters of the Onon, in Khentii province. An USDOD map on a scale of 1:500,000—the best map I could obtain—indicated that the distance from Möngönmort to the beginning of the Onon was just over fifty miles.

I chartered a jeep and at mid-August we—my translator, a woman in her thirties named Tuya, our driver, and I—left Ulaan Baatar on the main road heading east toward Öndörkhaan, the capital of Khentii aimag. Soon after the coal mining town of Nailakh the road is undergoing major reconstruction financed, according to Tuya, by the Japanese. From the looks of the nearly completed sections this will be one of the best roads in the country. In the meantime we take one of the many jeep trails running parallel to the new highway. These have been blazed by people avoiding the rougher sections of the old road. Ready-made detours are never in short supply in Mongolia. Almost every road has a couple—sometimes a half-dozen or more—parallel tracks.

Soon we drive up on two big East German army trucks parked on the steppe. These, Tuya informs me, belong to her regular employer in Ulaan Baatar, an outfitting company which specializes in group tours of the Mongolian countryside. In one truck are eight men on a sports fishing jaunt to the Kherlen River. Seven of them, it turns out when we are introduced, are expatriates living in Hong Kong six Americans and one Englishman. The eighth is a reporter for *USA Today*. Except for the reporter, who is in his early thirties, the men are in their forties and fifties. They plan to fish for a week and do a little horseback riding. The other army truck is a kitchen on wheels. They will stay in tents on the Kherlen, but their meals will be prepared by the staff in this mobile kitchen. Tuya now informs me that for convenience's sake she has made arrangements for us to spend the first night with this group on the Kherlen. The next day we will start out on horses for the Onon.

Tuya–short, medium build, hair cropped off at the back like a man's–speaks excellent, if somewhat strangely accented, English. Like most Mongolians Russian is actually her first foreign language. Just since 1990 has her interest shifted to English. I was lucky to get her as a translator. Most often she works for upmarket tour groups to the Gobi Desert or those with specialized interests like birding or ethnology. Her good English and pleasant yet forthright personality ensures that many return customers ask for her. She also gets some high profile clients. A month before she had translated for a "very big man" with *NBC News* named "Tom Broker"–only after questioning her some more did I realize this was Tom Brokaw. Thus her dance card is usually full during the summer, and she decided to come with me only after discovering that we had a mutual interest in the *Secret History*. She admitted that this might be her only chance to go to the source of the Onon north of Burkhan Khaldun, where scheduled tour groups never go. She is a native of Khentii Aimag–born in Öndörkhaan–and she felt she should visit this famous landmark in her home aimag.

About fifty miles from Ulaan Baatar we cross a low pass which marks the divide between the basin of the Tuul River, in which Ulaan Baatar is located, and the basin of the Kherlen River. This divide is also the boundary between two of three great drainage systems of Mongolia– the Arctic Ocean drainage and the Pacific Ocean drainage. Dropping through low hills we soon reach the edge of the vast Kherlen River basin, here twenty to thirty miles wide. It was in these immense pastures that the first tribes which made up the Mongols flourished.

The Kherlen, one of Mongolia's five longest rivers (676 miles within Mongolia), begins just southeast of Burkhan Khaldun Mountain, about twenty-five miles from the source of the Onon–some of its tributaries begin just a mile or two from tributaries of the Onon–and then flows almost due south to near the southern edge of Khentii Aimag before looping around to the northeast. Flowing through Öndörkhaan, the capital of Khentii aimag, it continues northeastward through Dornod aimag, crosses the border into China, and eventually flows into Khölön Nuur. Khölön Nuur normally drains via the Argun River (during dry periods it doesn't drain at all) which combines with the Shilka to form the Amur. Thus the waters which drain into the Onon from the slopes just north of Burkhan Khaldun and into the Kherlen to the south are finally united in the Amur.

Just west of the border between Töv and Khentii aimags we turn north on the road to the town of Baganuur. Off to the right, on the tablelands near the Kherlen River, can be seen the spoil piles and dragline booms of the strip mines which are the city's reason for existence. These mines, which reportedly produce 6 million tons of coal a year, supply most of the energy used by the power plants in Ulaan Baatar. Soon we pass through Baganuur, a cluster of Soviet-style apartment blocks plopped down in the middle of the steppe. Created from scratch in 1978, the town now has a population of about seventeen thousand. Except for the horses tied up to the light poles in front of apartment buildings it could pass for any bleak industrial suburb in the old Soviet Union.

From Baganuur a dirt road continues north up the Kherlen valley thirty-three miles to Möngönmort. After about ten miles the Kherlen River, which up until now has flowed out of sight on the far side of the valley, finally comes into view. For about ten miles we follow its left bank, then veer to the northwest. Möngönmort, a village of perhaps 800, is nestled beneath some hills along the edge of the valley, about eight miles from the river. Asking around, we soon track down our horse wrangler, a man in his late twenties named Bagabandi ("Just call me Bagi") who lives on the edge of town in a ger enclosed by a high wooden fence. He invites us in, and his wife quickly serves up salted milk tea followed by bowls of mutton and noodle soup. Bagi is currently unemployed—his usual job is unclear—but he has a couple of mouths to feed—there's a baby crawling about his ger—and he is quite eager to work as a horse wrangler and guide. His father, who lives in a ger fifteen miles up the Kherlen, has plenty of horses. Excusing himself,

Bagi explains that he must see the ranger of the Khan Khentii Strictly Protected Area, who is headquartered here in Möngönmort, and get permits for our trip. Created in 1992, the 4,786-square-mile nature preserve encompasses the upper Kherlen and Onon where we are headed, and supposedly permission is needed to enter this area, although Bagi admits that very few people actually bother getting permits.

When he returns we drive north along the Kherlen and finally catch up with the East German army trucks containing the fishermen from Hong Kong. They plan to camp just a couple miles upstream from the ger of Bagi's father. A local man with a jeep leads us all to a large clearing right next to the Kherlen. Soon a tractor pulling a wagon appears and a couple of local men begin to assemble a ger which will be used for the fishermen's dining room. Obviously these guys are traveling in style. It takes exactly forty minutes for six Mongolian men to set up a four-wall ger. While dinner is being prepared in the mobile kitchen a couple of the fishermen assemble fly rods and make a few exploratory casts. The Kherlen, however, is nearly over its banks from recent rains and it's soon obvious that the fishing is going to be slow. Tuya and I have our own fish to fry. We need to buy a sheep from Bagi's father and have it butchered that evening. Tuya agrees to go with Bagi and oversee this operation while I remain here in camp.

Fishing soon palls and the fishermen assemble around the campfire. Three or four bottles of excellent Australian and Californian wines materialize—merlots and cabernets. These guys are serious wine connoisseurs and there follows a long plaint about how difficult it is to get good wines in Hong Kong. As is my custom when going into the back country I had brought no alcohol on this trip—and I had certainly not expected to be doing any socializing this evening—so I just sit quietly by the fire and listen. Not until they have finished six or so bottles does one of them inquire if I might like some wine. None, of course, is offered to the several Mongolians scurrying around gathering firewood and setting up folding tables and chairs in the ger dining room. Soon we retire into the ger for dinner, which is served restaurant-style with two of the Mongol men acting as waiters. The fishermen seem a bit perplexed to find me, an apparently uninvited guest, in their midst, but Tuya has assured me that the meal was included in the overall fee I am paying for the jeep charter that day. I admit it is the first time I have been with one of these upmarket tour groups, and I find the experience a bit disconcerting. The main topic of conversation is various restaurants in Hong Kong where they have eaten, a subject to which I can add nothing. The unspoken corollary to the stories about Hong Kong food is the apparent inadequacy of the mutton, instant mashed potatoes, and canned vegetables we are being served. At least the wine begins to flow more freely–they have several cases–and soon a couple bottles of Scotch and Irish whiskey appear. Finally the group moves back to the campfire. A case of beer which has been cooling in the river is dredged up. It looks to be a long night. I retire to my tent early, even before Tuya had returned from her sheep-procuring trip.

Headwaters
of the Onon

ALL IS QUIET when I awaken the next morning. The only sign of last night's bash is a thin ribbon of smoke rising from the ashes of the campfire. Soon Tuya appears from her tent. All went well with the sheep; it was extremely fat and we should easily have enough mutton for the entire trip. She also announces that Bagi's father, Zevgee, wants to come along with us. He has lived in this area all his life and is extremely knowledgeable, she says, and he also has read the *Secret History* in Mongolian and is familiar with many of the places named in it.

After tea, bread, and blueberry jam in the dining tent–the fishermen slowly appear one by one, looking the worse for wear after last night's debauch–we take the jeep over to Zevgee's ger. Meeting him I am immediately reassured. In his early sixties, with close-cropped gray hair, he exudes self-confidence and aplomb. We retire to his ger, where his wife serves us milk tea and khaimag, the mixture of butter solids and flour for which I have grown fond. When I mention this she laughs and immediately begins to prepare a new batch for us to take along. We also buy three homemade cheeses, each weighing two kilos or more, and a large jar of thick cream the consistency of mayonnaise. The mutton has already been cut up into manageable chunks. The innards of the sheep, which I did not want, had been cooked up last night, and the remains of this feast rest in a large basin sitting by the stove.

Outside Bagi has driven a dozen horses into a corral. "Tell the American to pick out his horse," he yells to Tuya from among the milling herd. I see a long-legged chestnut standing alone in the corner of the corral. It is resting with its weight on one back leg and has a calm look in its eye. I point to it and shout, "That one!"

"Exactly so," cries Bagi, as Tuya translates it, "that's just the one I had picked out for him." With a *uurgaa*–a long pole with a loop of rope on the end–he snares this horse and four others. Another young man very cautiously slips bridles on them–the horses are always skittish until bridled–and then saddles them up. Bagi comes with us in the jeep back to the fishermen's camp and Zevgee brings the horses.

Zevgee has two pairs of huge leather saddle bags which greatly facilitate the loading of our gear on the pack horse. Two smaller pairs will be carried by him and Bagi. Still, it takes over an hour to get everything sorted and packed up. At 12:20 we finally mount up, bid farewell to the fishermen–they will be long gone by the time we return–and head north on the jeep track paralleling the Kherlen. Our horses are frisky to a fault, so to let off some steam we fast-trot and gallop them for the first five miles or so. Near the fishermen's camp the valley of the Kherlen is still almost ten miles wide, and except for some cottonwoods and willows along the river uninterrupted steppe stretches to the far ridges. About eight miles upstream the valley quickly narrows and tongues of larch forest lap down the encroaching ridges toward the river. Just to our left rise three peaks, sentinels guarding the approach to the upper Kherlen. The first, Zevgee tells us as we slow to a walk, is called Mönkh Jargalant (Eternal Happiness); the second is Dund Jargalant (Middle Happiness); and the third Baruun Jargalant (West Happiness, although it is in fact north of the other two). Next on the left is a mountain known as Khambyn Ereen. In the old days, says Zevgee, lamas often came here and camped in gers on the side of the mountain, which has numerous flat grassy benches. It was thought to be an auspicious place for reading the scriptures of Lamaism. Not far past Khambyn Ereen the jeep track we have been following veers to the right toward the Kherlen. A half mile away we can see a wooden bridge across the river. Zevgee explains that from there the main jeep trail goes up the opposite side of the Kherlen toward its source. We continue on the less traveled jeep trail on this side of the river.

Ahead and to the left looms a still higher bare-domed mountain. This is 7,531-foot Erdene Mount, which Zevgee says is mentioned in the Mongolian version of the *Secret History*. Although he is a herdsman without any higher education, Zevgee is, as I mentioned earlier, intimately familiar with this thirteenth-century history of the Mongols. Not only has he studied it himself, but he has worked with several expeditions of Mongolian and foreign historians, archeologists, and ethnologists who used the book as a starting point for their own researches into early Mongol history and especially into the life of Chingis Khan. The most notable of these, or at least the best funded and most aspiring, was the so-called Three Rivers Joint Mongolian-Japanese Expedition, which was largely funded by the Japanese. Using high attitude aerial photography and assorted remote sensing equipment supposedly capable of locating archeological remains—Zevgee is a bit hazy about the technical details—the expedition spent two and a half years in the Three Rivers Region looking for the grave of Chingis Khan, which for the Japanese is like the Holy Grail and the Ark of the Covenant rolled into one. Chingis eluded them, of course, but according to Zevgee they did succeed in antagonizing some Mongolians who believe that Chingis's final resting place should remain a secret, as Chingis himself obviously intended. He adds that many of the local people don't like foreigners poking around this area at all, and most especially not around Burkhan Khaldun, the mountain which Chingis himself worshipped.

Some Japanese, however, seem to believe that they have a racial affinity with Mongolians and thus are not in the same category as other foreigners. Chingis for them epitomizes the greatness of Asia—the Asia of which they see themselves at the forefront. Japan, attempting to establish a foothold here in the middle of the continent, invaded Mongolia in the late 1930s and was dealt a devastating military defeat at the hands of the Soviet and Mongolian armies. (Just this summer the remains of Japanese soldiers killed in the conflict were returned to Japan amidst great fanfare.) Now they dump tens of millions of dollars of aid, loans, and investments into Mongolia—one hundred of the big blue buses plying the streets of Ulaan Baatar are outright gifts from the Japanese—and spend millions more on projects like the Three Rivers Expedition. Zevgee tells us that this past June the honorary head of the Three Rivers Expedition–an eighty-four-year-old archeologist who once served as a tutor to the Japanese Emperor–was flown by helicopter from Ulaan Baatar to the summit of Burkhan Khaldun, the mountain worshipped by Chingis. Here he paid homage to the World Conqueror. Zevgee, as one of the expedition's guides, got to go along on the helicopter and witnessed the whole event.

As we approach closer to Erdene Mount Zevgee tells us that near the summit of this peak is a rock pinnacle, over fifty feet high and twenty feet wide at the top, which once served as a hitching post for Chingis's armies. How one would get a lead rope around such a hitching post and what a whole army would be doing near the summit of a 7,531-foot mountain are unclear to me, but I let the matter pass.

Just past Songino Creek, a small tributary of the Kherlen flowing out of the hills below Erdene Mount, and off to the right near the river can be seen some corrals partly hidden in a copse of larch. This, says Zevgee, is his winter camp, where he moves his ger and livestock after the snow starts flying. The spot is protected from the wind and relatively warm, he notes. Our horses jerk their heads toward the corrals and try to turn that way but we keep them on the path. "They recognize their winter quarters," says Zevgee, "They like it here."

A bit farther on Zevgee points to Erdene Mount. "There, on the horizon just to the left of the summit, is the hitching post Chingis used." From this distance it looks like a small nipple on the ridge. "And look other there," he adds, pointing to a mountain on the other side of the valley six or seven miles away. "That mountain is called Dash Norov. See on the ridge to the left? There is another rock used as a hitching post." Indeed, there was a small bump on the ridge. "Chingis's armies stretched a rope between the rock on Erdene Mount and the rock on Dash Norov and to this rope they tethered their horses." I burst out laughing. I had thought he was referring to actual hitching posts. Obviously this is a phantasmagoric legend. But when Tuya explains why I am laughing Zevgee replies enigmatically, "Who knows? Maybe things were different in those days."

We cross Yamaakhai Creek, another tributary flowing down off Erdene Mount, and where the creek flows into the Kherlen we stop for a late lunch. Gathering firewood in the grassy glades next to the river I'm amazed by the profusion of wild flowers still in bloom—various buttercups, purple asters, burnet, artemisia, forget-me-nots, silverberry, edelweiss, and most surprisingly, northern anemones, usually one of the first flowers to appear in the spring, often before the snow melts. With the exception of edelweiss I am familiar with these flowers from Alaska, where most would have flowered by mid-July at the latest. Here they are blooming in the third week of August. Perhaps the extremely dry early summer experienced by most of Mongolia had inhibited many plants, and only the plentiful rains of August had caused them to flower. Only fireweed, the unfailing harbinger of the seasons, has not been fooled. It has bloomed and dropped all its flowers, a sure sign that summer is indeed over.

While we are eating our cold mutton, cheese, and khaimag, Zevgee points out two more mountains on the far side of the valley—Baga Khorig and Ikh Khorig. Both, he says, are mentioned in the Mongolian version of the *Secret History*, and some Mongolian researchers he talked to years before believed that Chingis was buried somewhere near the base of Ikh Khorig. The Three Rivers Expedition, however, checked out this area thoroughly and found nothing. I pull out for the first time my copy of an English translation of the *Secret History* and check the index for these places. I can't find them, although they might well be listed by some other name. Zevgee asks to see the book. Of course he can't read English, but he is amazed that an English translation of the *Secret History* exists and intrigued that I should take an interest in it. He and Tuya put their heads together and page through the book. Zevgee asks a lot of questions and several times I hear the words "Burkhan Khaldun." Finally he asks, "Would to like to go to the top of Burkhan Khaldun?"

Now when planning this trip I had specified only that I wanted to go to the headwaters of the Onon. I knew we would have to cross a pass west of Khentii Khan Uul, which people in Ulaan Baatar had told me was another name for the mountain known as Burkhan Khaldun, but I had no idea how close we would get to its actual base. Although almost all Mongolian people I had talked to had heard of Burkhan Khaldun none had actually been there, and no one could give me any information about climbing the peak. Apparently it was climbable–after all the summit was only 7,724 feet high; I had been in valley bottoms in the Khangais higher than that–but I assumed the ascent would have to be made on foot, and I knew the great reluctance of Mongolians to go anywhere that can't be reached by horses. If we did get near enough to the base to attempt an ascent I would probably have to do it alone. But of course I did very much want to climb the mountain.

"Is it possible to climb to the summit?" I ask tentatively. "Yes," says Zevgee, "you can even take horses the whole way to the summit, although it is very difficult. You have to walk the horses up some of the steeper places, but it can be done in one day–if you leave very early in the morning. But there is a problem. Many local people don't like foreigners climbing this mountain. From reading the *Secret History* you know that Chingis himself worshipped Burkhan Khaldun. It is a very sacred place. Tomorrow we will see the mountain. Let's talk about it more then."

Four-wheel-drive vehicles can take the track we have been following as far as Yamaakhai Creek, at least if the weather is dry, but few venture beyond here. The Three Rivers Expedition went farther but they had specially equipped all-terrain vehicles outfitted (and donated) by a Japanese auto-maker, and they traveled in a convoy of seven vehicles, so that they could pull each other out when they got stuck. After the heavy rains of August the track is very wet, and we go through some boggy areas that would have stopped any vehicle. Straight ahead of us are three mountains in a row–Baldanch, Jakhüüjin, and Bayan Öndör. Zevgee explains that just in front of these mountains the Kherlen curves away to the right, eastward. We turn to the left and head up the valley of the Shirengetei River, a tributary of the Kherlen.

Entering the mouth the Shirengetei valley we pass out of the steppe zone completely. Thickets of willows line the banks of the river, and moist tundra dominated by knee-high dwarf birch carpets the rest of the valley bottom to the base of the encroaching ridges, which are mantled with thick forests of larch. Riding through a tongue of larch intruding into the valley we hear sharp barking which sounds exactly like a dog. This, says Bagi, is a musk deer. A little farther on a large patch of ground has been thoroughly uprooted. "Wild pigs," notes Bagi, "digging for roots." After following the left side of the river for about an hour we come to a dry bench overlooking the river bottom. Here we decide to spend the night. Over the closest ridge peeks the bare summit of Erdene Mount, almost 2,000 feet above us—the elevation of our campsite is 5,543 feet. As we eat our dinner of fried mutton and potatoes Jupiter appears over the ridge to the southeast, soon joined by red Mars to the southwest. By the time we turn in the Seven Wise Men, as Tuya calls them (the Big Dipper), are directly overhead.

Zevgee has a fire going and water boiling when I awaken at seven the next morning. I knock the ice out of my cup and have some instant coffee. Overhead is a solid dome of cobalt blue and my barometer has been rising all night. We should have a nice day. The others belatedly appear and we breakfast on the remains of the mutton and potatoes from last night. This is our first morning together and we have yet to establish a routine, so it's 10:30 by the time we break camp, load our pack horse, and get moving.

For a mile or two we follow a fairly dry trail along the edge of the ridge to the left of the river. Then Zevgee announces that we must cross the valley bottom, here about a half-mile wide, and pick up a track running along the base of the ridge on the other side. The moist tundra soon grades into marsh and swamp and our horses start floundering in the mud. Once my horse falls to its knees, and I have to jump off to allow it to get back on its feet. The river itself meanders between five-foot-high banks and is surprisingly deep. We battle through thick stands of willows higher than the heads of our horses for a quarter of a mile before finding a place where we can ford. After another bad patch of bog we emerge on the track along the base of the ridge. Zevgee tells us that a mere fifty years ago this river bottom was covered with steppe and that there are old-timers who can remember when people set up gers here and grazed livestock in the summer. He also maintains that Mongolian researchers he has been with say that the larch forests on the lower flanks of the mountains have appeared here only in the last two or three hundred years. The climate is changing, he opines, and the edge of the Siberian taiga is advancing relentlessly southward.

The track we are following is well-defined, although it appears no one has used it recently. It follows the right bank of the Shirengetei to its mouth and eventually joins the jeep track on the opposite side of the Kherlen. We had taken a shortcut and come upon it several miles above the mouth of the Shirengetei. The Three Rivers Expedition, with their specially equipped all-terrain vehicles, used this track, Zevgee says, and in late fall, after freeze-up and before heavy snows, some hunters come this way by four-wheel-drive truck. Now, after the recent rains, it is impassable by any vehicle. As an afterthought, Zevgee adds, "Zanabazar used this trail to get to the Onon Hot Springs."

"Wait a minute! Zanabazar, the first Bogd Gegen, used this trail?" I blurt out.

"Yes, you have heard of Zanabazar?" he innocently asks.

I explain that I am quite interested in Zanabazar, and that earlier that summer I had visited his birthplace and numerous other places connected with his life. "And what about these hot springs?" I ask. I knew that Zanabazar had investigated the medicinal properties of numerous hot springs, but nowhere in my researches into his life had I found any mention of such springs on the upper Onon, nor had anyone in Ulaan Baatar told me about them when I tried to get information about this area.

"Oh yes, these springs are quite well known among the local people. There is even a log guest house where people can stay. And just recently some people built a small Buddhist temple there. Listen. We can go to the beginning of the Onon, as you suggested, then go downstream to the hot springs. It's only a half day's ride. We can spend the night there." Of course I agree.

The valley of the Shirengetei, which we are ascending, serves as the main passageway between the valleys of the Onon and the Kherlen rivers. Time and time again in the *Secret History* we read about the early Mongol tribes moving between these two rivers, and indeed Chingis himself must have come just this way many times and seen the same sights we are seeing. We soon pass a mountain to our left topped by an assemblage of granite tors which seem to form a natural amphitheater. This is Ëldn Mountain, Zevgee says, adding that on its lower flanks are salt licks which attract many wild animals, including bear and elk. Hunters sometimes come here in search of easy prey. I long to make a detour and explore these interesting rock formations, but I know that Zevgee wants to push on and cross over into the drainage of the Onon by nightfall. Still farther on we see to the left a high, barren mountain called Davaatyn Uul. The lower vegetated flanks of this mountain and the forests at its base, Zevgee says, harbor an unusual variety of medicinal plants (404 different types, he claims, but this figure is probably symbolic). People come from as far away as Ulaan Baatar to collect them. Suddenly at the base of the mountain we see a flash of silver-gray knifing through the underbrush. "*Chono* [wolf]!" shouts Bagi. His hunter's instincts are aroused—he has a rifle slung over his shoulder—and now it is he who wants to take a detour. Zevgee nixes this idea and we push on. Soon we pass a dry, flat shelf along the mountains to the right. This spot is known to local people as Kharganat, and according to Zevgee Mongolian researchers he has guided have determined that Chingis himself camped here.

At three-thirty in the afternoon we reach a small stream flowing out of the mountains to the right. Nearby is a small stand of larch littered with dry firewood. This place, Zevgee announces, is called Maant, and here we will stop for lunch. As we prepare tea Zevgee explains that the mountain directly across the valley is known as Khonog Tolgoi. This was one of the places located and extensively investigated by the Three Rivers Expedition. They found over 150 graves of the Hsiung-nu who ruled Mongolia from 210 B.C. to A.D. 155 and over a dozen graves of Mongolian princes, probably from the Chingis era and immediately thereafter. On a cliff face above the gravesites someone at some unknown date, but apparently after the introduction of Lamaism into Mongolia by Abudai Khan in the 1580s, had carved the words *um ma ni bag mi khym*, the Mongolian version of the famous Buddhist mantra *om mani padme hum*.

During lunch of tea, fried bread, homemade cheese, and khaimag, Zevgee recounts a story about Abudai, who founded the Erdene Zuu

Monastery in 1585 and who was Zanabazar's great-grandfather. Abudai, along with his entourage, came to the upper Kherlen on a hunting expedition and had great success, killing many elk. While camped along the Kherlen Abudai dreamed that a bear came into his ger and tried to maul him. The next morning he said, "I had a bad dream that a bear tried to kill me. The spirits of the mountains must be angry with me because I killed so many animals." Hoping to appease the mountain spirits he had a statue of a horse made and gilded it with silver. This statue, supposedly life-sized, was placed on the summit of a mountain near present-day Möngönmort (*möngön* = silver; *mort* = horse). Zevgee assures me that this is not merely a legend. This statue stood up until the end of the last century and some old people in Möngönmort still have pieces of it.

Back on the trail at 5:30 we trot as quickly as possible on the soggy, muddy track and soon reach the headwaters of the Shirengetei. Veering off to the right we leave the valley and cross Baga Davaa (Little Pass) on a forested ridge. From just beyond the pass a marshy track follows a small creek down to the valley of the Elüür River, a sizable tributary of the Kherlen. Approaching the Elüür we notice an animal standing on an island in the river about 200 yards away. Getting closer we can see a big bull elk with an immense rack. Had the bull thrown back its head, the tines of its antlers probably would have touched its back rump. We ride to within 200 feet of the elk, but it makes no movement; it simply stands perfectly still with its front legs widely spread apart. We ford the river no more than a hundred feet below the animal and still it does not budge. Suddenly not sixty feet away two huge silver-gray wolves jump out of the underbrush and begin loping upstream. Hoping to get a better look at them we charge our horses up onto a high bench overlooking the river valley, but the wolves quickly disappear into the high willows. The elk still has not moved. Bagi opines that the wolves had been chasing the elk for a long time, perhaps all day, and that it was so exhausted it could no longer run. It had gone onto the island to make its last stand against its pursuers, who would have surely brought it down had we not arrived on the scene. We watch for about fifteen minutes, and finally the elk, having gathered its strength, slowly trots off down the valley, in the opposite direction from the wolves, and finally disappears.

Then Zevgee points off to the right. "See that big mountain, the one forested almost to its top? It is called March Mountain. The big barren mountain to its left is called Baatar Yan. See the saddle between them? That mountain behind the saddle, the one with what looks like a small crown on its top–that is the sacred mountain of Burkhan Khaldun. We could camp here on this bench tonight–this is where the Three Rivers Expedition camped when they were looking for the grave of Chingis–but I suggest we keep riding and cross the pass over into the drainage of the Onon before dark. After we visit the hot springs we will return and camp here. Since you are so interested in Chingis and the history of the Mongols I have decided to take you to the top of Burkhan Khaldun. If we start very early in the morning we can get back here before dark. There is one problem. Women are not allowed to go to the summit."

The moment Tuya finishes translating these words, she adds, "And he says that if he and Bagi take you to the mountain I will have to remain behind! No way am I staying here all day by myself!" Why not? I wondered. "Wild animals, wolves, bears, maybe some crazy people will come along!" she cries. Ask Zevgee if he and I can go by ourselves, I tell her. Bagi and she can spend the day resting in camp. "You're crazy! I'm not spending a day alone with Bagi!" she retorts. I really can't imagine what she thinks Bagi would do to her. True, he was quite a rougher piece of goods than his father, but Tuya seems like a woman perfectly capable of taking care of herself. Has there been some undercurrent of behavior going on that I haven't noticed? So just tell Zevgee his plan is fine, I finally tell her. When we get back here we'll figure something out.

We do not follow the valley of the Elüür, which trends off to the east, but instead head north through timbered slopes leading to Ikh Davaa (Big Pass) which separates the drainages of the Onon and the Kherlen. For a couple of miles I ride alongside Tuya. I ask her if she resents that she is not allowed to go to the summit of Burkhan Khaldun. "Oh no," she replies, "there are many places like this where women are not allowed to go. It's either prohibited by the lamas or by tradition. I don't want to upset anyone. You know, Zevgee is a very traditional person. Have you noticed, when he points to a mountain or a river he always has all his fingers stretched out? It's considered very rude to point at things, especially mountains and rivers, with a single finger. This made me think of when I was a small girl and my mother scolded me for this. You should only point at something with a single finger if you are mad at it. Zevgee is very respectful to nature, and to tradition, and I respect that. But still . . . I have heard about Burkhan Khaldun all my life; it is so important to Mongolian people. Yes, maybe I would like to go to the top of Burkhan Khaldun." We ride on farther in silence.

According to the *Secret History*, eleven generations or so after the Mongols settled in the upper Onon there was a chieftain named Duwa-Soqor who with his younger brother, Dobun-mergen, climbed one day to the top of the mountain Burkhan Khaldun. Looking far into the distance–according to legend he had an eye in the middle of head which enabled him to see the distance of a three days' journey–Duwa-Soqor saw a large band of nomads approaching and among them, riding in the front seat of a cart, was a young "girl of beauty." Duwa-Soqor, who was already married, suggested to his younger brother, Dobun-mergen, that he go and inquire about this girl. He discovered that she was a "girl of true beauty and good reputation" who had not been promised to any man and that her name was Alan-qo'a.[1] Her father, Qorilartai-mergen, was from the Barguzin lowland, the area along the eastern shore of Lake Baikal between the Barguzin and Selenga rivers. He had fallen out with other members of his tribe over a ban they had imposed on hunting sables and other animals and had decided to move his family and followers southeast toward the source of the Onon. They were particularly attracted to the area around Burkhan Khaldun because of the plentiful wildlife.

Dobun-mergen married the beautiful girl in the cart, Alan-qo'a, and they had two children, Bügünütei and Belgünütei. Dobun-mergen soon died and Alan-qo'a, who did not remarry, had three more sons, Buqu-qadagi, Buqatu-salju, and Bodunchar-mungqaq. Later the first two sons came to resent the three other sons, whom they considered illegitimate. Alan-qo'a brought her sons together and chastised them, saying, "You five sons were all born of my one belly." Then she handed each an arrow and told them to break it. They did so easily. Then she bundled five arrows together and told her sons to break them. They couldn't. "When you are by ourselves, like the five arrow shafts just now, you can easily be broken by anyone. When you are together and united, like the bound arrow-shafts, how can anyone easily overcome you?"[2]

Soon thereafter Alan-qo'a died. Her sons did not entirely heed her words. Four of them split her property among themselves and cast out the fifth, Bodunchar, who they thought was dull and stupid. After wandering by himself in the valley of the upper Onon and suffering many tribulations, Bodunchar finally met up with his brothers again. Hardened by his experiences Bodunchar was now considered the strongest and under his leadership the brothers plundered neighboring tribes and took control of the upper Onon valley. All the brothers prospered. Eventually each formed his own clan. Bodunchar's clan was called the Borjigin. Eight generations later, Temüjin, the future Chingis Khan, would be born into this clan.

The *Secret History* recounts another story about Burkhan Khaldun. In a confusingly worded passage a shaman named Shinchi-bayyan, apparently a follower of Qorilartai-mergen, the father of Alan-qo'a, went to the summit of Burkhan Khaldun and invoked the spirits of his ancestors. These spirits then became the "spirit owners" or "Lords of the Earth" who thereafter held dominion over the mountain. Indeed, one translator of the *Secret History*, Urgunge Onon, maintains that the correct name of the mountain is Burqan Qaldun and that burqan (pronounced barken) means, in one Mongolian dialect, "spirit of a shamanist." He notes that this should not be confused with the word *burkhan* (a Buddhist idol) by which the mountain is signified in most modern Mongolian and Western literature. He also maintains that the word *qaldun* means "rocky mountain or cliff." According to this interpretation the name *Burqan Qaldun* therefore seems to refer to the spirits of shamans who dwell on this high, rocky mountain. "A Mongolian tradition has this to say about these protective spirits," adds scholar of Mongolian religion Walter Heissig. "'The souls of shamans and shamanesses who died long ago become the Lords . . . that is protective spirits and demons, of . . . mountains, streams, lakes and brooks and forests, and they are both helpful and harmful to living beings."[3] Many years later the young Temüjin sought refuge from his enemies on Burkhan Khaldun (I'll stick with the conventional spelling) and he came to believe that it was these protective spirits which saved his life.

The trail to Ikh Davaa climbs through mixed tundra and taiga vegetation–dwarf birch and willow interspersed with stands of larch. On a slope not far below the pass Zevgee points off to the right. "Over there about a hundred meters, by that stand of larch, are the graves of many Hsiung-nu and at least fourteen Mongol princes," he says, adding that this site was long known to local people and has recently been examined by Mongolian researchers. He spoke with some of the scientists, and they claimed that around the time of Chingis–the twelfth and thirteenth centuries–this area was vegetated by steppe, indicating a much dryer climate. I want to ride over and take a look, but Zevgee says there's really nothing to see; the grave mounds are now covered with thick mats of moss and dwarf birch.

We soon top the forested ridge. Ikh Davaa, which marks the boundary between the watersheds of the Onon and the Kherlen, is unimpressive. A small ovoo of brushwood draped with a few blue prayer scarves marks the spot. Nevertheless we dutifully dismount and walk around the ovoo three times. On the other side the trail drops steeply through a ravine flanked by heavily forested ridges. We walk our horses down and although Zevgee says we must hurry–the sun has already set–we can't resist stopping several times to gorge on huckleberries dripping from the bushes along the trail.

At the bottom of the ravine we remount and follow Davaa Creek down to its confluence with Tsonj Chuluu Creek, which flows out from between steep forested ridges to our left. We hurry through the dense woods in the narrow valley of Tsonj Chuluu Creek until it is almost too dark to see. Amidst the thick stands of larch we finally find a small clearing not far from the creek where we can camp. A big blaze soon cuts through the cold mist which has hunkered down into the valley. Supper is simple: Zevgee cuts up some mutton which, along with some big bones, he throws into our cooking pot. After they boil awhile he tosses in a couple handfuls of rice. It's been a long day and we all huddle quietly by the fire with our bowls of rice stew. Bagi cracks open the bones between two rocks and sucks out the marrow, his greasy face gleaming in the firelight. It's almost midnight before we retire.

I had told Bagi and Zevgee earlier that one of my goals of this trip was to locate the source of the Onon. From my past experiences in Mongolia I had doubts as to whether they understood what I meant by "source." We discuss this the next morning over our warmed-up rice stew. Zevgee maintains that the source of the Onon is where Tsonj Chuluu Creek, on whose banks we are camped, and Ongoljin Creek, which flows out of the west, come together a few miles down downstream from here. "This is the beginning of the Onon. All local people know this, and it is a very famous place in Mongolian history. It is clearly mentioned in the *Secret History*, where it is called Botoqan-bo'orji. I was there once with a well-known Mongolian historian who confirmed that this was the place where Chingis, then still a teenager or in his early twenties, met with other Mongol chiefs–To'oril and Jamukha–to plan his attack on the Merkits, who had kidnapped his wife, Börte."

It is hard to argue with this. Even my English translation of the *Secret History* describes the three men setting out with their followers "for the Onon's source at Botoqan-bo'orji."[4] I tell Zevgee that in light of its historical associations I am very interested in visiting this place, but add that while it may be the beginning of the river known as the Onon, it is not, in the sense I used, the source of the Amur-Shilka-Onon river system. After giving him a brief rundown of my previous attempts to find the sources of the Lena and the two trunks of the Yenisei I ask him which of the two creeks which combine to form the Onon is the bigger. "Ongoljin Creek is bigger," he replies. Then, I say, the very beginning of Ongoljin Creek, where it first flows out of the ground, is the beginning of the river system. That is where I would like to go.

"Impossible," Zevgee announces with surprising finality. "Upstream from Botoqan-bo'orji it is very swampy. You cannot take horses there. Also, I understand now what you mean by the source of a river. Upstream from Botoqan-bo'orji Ongoljin Creek breaks up into many smaller branches–ten or fifteen or more. It would be impossible to tell which one was the "source," as you call it. Believe me, Botoqan-bo'orji is the source of the Onon. This is where you want to go."

Well, I press on, let's go and camp at Botoqan-bo'orji. I will walk by myself upstream and try to find the source of Ongoljin Creek.

"Impossible! There is no place to camp at Botoqan-bo'orji. And it is too swampy to go on foot. Also, I cannot allow you to go alone. There are bears, and what if hurt yourself or got lost and didn't come back? If we had to go back to Möngönmort without you we would have to answer to the authorities. They might accuse us of something . . . Anyhow, we do not have time for this if we are going to Burkhan Khaldun. I will take you to Botoqan-bo'orji, although it is difficult to get even to there. Then we will go to the hot springs; then, as I promised, to Burkhan Khaldun."

Up until now Zevgee has been the soul of accommodation, and I am rather surprised by his firm refusal to proceed upstream on Ongoljin Creek. I am afraid if I press the issue he might not even take me to Burkhan Khaldun, and an ascent of this sacred mountain has already taken precedence in my mind. So let's go to Botoqan-bo'orji, I tell Zevgee.

By 9:30 we are back on the trail down the Tsonj Chuluu Creek Valley. From the thick larch forest we pass into high bush tundra and scattered stands of larch and birch. Zevgee soon explains that the trail we are on cuts over the spurs to our right and continue on to the Onon Hot Springs. We will have to turn to our left across the valley of Tsonj Chuluu Creek, then continue down the far bank to Botoqan-bo'orji. The valley here is almost a mile wide and covered with thickets of dwarf birch, mats of spongy moss, and swampy muskeg. Several places our horses sink up to their knees in muck. Once my horse flounders completely and I have to jump off to allow it to get back on its feet. Finally we emerge on some higher, forested ground on the far side of the valley and proceed downstream, but we still have to fight our way through a tangle of down timber and thick stands of willow. Emerging suddenly from one dense thicket we find ourselves at the confluence of Tsonj Chuluu Creek and Ongoljin Creek–Botoqan-bo'orji, the beginning of the Onon.

Upstream on the Ongoljin, not more than six or eight miles away,

I can see a bowl rimmed by gray ridges which are topped by several conspicuous peaks. The source of the Ongoljin, and thus the source of the river system, has to be somewhere on the flanks of those gray ridges. By now, however, I have resigned myself to simply standing here at Botoqan-bo'orji, the beginning of the Onon itself. My altimeter gives a reading of 5,410 feet, a relatively low altitude for the beginning of one of the world's longest river systems. (The source of Yenisey-Angara-Selenge-Ider, it will be remembered, was at an elevation of 9,880 feet.)

We all take a ceremonial drink from the river at this historic spot. Zevgee asks me if I know what the word *onon* means. I tell him that according to one of the translators of the *Secret History*, who by coincidence is named Urgunge Onon, the word may mean "boy"; however, Urgunge Onon provides no explanation why this river should be named "boy." Zevgee scoffs at this idea. He claims the name is based on the archaic Mongolian word *on* which he says is the point where the slats making up the walls of a ger intersect. The name refers to the many small creeks which join together upstream from here to form the Onon. Tuya says she has never heard of the word *on*, and the two get into a spirited discussion on this subject, most of which she doesn't bother to translate.

Finally interrupting, I ask Zevgee why Chingis and other Mongol leaders chose to rendezvous here with their armies. As Zevgee had pointed out earlier there isn't any place to camp here amidst all the brush and swamp. Zevgee explains that according to Mongolian scientists he accompanied here, this valley bottom was covered by steppe in the twelfth century. The higher elevations, as documented in the *Secret History*, were covered with thick forests, as today. At that time this area would have been very similar to the mixed mountain-steppe environment of central Mongolia today, with dry, open places to camp in the valleys and plentiful grass for horses. Many of the Mongol tribes of the twelfth century roamed in the valleys of the Onon and the Kherlen, and here at the headwaters of the Onon, not far from the pass leading to the drainage of the Kherlen, was a perfect place to meet.

Zevgee says we must hurry if we hope to get to the hot springs before dark. We ford the Onon and head downstream. The valley bottom itself is too brushy and swampy for the horses and we're forced up onto the flanks of the hills on the left side of the valley. I can understand why Zevgee was not eager to come this way. There are only game trails meandering through down timber, thickets, and boulder fields. Zevgee's horse gets a leg caught in a crevasse between two boulders and flounders, flinging him off. A bit later the pack horse slips to its knees and rolls over on its side. Struggling to get back on its feet it throws off its load. Then my horse gets a leg caught in a hole and I have to jump off. For a sickening moment all its weight goes forward against its shin bone, which is wedged between rocks. It bucks wildly, trying to free its leg. Zevgee runs up, grabs the bridle and jerks the horse's head around. It rears backward and the leg pops out. Zevgee runs his hands up and down the leg, but it appears unhurt. A bit later Tuya's horse stumbles into a nest of wasps. It bucks madly, almost dismounting her, then charges off for a couple hundred feet before Tuya, an expert horse-person, finally gets it back under control.

After an hour or more of this, we emerge out of the forest and thickets into more open terrain carpeted with dwarf willows and soggy grass. We cross the Onon to the other side of the valley and pick up the trail to the hot springs that we had left earlier. Off to our right are high ridges topped by several barren peaks. As we ride down the valley the crowned summit of Burkhan Khaldun peeks out several times from between the mountains in the foreground.

It was here, on the upper Onon basin, just north of Burkhan Khaldun, that the people known as the Mongols first settled in the latter part of the eighth century. "Chingis Khan was born with his destiny ordained by Heaven," reads the opening line of the *Secret History*.[5] His ancestors who first came from "across the lake" here to the Onon, continues the *Secret History*, were Börte Chino (Wolf) and Qo'ai-maral (Beautiful Doe). The lake mentioned is usually assumed to be Khölön Nuur, in present-day China just east of Mongolia. Other sources confirm that during the Chinese Tang Dynasty (618-907) a tribe known as the Meng-ku (or Mengwu) nomadized in the mixed forests and grasslands to the northeast of Khölön Lake on the borders of present-day Manchuria. According to Chinese sources they were wild, warlike people who lived primarily by hunting and raiding neighboring tribes. They had no iron and fashioned their weapons from bone. Only later did they take up animal husbandry and begin to raise horses and livestock. Why they migrated is unclear, but it might be surmised that as animal husbandry became more important to them they began seeking better grasslands than could be found in their original homeland. Moving to the southwest they found these pastures in the upper Onon basin.

Batachi-qan, the first son of Börte Chino and Qo'ai-maral, was born here on the Onon, probably in 786. As I have already recounted, ten generations later a descendant of Batachi-qan, Dobun-mergen, married Alan-qo'a, whose son Bodunchar was the founder of the Borjigin clan into which Temüjin was eventually born. By the eleventh century these people were known as the Mangqol or Mongqol: Mongols. They were still a relatively minor tribe with a tentative hold on the upper basins of the Onon, the Kherlen, and the Tuul rivers, one of many groups jockeying for power in what is now Mongolia.

Anarchy had reigned on the steppe for the three hundred years following the fall of the Uighurs. In 840 of the Uighur capital of Karabalgasun, whose ruins I had visited earlier in the summer, was sacked by Kirghis from the Upper Yenisey region, and the Uighur Empire (745-840), which at its height controlled most of current-day Mongolia, disintegrated. The Kirghis, then a relatively primitive tribe with little social organization beyond the clan level, could not replace the Uighur Empire. They were interested only in plunder, especially coveting the wealth accumulated by the Uighurs at their capital of Karabalgasun. By the year 920 they were forced to retreat back to the fastnesses of Siberia by the Khitans, a rising power in Manchuria to the east; and the Naimans, a lesser tribe who ruled in the Altai Mountain region to the west. The Khitans, who established the Liao Dynasty (907-1124) in northeast China, used the time-tested technique of divide-and-conquer in Mongolia. According to the historian Thomas Barfield, "They threw their weight behind lesser tribes in order to destroy greater ones, who in their turn would be betrayed. Their basic policy was to keep the steppe in anarchy by preventing the rise of any powerful figure."[6]

By the end of the eleventh century the Mongols were prospering.

Kaidu, a descendant of Bodunchar, defeated the Jalairs, a Manchurian people who had invaded the Three Rivers Region, and began to unite the various Mongol tribes. "Gradually his power grew; the clans and tribes who submitted to him became more numerous," says one Chinese source.[7] His grandson, Khabul Khan, finally achieved hegemony over most of the Mongol tribes. Such was his power that in the year 1125 he was invited to the coronation of Xi-zong, the emperor of the new Chin Dynasty, founded by the Jurchens of Manchuria, who the year before had overthrown the Liao Dynasty and taken control of China. There, Khabul Khan, deep in his cups, had the audacity to playfully tug at the emperor's beard. The Emperor Xi-zong forgave this prank, but enraged officers in the imperial court later tried unsuccessfully to kill Khabul Khan on his way back to Mongolia. Relations deteriorated and a Chin army was later sent to Mongolia with orders to smite the unruly, disrespectful Mongols. Smitten itself, this army was chased back into China by the Mongols and trounced near the city of Hailing. Another Chin campaign against the Mongols in 1146 also failed ignominiously. In exchange for peace the Chin finally agreed to make huge annual payments of cattle, silk, rice, and beans to the Mongols.

Humiliated by their defeat and burdened by the big bribes they had to pay for "peace," the Jurchens eventually sought allies for an attack on the Mongols. From the lower Kherlen and Onon basin eastward to the Khingan Mountains, including the vast pasture lands about Khölön and Buir lakes, dwelt the Tartars. A relatively rich tribe known for their silver utensils and tools, they were also much-feared warriors who had earlier subjugated the Mongol tribes in their midst and who themselves regularly extorted huge bribes from the Chin Dynasty. The Tartars and Mongols had long been involved in bloody feuds and by then were sworn enemies. The Mongols under Khutula, the son of Khabul khan, launched more than a dozen raids against the Tartars but were unable to decisively defeat them. Finally by the early 1160s, when the Mongols were weakened by internal dissensions among the various tribal and clan leaders, the Jurchens of the Chin Dynasty saw their chance. They formed an alliance of convenience with their erstwhile enemies the Tartars and together they launched all-out attack on their mutual foes. The Mongol army was crushed near Lake Buir, the Mongol confederation destroyed, and the individual tribes fell under the control of either the Tartars or the Keraits, a tribe who roamed in the area between the Three Rivers country and the Orkhon River. Bereft of their leaders, subjugated, and reduced to abject poverty, the fortunes of the Mongols were at their lowest ebb. It was at this time that Temüjin, the future World Conqueror, was born.

Onon Hot Springs

SHADOWS ARE FALLING across the Onon valley by the time we see the huge ovoo of logs and brush that marks the location of the Onon Hot Springs. Hurrying on we cross the river at the ford just below the steaming springs and ride up a high bank to the large log cabin that serves as a guesthouse. The cabin has doors at each end and is divided into two separate parts. Along the walls are sleeping platforms of roughly planed logs. A dozen or more people could easily sleep in each compartment. There are stoves in each section, stacks of firewood, and a hodgepodge of pots, skillets, plates, and utensils, but it doesn't appear that anyone has been here recently. Zevgee explains that nowadays most people visit here only in the wintertime. When the river and ground are frozen solid it's possible to drive here in big all-terrain-four-wheel-drive Soviet army trucks (GAZ) from the villages far downstream on the Onon that are linked to the road system.

While Bagi tends to the horses, Zevgee, Tuya, and I walk down the high bank to the hot springs complex, which consists of at least fourteen different springs spaced out for about one hundred and fifty feet along the riverbank. Two of the springs, holes in the ground the size of a small cooking pot, are boiling hot. Another, the size of a large wash basin, has water in it hot enough to be uncomfortable to the touch. Nine of the springs are enclosed in small log bathhouses. Inside these huts pits have been dug around the springs and lined with boards and logs. Most of the bath pits are three or four feet deep and a couple are big enough to hold several people at once.

Some of the bathhouses have collapsed and the pits have fallen in, but about half a dozen are in fairly good shape and appear to be used regularly. At the lower end of the complex are two bathhouses in better condition than the rest. On the door of one is a carved wooden sign reading "Ikh Tsenkher" (Big Blue) and on the other a sign reading "Baga Tsenkher" (Little Blue). These, says Zevgee, were the favorite baths of Zanabazar, the first Bogd Gegen of Mongolia, and he himself named them. Zanabazar, an indefatigable polymath, was very interested in the medicinal properties of hot springs. I knew that Zanabazar regularly visited hot springs—Yestii, elsewhere in the Khentii Mountain, the now well-known complex at Khujirt in the Orkhon valley, and others—and studied their composition, but as I mentioned before nowhere in my researches had I encountered any references to these springs.

Zevgee says that the springs here are famous for treating diseases and afflictions of the lower body: knees (mud packs taken from near the springs are especially good for knee joints), lower back pain, kidney and liver problems and also rheumatism and sore muscles in general. In fact, according to a wooden sign on a nearby bathhouse, the springs can cure 404 different ailments. (It will be remembered that this is exactly the number of medicinal plants that supposedly grow on Davaatyn Uul; as mentioned, this number has a symbolic significance in the Lamaist religion.) If you want the full effect of the springs you should take a complete course of baths over a period of about ten days. The bathhouses are numbered and there are prescribed series of baths for the treatment of various ailments.

A few hundred feet from the hot springs is a small log Lamaist temple which had been built just two or three years ago by people from one of the villages on down the Onon. The inside of the temple is sparsely furnished. On a rough plank which serves as an altar is an assortment of offerings: moldering cookies, small jars of grain, bowls of rancid butter, cigarettes, coins and bills, and other ephemera. Above the altar are several small thangkas, the kind you can buy in any tourist shop, and two pictorial reproductions, apparently torn from books, of Zanabazar's famous White Tara.

Zevgee and Tuya wander back to the guesthouse but I remain behind. Of course I must take baths in Zanabazar's favorite springs. I test the water in Ikh Tsenkher with my hand and it doesn't seem too hot, but after stripping off my clothes I find that I have to ease my way into the bath very slowly. I sit up to my neck for fifteen minutes, fresh water from the spring bubbling up between my legs, then move over to Baga Tsenkher, which is just pleasantly warm. The soothing water does indeed seem to be soaking away the aches and pains accumulated over three days of horseback riding.

Back in the guesthouse, Tuya, who up until now has not demonstrated any great enthusiasm for culinary endeavors, is rolling out dough for homemade noodles. Bagi is cutting up mutton into bite-sized pieces. Would I help cut up the mutton? he asks. I reach for my knife, which I keep in my coat pocket, and find nothing. Both snaps on the pocket are open and the sheath knife is gone. Bagi stares at me for a few moments, then smiles and hands me my knife. "When I was riding behind you on the trail I saw your knife on the ground. It fell out of your pocket," he explains, and adds chidingly, "No Mongol would ever lose his knife." I thanked Bagi profusely. A Siberian girlfriend of mine had given me that knife and I had carried it for five years. I had lost it on three other occasions and it had always come back to me. I consider it my lucky knife.

Over our candlelight dinner of fried mutton and noodles Zevgee spins yarns. One concerns a man named Red Mountain Tsend, a Mongolian Mountain Man who lived alone here in the mountains at the headwaters of the Onon. The story begins around the turn of the century when a Japanese monk came to Mongolia and became very interested in the Lamaist form of Buddhist. He learned the Mongolian language and assumed the Mongolian name of Damdinbazar. He was considered a very holy man and eventually gathered around him a flock of Mongolian acolytes. One of them was named Tsend. Then came the revolution in Russia, which soon spread to Mongolia. At first religion was tolerated, but Damdinbazar warned his followers that the day would come when Lamaism would be ruthlessly stamped out by the atheistic communists. Finally the authorities did come to the monastery where Damdinbazar and his followers lived. Some were seized on the spot;

others fled into the hills where they were eventually tracked down and arrested. Some were sent to prison camps in Mongolia and Siberia and others were executed. What happened to Damdinbazar is unknown. His disciple Tsend hid in the remote mountains at the headwaters of the Onon. Living here by himself at a place called Red Mountain he managed to elude the authorities. Assuming the life of a hermit, he avoided contact with civilization and eventually the government lost interest in him.

He became a skilled hunter and fashioned his own clothes from the furs and hides of wild animals. Occasionally he came out of the mountains and approached the local herders. They were happy to take his furs and wild meat in exchange for dairy products, flour, and other essentials. He was also able to trade an amazingly strong glue he made from the hooves of elk and other secret ingredients for what other supplies the mountains did not provide. Zevgee says that even now there are saddles and other leather goods in Möngönmort made with this glue. No one has ever been able to duplicate it.

Red Mountain Tsend lived into the 1950s. He had been married in his early life and had a son. Not wanting to get this son in trouble with the authorities he had avoided contact with him, but sensing the approach of death he sent a message asking the son to come to him. Tsend died before the son arrived. Another legend was spawned. The monastery of Damdinbazar and his followers supposedly had many gold and silver statues and other valuable works of art. Most of this treasure trove disappeared before the communists came and destroyed the monastery. Some said it was hidden in the mountains at the headwaters of the Onon and that only Red Mountain Tsend knew where it was. He had summoned his son to tell him where the treasure was located, but his secret died with him. The treasure, if it indeed existed, is still hidden somewhere in the mountains around here. Even today hunters and plant gatherers who wander into this area keep an eye out for it, but no one has ever found anything, or so they say.

Zevgee goes on to say that these mountains used to also harbor bands of Russian prisoners who had escaped from communist labor camps in Siberia, the border of which he says is only about thirty miles away. In fact, just before I left Ulaan Baatar a Mongolian acquaintance had warned me that even now Russian escapees were hiding out the Khentii Mountains near the border and strongly advised me to stay out of this area. These Russians, he claimed, were cutthroats who would kill you for the clothes off your back. When I tell Zevgee this story Tuya pipes up and says that the jeep driver who had driven us to the Kherlen River had told her exactly the same story. He had assured her that she was crazy to go into these mountains so close to the Russian border. Zevgee shakes his head and laughs. "Fifteen or twenty years ago that may have been true, but I haven't heard about any escapees in this area recently," he says. By now I trust Zevgee implicitly, but I notice that before we blow out the candles Bagi puts his loaded rifle right beside him on the sleeping platform, whether out of fear of bears, or of Russian desperadoes, or of the spirit of Red Mountain Tsend, I don't know.

After awakening in the gray predawn morning I tiptoe out of the guest house where my companions are still sleeping and walk a hundred yards up the hill to the huge log and brush ovoo which honors the hot springs. Directly to the south across the valley of the Onon, here at least five miles wide, is a long ridge which Zevgee had called Tushlegt Yan Uul. The crown of Burkhan Khaldun is hidden somewhere behind this massif. I sit by the ovoo and watch as the rising sun floods the Onon Valley with pellucid light. For the present-day traveler it's a peaceful scene of heart-rending beauty. For Temüjin, the future World Conqueror, the upper Onon was the merciless stage on which was played out his struggle for survival as a young man.

Temüjin's father was Yesükhei-baatar, the nephew of Khutula Khan, who had led the Mongol attacks against the Tartars in the 1150s. Khutula Khan belonged to the Borjigin clan founded by Bodunchar, the son of Alan-qo'a. During an internal struggle for power among the various Mongol tribes Khutula was killed. A tribe known as the Tayichi'ut attempted to assume leadership of the Mongol people but failed and, as we have been, the Tartars and Jurchens were eventually able to defeat the dissension-torn Mongols. At that point the Mongols had no real leader, but Yesükhei-baatar was to provide them with one.

Yesükhei-baatar was out hunting with hawks one day somewhere on the upper Onon when he saw a beautiful young woman in a cart being led by her husband, Chiledü, a member of the Merkit tribe that lived in the lower Selenga Valley to the south of Lake Baikal. Yesükhei-baatar was immediately attracted to the young woman. He went home, got his two brothers, and came back for her. Realizing that she was about to be kidnapped she herself advised Chiledü to flee for his life. The young woman's name was Hö'elün. She came from a tribe of Mongols known as the Onggirat that dwelt around the lakes Khölön and Buir to the east. Hö'elün resigned herself to her fate and became Yesükhei-baatar's wife. Just after Yesükhei-baatar returned home from a campaign against the Tartars their first son was born. According to tradition the boy was born clutching a clot of blood the size of a knuckle bone in his right hand. While fighting the Tartars Yesükhei-baatar had captured a Tartar chieftain named Temüjin-uge, and in accordance with a Mongol tradition he named his son after the enemy he had defeated. The year of Temüjin's birth is uncertain. Dates from 1155 to 1167 have been put forth, but several recent publications, including an almanac published in Mongolia, favor the year 1162.

When the boy, Temüjin, was nine years old Yesükhei-baatar took him to visit Hö'elün's tribe, the Onggirat, in hopes of making a marriage alliance. The Onggirat was famous for their beautiful women, and the Borjigin clan frequently sought wives among them. While traveling to the Onggirat camps to the east of Lake Buir they met up with the Onggirat chief Dai-sechen. He took a liking to Temüjin. "That boy of yours has fire in his eyes and light in his face," he told Yesükhei-baatar. Dai-sechen led Yesükhei-baatar to his ger and showed him his daughter, Börte, who was a year older than Temüjin. She too "had light in her face and fire in her eyes," and Yesükhei-baatar liked her immediately.[8] (The *Secret History* does not comment on Temüjin's opinion, which in any event was unimportant.) It was decided to leave Temüjin with Dai-sechen as a future son-in-law. On the way back, however, Yesükhei-baatar met some Tartars he had robbed earlier. Remembering the insult, they feigned friendliness but gave him poisoned food. Yesükhei-baatar was able to return to his ger but died not long after. Before dying he gave instructions that his friend, Mönglik, should go and bring Temüjin back so he could look after Mother Hö'elün and the rest of the family.

At this time some members of the Borjigin clan were camped with the Tayichi'ut tribe. The Tayichi'ut scorned Mother Hö'elün's family, whose oldest male member, Temüjin, was a mere boy. When the Tayichi'ut moved their camp, they decided to leave Mother Hö'elün and her family behind. Members of her own clan, bereft of a leader, chose to throw their lot with the Tayichi'ut. When they left, Mother Hö'elün rode after them on horseback and managed to persuade some of them to return. But soon they too drifted away and followed the Tayichi'ut. Mother Hö'elün was left alone with her family–Temüjin, his three brothers and a sister, and his two half-brothers, Bekhter and Belgutei, sons of Yesükhei-baatar's other wife.

They came to the upper Onon and eked out a living as best they could. Mother Hö'elün dug up roots and wild onions with a stick of juniper. "Her cap firmly on her head and dress girt around her knees, she ran up and down the Onon River collecting rowans and bird cherries, feeding her chicks night and day," according to one version of the *Secret History*.[9] The boys shot marmots, steppe rats, and birds with their bows and caught fish from the Onon. And so the family managed to survive.

But even within this little group there were dissensions. One day Temüjin and his brother Kasar caught a fish, and Bekhter and Belgutei snatched it away from them. Temüjin and Kasar complained to Mother Hö'elün. Scolding the boys, Mother Hö'elün reminded them of what Alan-qo'a had told her five sons: they were like arrows that separately could be broken quite easily, but united they would be unbreakable. If they ever wanted to gain revenge against the Tayichi'ut who had deserted them they must cooperate, she told the boys. Temüjin and Kasar didn't listen. After Bekhter and Belgutei snatched from them a lark they had shot they made their move. Sneaking up on Bekhter while he was watching their horses they shot him dead with arrows.

"You destroyers!" Mother Hö'elün screamed, then voiced her famous lament: "Apart from our shadows we have no friends. Apart from our tails we have no fat."[10] But if the family was to survive Mother Hö'elün had to make peace with her boys. The other half-brother, Belgutei, reconciled himself with Temüjin, and later he would become one of the World Conqueror's greatest generals.

Temüjin was probably fourteen or fifteen when he killed his half-brother Bekhter. Not long afterward the Tayichi'ut came looking for him. Despite the impoverishment of his family he was still a descendant of the great chieftains like Khabul Khan who had united the Mongol people under the banner of the Borjigin clan. He was on the verge of manhood and he might attempt to regain the positions of leadership held by his father and his ancestors. As such he posed a threat to the Tayichi'ut, and they decided to eliminate him.

There are several different versions of Temüjin's capture by the Tayichi'ut. According to the most prevalent, when a band of Tayichi'ut led by the chieftain, Tarkutai, came for Temüjin the family hid in the forest and the brothers tried to fight them off. The Tayichi'ut announced that they wanted only Temüjin; if he surrendered the rest could go free. Temüjin escaped on horseback and the Tayichi'ut followed him. Hiding in the thickets on a hilltop, he managed to evade the encircling Tayichi'ut for nine days, but finally hunger forced him out and he was captured.

Temüjin was imprisoned—according to some versions, in a wooden cage—and he was forced to wear a large wooden cangue around his neck. But then while the Tayichi'ut were busy feasting on the sixteenth day of the fourth lunar month—the time when the steppe again turns green—Temüjin managed to escape. He was discovered hiding up to his neck in the waters of the Onon by Sorkan-shira, a member of the Suldu tribe who was living with the Tayichi'ut. Sorkan-shira was so impressed by Temüjin's cleverness and will to survive that he helped the young man elude his pursuers and return to his family. Sorkan-shira was one of the first, but certainly not the last, to succumb to Temüjin's charismatic spell. He eventually deserted the Tayichi'ut and became of follower of Temüjin.

By then Temüjin was sixteen or so. His thoughts turned to women, specifically to Börte, the beautiful Onggirat girl to whom he had been betrothed five or six years earlier, and he set off down the Kherlen River to look for her. Dai-sechen, Börte's father, had almost given up hope that Yesükhei-baatar's son—the one with light in his face and fire in his eyes—would ever return, and he was overjoyed when Temüjin appeared in the Onggirat camp to claim his bride. With Dai-sechen's approval the marriage was consummated. Temüjin brought his new bride back with him to the Onon, and in accordance with tradition Börte presented her mother-in-law with a gift–a magnificent black sable coat.

Temüjin soon moved his camp, which at that point included his wife, mother, brothers, sister, and several followers, including Bo'orchu and Jelme, to a place called Bürgi-ergi (Muddy Banks) on the upper Kherlen. (This place, still well known today, is on the Kherlen River between Baganuur and Möngönmort. Zevgee says Tuya and I drove right by it on the way to Möngönmort, although of course I was not aware of it at the time.) Here they were attacked by the Merkits. It will be remembered that Temüjin's father, Yesükhei-baatar, had kidnapped Mother Hö'elün from her first husband, the Merkit Chiledü. The Merkit chieftains, Toqto'a, Dayir-usun, and Qa'atai-darmala heard that Temüjin had taken a wife, and now they and three hundred of their men came seeking revenge for the insult suffered by Chiledü, who had since died. It was early morning when the Merkits struck. Temüjin and most of the camp escaped on horseback, but inexplicably Börte was left behind. How was it that Temüjin abandoned his new wife? The *Secret History* says that there was no horse for her, a seemingly insufficient excuse. After capturing Börte, who had hidden under a pile of wool on a cart, the Merkits picked up Temüjin's trail and chased him up the Kherlen valley. He finally sought refuge on the mountain known as Burkhan Khaldun.

Burkhan Khaldun

ZEVGEE AND BAGI are lounging on the sleeping platforms when I return to the guest house. Zevgee has already soaked himself in Ikh Tsenkher and Baga Tsenkher. Now Tuya is bathing. She soon appears, her cheeks flushed from the hot water and her black hair glistening. Mutton and noodles, along with wild onions—presumably the same kind Mother Hö'elün fed to her chicks—are served up for breakfast. Bagi is amazed to find the onions still edible this late in the year. After breakfast and some rest—to let the mutton settle—I take long soaks in four of the springs. When I return to the guesthouse the horses are saddled and ready to go.

Shortly after eleven we cross the Onon and head back up the valley. We will stay on the trail the entire way back to the Elüür River, instead of detouring via Botoqan-bo'orji as we had done on the way here. The track through the low bush tundra is wet and boggy, and there are treacherous mud holes where the numerous creeks flowing out of the mountains to the left cross our path. As we veer to the left out of the valley of the Onon and cross some forested spurs, thunder cracks and booms in the mountains and several times we have to duck into thick copses of larch to take cover from sudden rain showers. We drop down into the valley of Tsonj Chuluu Creek and by five have reached the clearing where we overnighted on the way in. I am all for heading on but Bagi and Zevgee insist on a pot of hot tea and a late lunch of boiled sheep ribs. Eventually we climb toward Ikh Davaa, lingering for over an hour to gorge again on the huckleberries in the thickets just below the pass, then hurry down the other side. We reach the grassy bench above the Elüür River just as the sun is setting over the hills to the left of the valley. To the east its last rays illuminate the crowned dome of Burkhan Khaldun. Here we make camp.

It's dark by the time our mutton stew is ready. Over dinner we discuss the ascent of Burkhan Khaldun. Zevgee says that from here to the summit there is no real path, and it's necessary to climb through thick woods and boulder fields that are difficult and dangerous for the horses. Instead of going to the mountain and returning here via the same arduous route he now suggests that we take our gear with us to the summit, then drop down the east side of the mountain to the valley of a small stream which flows into the Kherlen. Once on the summit this is the easiest way back down, he claims. From the upper Kherlen we can then ride downstream and eventually pick up the jeep trail back to his ger. I am all for returning a different way and seeing some different country–I don't like backtracking–but there appears to be a problem. What about Tuya, who is supposedly not allowed on the mountain? If we don't return here we will have to take her with us to the summit. Sagacious Zevgee has a solution. Tuya already has short hair cropped like a man's and is wearing a man's baseball cap. Tomorrow she will wear Bagi's deel and also carry Bagi's gun strapped over her shoulder. Surely, then, no beasts, men, or gods will realize that she is actually a woman, opines Zevgee. Tuya will come with us and from the summit we will go down the other side of the mountain. Tuya appears pleased by this solution. Saying she must rest up for the morrow she soon retires to her tent. The two men and I sit silently by the fire. Jupiter glows in the sky to the right of March Mountain, and as we sit red Mars rises just above the horizon to the south-southwest and then sets again. In the north glitters the Big Nail (the polar star) and directly overhead wheel the Seven Wise Men (Big Dipper). Several meteor streak across the horizon on the far side of the Elëër. Zevgee and Bagi turn in but I sit up a while longer, until scudding clouds start to obscure the stars. Even in my tent I can't fall asleep. In the morning we will climb the mountain worshipped by Chingis Khan.

High cirrus clouds are still streaking the sky when I rise the next morning and there's a chill, moaning wind. Zevgee is anxious to get moving. After tea and cold mutton the pack horse is quickly loaded. We ride across a broad swampy meadow and begin our climb up the flanks of March Mountain. It's soon obvious what Zevgee meant when he said this was a difficult route. For two hours we fight our way upwards through thick woods and fallen timber bristling with nasty snags, around huge boulders, and over fields of treacherously loose rock. Amazingly, not once do any of our horses flounder or fall, and not once does Zevgee suggest that we get off and walk. Finally we emerge on the broad open saddle connecting March Mountain and Baatar Yan Mountain. Directly in front of us, across a deep, narrow valley, looms Burkhan Khaldun, topped with its distinctive black crown.

With the Merkits in pursuit Temüjin had hidden in the dense forests around Burkhan Khaldun. Three times the Merkits rode around the mountain looking for Temüjin, but he continued to elude them. Finally the Merkits tired of the chase through the trees and thickets, the down timber, and the mud holes. They had captured Temüjin's wife, Börte, and they decided this was sufficient revenge for the kidnapping of Mother Hö'elün. With their prisoner they headed back toward their camps. Temüjin cautiously descended from the heights of Burkhan Khaldun. Afraid that the Merkits had only feigned leaving and were instead waiting in ambush for him he sent Bo'orchu and Jelme on their trail. They followed them for three days; finally convinced that the Merkits had indeed left they returned. The protective spirits of Burkhan Khaldun had saved Temüjin and once again he had escaped with his life. According to the *Secret History*, he proclaimed:

> On Burkhan Khaldun,
> My life like a louse's,
> I was hunted.
> My life, the only one, was spared.
> With only a horse
> I followed the elk trails.
> I made a yurt of willow twigs.
> I climbed up on Khaldun,
> On Burkhan Khaldun,

My life like a swallow's,
I was protected.

In thanks he added, "I will honor Burkhan Khaldun with sacrifices every morning and pray to it every day. My children and my children's children shall be mindful of this."[11] The *Secret History* continues: "With these words he turned toward the sun, his belt around his neck and his hat hanging over his hand, beat his breast and knelt nine times to offer a libation and prayer to the sun."[12] Because he had miraculously escaped on Burkhan Khaldun Temüjin began to believe in his own special destiny. He was on his way to becoming Chingis Khan, the World Conqueror. But first, of course, he had to get his Börte back.

From the ridge line we ride up the eastern flanks of Baatar Yan Mountain. The larch and dwarf cedar thin out completely and we pass through dry low bush and alpine tundra. Finally we cross a short, knife-edged ridge which connects the massifs of Baatar Yan and Burkhan Khaldun. On both sides cliffs and steep slopes drop off precipitously for a thousand feet or more. At the end of the ridge is a sharp bluff up which we have to walk our horses. From the lip of the bluff a flat expanse of alpine tundra stretches off to the crown of Burkhan Khaldun less than half a mile ahead. From our campsite the crown had not looked that imposing, but now it appears as a black mass of loose black rock three hundred feet or more in diameter and over sixty feet high. Riding closer I can see that the rim of the crown is lined with dozens of small ovoos. We walk our horses up the last sixty feet of crumbling black rock and at last are standing on the summit of Burkhan Khaldun. "You know," says Zevgee somewhat anticlimactically, "I don't think anyone was ever brought a pack horse up here before."

The level top of the crown is dotted with hundreds of small three-foot-high ovoos built by Mongolians who have come here to follow Chingis's injunction that this mountain should be worshipped forever. On the northern edge of the crown is the main ovoo, a ten-foot-high pile of rocks topped by a carved wooden post draped with hundreds of blue and white prayer scarves. Resting on the sides of the ovoo are wooden statues of horses and a black stone bas relief of Chingis himself.

At its base are scattered offerings–whole bricks of tea, packets of cigarettes, coins and bills, rifle cartridges, and various other bric-a-brac. Zevgee digs out some cold mutton, cheese, and the last of the fried bread and the three Mongolians sit down for a snack in front of the ovoo. I wander off by myself to the southern edge of the crown. The weather has been threatening all day, and while there is still blue sky directly overhead dark clouds hang over the mountains on all horizons and long, low grumbles of thunder can be heard from the distant peaks.

Temüjin had to rescue Börte and for that he needed help. Shortly after marrying Börte he had approached To'oril, chieftain of the Keraits, who ruled over a confederation of tribes stretching from the upper valleys of the Onon and the Kherlen in the east to the valley of the Orkhon in the west. Temüjin's father, Yesükhei-baatar, had earlier helped To'oril rise to power, and the two had sworn a pact of friendship. Now Temüjin reminded To'oril of this pact and added that since his own father was dead he looked upon To'oril as a father. To prove his devotion he gave To'oril the magnificent sable coat Börte had given his family as a wedding gift. Having no father Temüjin needed a patron, and To'oril, who had seized the leadership of the Keraits by murdering his own brothers and thus could not count on the support of his own family, needed loyal followers. The two entered an alliance of convenience. In exchange for Temüjin's support To'oril promised he would help the young man reunite his scattered clan.

Now with Börte in the hands of the Merkits, he and his brother, Kasar, and half-brother, Belgutei, traveled to To'oril's camp on the Tuul River. The Kerait chieftain hated the Merkits, who had kidnapped him as child–he later escaped–and he now had an excuse to attack them and reward his vassal, Temüjin, at the same time. According to the *Secret History* he announced: "In gratitude for the sable cloak I will find your Börte for you, even if I have to destroy all the Merkits. In gratitude for the black sable cloak we will rescue your wife Börte, even if we have to massacre every Merkit!"[13]

The brothers also called on the chieftain, Jamukha, who had been one of Temüjin's few friends during his early boyhood on the Onon. The two had skated on the ice of the Onon together and had sworn a pact of friendship. By now Jamukha was a powerful man with a considerable following of his own, although like Temüjin he recognized To'oril as an overlord. As a young man he had been robbed of all his possessions by the Merkits and he too wanted revenge. Such was his standing among the tribes that To'oril gave him overall command of the campaign against the Merkits. Jamukha, To'oril, and Temüjin, along with their men, agreed to rendezvous at Botoqan-bo'orji, where Tsonj Chuluu and Ongoljin creeks come together to form the Onon. The assembled army was not inconsiderable. To'oril and Jamukha each brought twenty thousand men. Together they rode northward against the Merkits.

Toqto'a and Dayir-usun, two of the three Merkit chiefs who had chased Temüjin around Burkhan Khaldun, were camped with their followers on the Khilok River, a tributary of the Selenga. Warned in the middle of the night that the Mongol force was approaching, they with some of their men fled in the dark down the Selenge, eventually reaching the Barguzin lowland just east of Lake Baikal. The Merkits who were left behind were cut down or captured and their camps looted. Temüjin ran among the panicked Merkits crying, "Börte! Börte!" From her hiding spot Börte recognized his voice and she ran to him. Under the light of the moon they hugged each other. Temüjin had his Börte back. There was only one problem: Börte was pregnant.

Gray clouds scud over Burkhan Khaldun and big raindrops spatter on the black rock. Massive bolts of lightning rattle off the summit of Baatar Yan Mountain just to the northwest. I hurry back to the main ovoo where Zevgee has all the horses assembled. He suggests we leave immediately rather than get caught in a thunderstorm here on the summit. I agree. I had once been caught in a thunderstorm like this on the summit of a mountain in the Baikal region and it was a truly nerve-shattering experience. We walk our horses down the black crown, and ride down a rounded ridge leading away from the mountain to the southeast. Dropping through alpine tundra we're soon back at the timberline. From here we have to walk our horses down a well-marked but very steep trail that switchbacks along the side of the ridge to the valley of the Bogdiyn River.

On a flat bench just above the valley bottom we emerge into a small clearing in the larch forest. Right by the trail is a large brush ovoo and an immense iron kettle. At the base of the ovoo are more than a dozen whole bricks of tea, Mongolian and Russian bills and coins, and other offerings. The pot, which could hold at least fifty gallons, was the teakettle of a monastery which once existed here. This monastery, says Zevgee, was built by Zanabazar, and he used it as a retreat when he came to pay homage to Burkhan Khaldun. Most people who go to the summit of Burkhan Khaldun, he explained, come this way, and not via the route we had used. We had ascended from the west because, of course, we were coming from the Onon Valley. In the past people always stopped at this monastery to make offerings before starting up the mountain. Kicking around in the thick moss he soon uncovers a ceramic roof tile, some bricks, and other building remnants. He does not know the name of this monastery, nor have I found any reference to it in my researches. It was probably destroyed by the communists in the 1930s, but he's not sure of the exact date. Mongolian scientists he has accompanied here say that in the time of Zanabazar, three hundred years ago, there were no trees on this bench, and that it was covered with steppe.

Zevgee goes out ahead on the trail and we follow slowly behind with the pack horse. He soon hurries back and he and Bagi have a whispered conference. Then he tells Tuya and me that we must go and hide in the woods. He has heard someone approaching and he doesn't want them to see us. He rides off and returns fifteen minutes later. Before leaving on this trip he had heard that some Mongolian scholars from Ulaan Baatar were planning a pilgrimage to Burkhan Khaldun and now he is afraid that we might encounter this group. He doesn't want them to know that he has taken both a foreigner and a woman up on Chingis's sacred mountain. It's a false alarm; there is no one.

While we were coming down the mountain the rain clouds had blown over completely and now the skies are burnished a cobalt blue. Although it's only a little past seven we decide to camp in a large grassy clearing along the Bogdiyn and enjoy the evening. A fire is soon blazing and we relax with hot tea. When Bagi goes to cut up mutton for our dinner he discovers that his knife is missing. His knife was handmade and one-of-a-kind, with a ten-inch blade of finely tempered steel and an elaborately engraved bone handle. Now he remembers that he used it while eating lunch at the ovoo on the top of Burkhan Khaldun. He apparently left it there. He stares ruefully back at the massif of the mountain—the summit is not visible from here—as if considering riding back up to get it. But of course there isn't time for that. I am tempted to remind him of what he said when I lost my knife, but I don't.

Upper Kherlen Valley

T HE NEXT DAY dawns clear and still. Zevgee announces that if we start early we can get back to his ger tonight. He's anxious to see his family. After a quick breakfast we hurry down the Bogdiyn valley. There's a good trail, a jeep track actually, and if the weather has been very dry or the ground is frozen solid four-wheel-drive jeeps can make it up to our camping spot in the Bogdiyn Valley, Zevgee says, adding that the scholars from Ulaan Baatar may not have come because the track is now, after a damp spell, impassable by vehicle. We reach the mouth of the Bogdiyn Valley and turn right down the valley of the Kherlen. The others quickly trot on ahead but I stop for one last look at the massif of Burkhan Khaldun before we lose sight of it behind the foreground ridges along the Kherlen.

Temüjin's campaign against the Merkits was his first real military success. Although he had probably just turned twenty, he had proven himself as a man to be reckoned with. He began to attract more followers and by the time he was twenty-three or so had recovered the leadership of the Borjigin clan. Still, he was just one of many local chieftains who aspired to power in Mongolia. He soon came into competition with his erstwhile ally, Jamukha, who had his own considerable following. After a series of clashes Jamukha finally routed Temüjin's forces at the Battle of Dalan Baljut, killing many of the prisoners he had taken by boiling them alive in seventy huge pots. Temüjin's star seemed to wane. There follows an almost ten-year hiatus in his career about which very little is known.

The *Secret History* here has a very noticeable gap. Other accounts hint that he fled to China and sought the protection of the Chin Dynasty, but instead was taken prisoner and held in captivity for many years.

Temüjin had not yet used up all his lives, however, nor had he lost his charismatic powers. Around 1195 he reappeared in Mongolia and managed to rally around him a new following. By then To'oril, his original patron, had been ousted as the head of the Keraits by disgruntled relatives and was in exile among the Kara-Khitai in Turkestan. He attempted to enlist the Kara-Khitai in a campaign to regain his lost throne, but their leader, the Gur Khan, refused. To'oril and a few of his followers wandered back to Mongolia and eventually turned up in Temüjin's camp virtually destitute. Temüjin, remembering To'oril's assistance to him as a young man, welcomed him back, and the two once again became allies.

It will be remembered that the Chin Dynasty had earlier united with the Tartars to crush the Mongol confederation founded by the khans Khabul and Khutula. Now the Tartars had become too powerful and posed a threat to the Chin. Using the old-age tactic of "fighting barbarians with barbarians" the Chin decided to enlist Temüjin and To'oril in a campaign against the Tartars. Temüjin, whatever his earlier experiences with the Chin may have been, was only too glad to oblige. After all, the Tartars had killed his father. "They are the ones who destroyed our ancestors and fathers," he proclaimed, according to the *Secret History*. "Let us jointly attack the Tartar!" To'oril agreed: "My son is correct to send these words. Let us jointly attack."[14] Caught between the Mongols and the Chin the Tartars were crushed. Among the war booty Temüjin seized for himself was a much-prized solid silver cradle and a quilt decorated with pearls. In gratitude the Chin emperor awarded the title of Ong Wan (King) to To'oril and a lesser title to Temüjin. In using Temüjin to eliminate the Tartars, however, the Chin had made a fatal mistake. When Temüjin eventually became Chingis Khan there would not be any other "barbarians" strong enough to oppose him, and he and his sons would destroy the Chin Dynasty.

To'oril was once again proclaimed leader of the Kerait confederation with Temüjin as a junior partner. Temüjin's old nemesis, Jamukha, and his followers were also accepted into the alliance, and the crafty To'oril played off one against the other, allowing neither to became too powerful and thus threaten his own power. When the Naiman, who led a confederation of tribes stretching from the valley of the Orkhon west to the Altai, fell into dissolution after the death of one of their rulers, To'oril enlisted the forces of both Temüjin and Jamukha and organized a campaign against them. Jamukha saw his chance. On the night before the crucial battle with the Naiman Jamukha persuaded To'oril to abandon Temüjin. They and their forces retreated, leaving Temüjin to face the Naiman alone. Jamukha, of course, hoped his longtime rival would be destroyed. He also appears to have deserted To'oril. The Naiman, instead of attacking Temüjin, pursued To'oril forces. The irresolute To'oril, facing defeat at the hands of the Naiman, had no choice but to once again call upon Temüjin to rescue him. As a reward Temüjin proposed a marriage between To'oril's daughter and his eldest son, Jochi. According to one account this presumptuousness on the part of someone whom he still considered an underling infuriated To'oril. "Go back and tell him that I would rather burn my daughter than give her to his family in marriage," he fumed.[15] His son, Senggum, believed that Temüjin's maneuvers were an attempt to ultimately seize control of the Kerait confederation when the now elderly To'oril died, and thus deprive him of his inheritance. His distrust of Temüjin was inflamed by the ever-persistent Jamukha, who, reappearing back on the scene, saw yet another chance to undermine his nemesis. A plot was hatched. Temüjin was told the marriage proposal was accepted and invited to celebrate at a feast. There he would be assassinated.

En route in the celebration, however, Temüjin took counsel with Father Möngke, the man his dying father had sent to bring him back from his in-laws, Börte's parents. This venerable personage, the father of the celebrated shaman, Teb-Tengri, who had once predicted Temüjin's destiny as World Conqueror, warned him away from the feast. Temüjin escaped the trap, but many of his followers, sensing that his star was waning, deserted him. Senggum then led the Keraits on a campaign against Temüjin and his remaining followers. After a series of bloody battles, in one of which his own son, Ögödei, was seriously injured in the neck, Temüjin was finally forced to retreat to Lake Baljuna near the Chinese border.

Only 2,600 of his warriors remained, according to the *Secret History*. Temüjin's fortunes appeared to be waning, but still he had not lost faith in his own destiny. Patiently he began gathering allies. He appealed to the Onggirat, reminding them that both Mother Hö'elün and his wife, Börte, came from their tribe. They sided with him, and several other tribes followed in their wake. The Khitans rallied to him in hopes that someday he would help them in their struggle against the Jurchens (Chin Dynasty) who had replaced them as the rulers of China. Defectors from the Keraits drifted into his camp. Soon he felt strong enough to send To'oril a message, asking one last time for an alliance with the Kerait leader. "If a two-shafted cart has a broken shaft the ox cannot pull it. Am I not your second such shaft? If a two-wheeled cart has a broken wheel it can travel no further. I am your second such wheel," he pleaded.[16] With To'oril's son, Senggum, and the ever-conniving Jamukha, both of whom coveted To'oril's throne, Temüjin could accept no compromise. Some accounts say that To'oril nevertheless attempted a reconciliation between himself and Temüjin; others say the now old and irresolute man allowed Senggum to decide how to treat with him.

With no satisfactory answer forthcoming, Temüjin decided to take the offensive. Informed by spies that To'oril and his followers were feasting in his encampment on the lower Kherlen, Temüjin and his forces rode all night and attacked them by surprise. The battle seesawed for three days but finally the Keraits were defeated. Attempting to flee in the night, To'oril, apparently mistaken for a common soldier, was killed. His son, Senggum, fled to Tibet, and later to Turkestan, where he was murdered. The shifty Jamukha had decamped before the battle and sought asylum among his erstwhile enemies, the Naiman.

Thus by the year 1203 Temüjin was in control of most of Mongolia east of the Orkhon River. Many of the tribes that still opposed Temüjin rallied around the Naiman, who ruled western Mongolia from the Orkhon to the Altai. In 1204 Temüjin's combined forces turned on the Naiman and drove them to the foothills of the Altai where they were annihilated. "They died, packed close together like felled trees," comments the *Secret History*.[17] The tribes that had allied themselves with the Naiman now submitted to Temüjin. In the autumn of 1204 Temüjin's men also tracked down the remaining Merkits. Only Tokto'a, the chieftain who had chased

Temüjin around Burkhan Khaldun, and a handful of his followers managed to escape the slaughter.

With the defeat of the Naiman, among whom he had sought refuge, Jamukha fled to the Tannu Uul on the northwest border of Mongolia, but he was eventually betrayed by his own followers and handed over to Temüjin. He had one last request of Temüjin, with whom as a boy he had played together on the ice of the Onon and whose wife, Börte, he had helped rescue from the Merkits: "If my friend, you are pleased to kill me, do so without shedding any blood. Then, when I am dead and if you place my corpse on a high place, I will watch over you, your grandsons and their grandsons, into the distant future. I will be your spiritual protector!"[18] According to some accounts Chingis honored this last request by having him rolled up in thick carpets and then trampled to death by the horses of his soldiers.[19] According to others he had Jamukha killed by slow, bloody dismemberment.

From Lake Khölön to the Altai there was no one of any consequence left to oppose Temüjin, by then forty-four years or so old. In 1206 the Mongol tribes met in a great assembly on the upper Onon River. They proclaimed Temüjin their leader and gave him a new title by which he became known all over the Eurasian continent in the thirteenth century and by which we know him today: Chingis Khan.

By now the others have fast-trotted down the Kherlen valley several miles. Galloping down the grassy track I finally catch up with them at a ford across the Kherlen, which here is no more than fifty feet wide and not over a foot deep. The river goes to the right and disappears between some high bluffs. The track swings left and climbs a steep muddy hill to a low pass marked by an ovoo. This place, says Zevgee, is called Bogdyn Pass in the *Secret History*. On the far side the trail goes down a long gradual incline. A half mile or so below the pass, in the middle of a grassy slope here a quarter of a mile wide, appears a mound perhaps sixty feet long and up to ten feet high. Although the mound is itself covered with grass and even a few aspen saplings–there aren't any other trees in sight anywhere near–it's obvious even to me, untrained as a geologist or archeologist, that this is not a natural feature of the landscape but instead a man-made structure. Curious, I gallop ahead to

Tuya, and together we trot up to Zevgee. What's that mound over there, I ask him. "I don't know," he answers shortly. "Oh come, Zevgee, you know about everything around here. What is it?" Tuya chides. "It is connected with Chingis," he brusquely retorts, "But local people never talk about this place." With that he kicks his already fast-trotting horse into overdrive and moves on ahead.

Inevitably my thoughts turn to the grave of Chingis, which is of course widely believed to be somewhere in this area. But this obvious monument is in plain sight only a hundred yards from the trail and must have already attracted the attention of any number of researchers, including those of the exceedingly determined Three Rivers Expedition. So what is this mound? I still don't know.

Far ahead and to our right appear the three mountains we had seen on the way in—Baldanch, Jakhüüjin, and Bayan Öndör. Just in front of them, I remember, we had turned to the left and gone up the valley of Shirengetei River on our way to the Onon. I for one would be happy just to get to their base today and camp there tonight, but from the way he's pushing the horses Zevgee apparently still thinks we can get back to his ger tonight. All afternoon we ride down the Selenga Valley and in our hurry I think we are even going to forego lunch; but no, at five we stop, unload the pack horse, unsaddle the horses to let them dry—they have worked up a sweat—build a big fire, and spent an hour and a half over tea, cheese, mutton and noodles.

Pressing on, we pass by Baldanch, Jakhüüjin, and Bayan Öndör mountains and eventually arrive at the wooden bridge across the Kherlen which we had seen on the way in. Parked here is a jeep with three men and a woman from Möngönmort—the first people we have seen since leaving the fishermen six days before. They have spent the day in the nearby hills picking cranberries. After confabulating with these people for fifteen minutes Zevgee, Bagi, and Tuya come up with a plan. Bagi will go back with them by jeep to Möngönmort and thus be able to spend the night in his own ger with his family. Also, Tuya had originally planned to call our jeep driver from Möngönmort when we arrived, but this way Bagi can call him late tonight, catching him at home, and tell him to come pick us tomorrow at Zevgee's ger. This, she decides, will save us a day or even two of waiting for our ride back to Ulaan Baatar. Bagi is wreathed with smiles as he pulls away in the jeep.

With Zevgee leading both the pack horse and Bagi's horse we continue on, but instead of taking the jeep trail, which swings over toward the flanks of the mountains, we follow a horse trail along the right bank of the Kherlen. Below the bridge the valley begins to widen, and soon we are back on firm, dry steppe. Even after five and a half days of riding my chestnut is still full of oats. Leaving the others behind, I gallop on, alone, across the flat steppe for several miles. Shadows are falling across the Kherlen, the heat of the afternoon has dissipated, and a cool breeze laden with the scent of sage wafts up the valley. My chestnut knows this is the home stretch and finally I have to pull him up. Eventually Tuya and Zevgee appear and we continue on as dusk fades into darkness. The sickle moon that rises over the mountains to the northeast provides no real light at all and finally I can't see the ground beneath my horse's feet. I get right behind Zevgee's horse and let my horse follow his. Does Zevgee know where he is going? I ask unnecessarily, just wanting to be assured. He says not to worry; he could find his way back to his ger blindfolded. On and on we ride completely enfolded in darkness, the silence broken only by an occasional grumble from Tuya, who I gather is not too pleased with this forced march. I slump in the saddle, exhausted, putting all my faith in the surefootedness of my chestnut. It seems like the sun has set hours ago when we finally hear dogs barking. Someone senses our approach and a faint light flickers across the steppe. We ride toward the light and at twenty minutes after midnight dismount in front of Zevgee's ger.

We duck inside while some boys see to the horses. It's soon clear there's no room for Tuya and me to sleep in the already crowded ger. I go out and like an automaton set up both tents in the utter darkness. Back inside Tuya appears to have resuscitated herself with hot milk tea, cheese, and khaimag. I do likewise. I ask Zevgee if he is tired. "This guy never gets tired," his wife answers for him. I myself am longing for my sleeping bag, but there is one last problem. From beneath a pile of blankets on the darkened side of the ger comes the crying and whimpering of a small boy. He had stepped on some broken glass, cutting his foot, and now the cut is badly infected. Do I have any medicine? asks Zevgee's wife. Going out to my pack and rooting around I find some penicillin and over-the-counter pain killers. Tuya provides an elaborate translation of how to use these medicines, and Zevgee's wife thanks me profusely.

The sun is sparkling on the ripples of the Kherlen directly in front of my tent when I awaken the next morning at nine o'clock. Tuya, amazingly, is already up and chatting with Zevgee's wife on the riverbank as they scrub some clothes in a wash basin. After I have performed my ablutions in the river Zevgee waves us into the ger for tea. Finally I can take stock of his family. There appear to be over a dozen in all: sons, daughter, grandchildren–including a six-month-old who monopolizes everyone's attention–and some nieces and nephews from the city here for the summer. The overflow sleeps in another ger nearby. I ask after the horses, and Zevgee says they are fine, but he has put them on the best grass and won't ride any of them for the rest of the year. He opines that the day before we rode about seventy kilometers (forty-two miles), which from my map seems about right. It was the longest day I ever spent in the saddle. I figure we rode a total of 135 miles.

Finally I wander off by myself and end up lazing in the sun on the grassy banks of the river upstream from the gers. The trip, I realized, had taken an unexpected turn. As hoped I had reached the headwaters of the Onon–the birthplace of the Mongols–but I had also been rewarded with an unexpected ascent of the mountain which had played such a consequential role in Chingis Khan's early life and which he worshipped to the end of his days.

Chingis never forgot that the protective spirits of Burkhan Khaldun had saved his life, and on his path to becoming the World Conqueror he would often reenact the seminal experience he had there. Eventually he would no longer call only on the localized spirits of the mountain, but on Tengri, the Eternal Blue Heaven which ruled over the entire earth. In 1211, before he began his campaign against the Chin Dynasty in China, Chingis again climbed to the top of Burkhan Khaldun and there, "his belt hanging around his neck, communed with the Eternal Heaven." He spent three days and nights meditating–just as he had spent three days and three nights hiding here from the Merkits–and on the morning of the fourth descended, proclaiming, "Heaven has prepared me victory. Now we must prepare ourselves to take vengeance . . . ."[20] This was just the opening thrust again the Chin. The dynasty would finally be destroyed by the Mongols in 1234, and in 1260 Chingis's grandson Khubilai Khan would found the Yüan Dynasty which eventually ruled almost all of China.

While his generals fought the Chin, Chingis turned his attention westward. In 1218 he launched a campaign against the Sultan Muhammad of Khwarazm, whose Islamic empire stretched from the Pamir Mountains in the east to the Aral Sea in the west, and south to the Persian Gulf, including an area that covers much of present day Inner Asia, Afghanistan, and Iran. Before he went into battle against the Sultan Muhammad he again "climbed to a top of a hill, bared his head, raised his face . . . and prayed to Heaven for three days."[21] We do not know if this hill was Burkhan Khaldun or some other mountain, but we do know that Tengri again favored Chingis. The fabulously rich cities of Inner Asia–Samarkand, Bokhara, and others–were looted and razed, and the great Islamic empire of Sultan Muhammad shattered.

Lying here on the banks of the Kherlen something else occurs to me. Not far downstream from here, at Bürgi-ergi, Chingis's wife, Börte, was kidnapped by the Merkits. After he escaped by hiding on Burkhan Khaldun Chingis, with the assistance of To'oril and Jamukha, rescued Börte from the Merkits, but as I mentioned, she was pregnant when he found her. Chingis's oldest son Jochi was born not long afterwards. Was Börte pregnant when she was kidnapped, as some sources suggest, or had she became pregnant afterwards? As a prisoner of the Merkits she had been given to the Merkit Chilgerbökö, the brother of Chiledü, from whom Chingis's father had stolen Mother Hö'elün. It would have been a supreme irony if Jochi was actually Chilgerbökö's son. Although Jochi's paternity was thus in doubt Chingis seemed to accept him. He entrusted his eldest son with the leadership of several armies and Jochi played a crucial role in the campaigns against the Chin and the Sultan Muhammad of Khwarazm. Yet when it came time to declare a successor Chingis was all too aware the Mongols might not follow someone they considered illegitimate and not a true representative of Chingis's own line. Thus he left his empire to his third son, Ögödei.

Jochi died when he was forty. According to one account Chingis had him poisoned, thus eliminating one source of contention among his successors. Jochi's son, Batu, however, went on to become one of the most successful of the Mongol generals. After the defeat of the Sultan Muhammad of Khwarazm the gate to the West was open. In 1237, a decade after Chingis's death, the Mongol armies under the command of Batu launched a great raid into the principalities of northern Russia. Moscow was burnt to the ground in February of 1238, and in December of 1240 the Mongols sacked Kiev, then the greatest center of medieval Slavic culture, thus effectively subjugating most of Russia. Batu had accomplished all this, but yet he had been left out of the line of succession because of the doubts about his father's paternity. Realizing that he could never rule as Khan of all the Mongols he carved out his own khanate on the Russian steppe—the so-called Golden Horde. This was one of the first of the cracks in the foundation of the Mongol Empire, the beginning of the schisms which would eventually destroy Chingis's Pax Mongolica.

So it was here, at the headwaters of the Kherlen and the Onon, that it all began—the kidnapping of Mother Hö'elün, the murder of Chingis's father, the abduction of Börte, the escape of Chingis on Burkhan Khaldun, and the raising of his first army—and it was here that the seeds of dissension were sown among his successors, and the fate of the largest land empire in history sealed.

We don't know if Bagi got through to our jeep driver. We eat a leisurely lunch of mutton soup and homemade bread slathered with thick cream. After lunch Zevgee takes us to a nearby ger which, it turns out, has nothing in it but a large sleeping platform and a crude still. By the still are big pots of yogurt used to make the moonshine. The still is fired up and arkhi—milk vodka—is dripping into a collection basin. From under the sleeping platform Zevgee pulls out a big jar of the clear arkhi, and we all taste samples out of a silver-lined bowl. Then he and I split a bowl. Then we each drink a whole bowl by ourselves. Then, I think, another. I have forgotten about our jeep by the time we finally hear its horn blowing outside the ger. The driver is in a hurry and we quickly throw our gear in the back and make our farewells. Zevgee gives me a big hug and his wife shakes my hand. The whole encampment lines up to wave as we drive away. After a brief stop in Möngönmort to say good-bye to Bagi we head straight back to Ulaan Baatar. We arrive at my hotel at twenty minutes after midnight, the exact time we got to Zevgee's ger the night before. I have a roaring headache from the arkhi and go straight to bed.

Burkhan Khaldun Revisited

THIS STORY DOES have an addendum. In the spring of 1998, eight months or so after I had been to the Onon River and Burkhan Khaldun, the Geographical Research Institute, a division of the Mongolian Academy of Sciences, published a remarkable book entitled the *Chinggis Khaan Atlas*. It contained thirty-seven maps (including insets) depicting in great detail the locations of many of the places and events mentioned in the *Secret History* of the Mongols and other chronicles of Chingis Khan's life. Flipping to the map entitled "Temüjin Attacked by the Merkits," I was disconcerted to discover that the map makers had given the name of Burkhan Khaldun to the mountain known as Erdene Mount. It will be remembered that during my trip to the Onon we had passed close by the base of Erdene Mount and that Zevgee's winter camp was located nearby. The map even showed the clockwise path the Merkits had taken around the mountain while searching for Chingis. Had I in fact visited the wrong mountain?

To confuse matters even further, another map in the *Atlas* showed not one but three Burkhan Khalduns: the Burkhan Khaldun of the Qamag Mongols, which is also called Khentii Khan Uul (the mountain to which I had been with Zevgee); the Burkhan Khaldun of the Uriankhai, also called Erdene Mount; and the Burkhan Khaldun of the Kereyids, also called Asralt Khairkhan Uul. The latter mountain is well known as the highest peak in the Khentii Mountains, but I had not realized that it was in any way connected with the life of Chingis Khan. Further study of the maps also revealed that Botoqan Bo'orji was, in the opinion of the map makers, not where Tsonj Chuluu and Ongoljin creeks come together to form the Onon, as Zevgee had claimed, but on the Minj River just across the border in Russia. Just what was going on here?

I reviewed what I knew about the Burkhan Khaldun I had visited. Zevgee, who had accompanied many expeditions of Mongolian and foreign scientists and who seemed extremely knowledgeable about the *Secret History*, apparently believed that this mountain was the real Burkhan Khaldun. And as I mentioned, the honorary head of the joint Mongolian-Japanese Three Rivers Expedition had been flown to the summit of this mountain to pay homage to Chingis. Surely the Mongolian scholars involved with the Three Rivers Expedition would not have taken this illustrious personage to the wrong mountain. I myself had seen the huge ovoo and hundreds of smaller ovoos on the top of the mountain, all placed there by Mongolians who apparently thought they were heeding Chingis's injunction that this mountain should be worshipped by his descendants' descendants forever. Passing by the base of Erdene Mount I had no good reason to closely examine its summit, but as I could recall there was no assemblage of ovoos visible on the top. Then there was the temple, the ruins of which I had seen, that supposedly had been established by Zanabazar as a place where pilgrims on their way to Chingis's sacred mountain could stop and make offerings. Why was this temple built here if the mountain was not in fact Burkhan Khaldun? Were Zanabazar–assuming the story of the temple's provenance was correct–and all the pilgrims who had come this way also deluded? Why were the Mongolian scholars that Zevgee was so determined to avoid coming to this mountain if it was not Burkhan Khaldun? Why was Zevgee so determined to avoid them if this was just an ordinary mountain and not Chingis's sacred mountain where foreigners and women were not supposed to go? I'll admit to being puzzled.

Also, shortly after returning from my trip to the birthplace of the Mongols I came across a lavishly produced book entitled *Chinggis Khaan* which apparently had just been published (the book is undated). It contained excerpts from the *Secret History* and excellent–with one exception–photographs of many of the places mentioned. The exception was the photograph captioned: "Burqan Qaldun [Burkhan Khaldun] mount which Temüjin reached safely uncaptured after escaping from Merkits." The photograph had been taken on a very overcast day and the mountain was shrouded in fog–I was reminded of the widespread Mongolian belief that certain mountains do not like to be photographed–but as near as I could tell it was indeed Khentii Khan Uul, the mountain I had been on. It certainly was not Erdene Mount, because on the next page was a very clear photograph of that mountain captioned: "Erdene Mount–Sentry Post." The authors of *Chinggis Khaan* were D. Bold and N. Ayuush. The editors were listed as D. Bazargür and D. Enkhbayar. A quick check back to the *Chinggis Khaan Atlas* revealed that it had been compiled by the very same D. Bazargür and D. Enkhbayar. Had they changed their minds as to which mountain was Burkhan Khaldun? Now I was more than puzzled, I was mystified.

I arranged an interview with Dambyn Bazargür and Dambyn Enkhbayar, editors of *Chinggis Khaan* and the compilers of the *Atlas*. Needing a translator, I met with Tuya, who was now employed by an even more upscale tourist agency than the one she had worked for the summer before. Over pasta in one of Ulaan Baatar's ubiquitous Italian restaurants I learned that just six weeks earlier she had returned with a small group to the upper Onon and Burkhan Khaldun, using Zevgee as a guide. They had gone to the summit of Burkhan Khaldun–the mountain we had been on earlier–via the Bogdiyn Valley and returned the same way. The trip to the summit was much easier now, she said, because a group of over three hundred Mongolians who had made a pilgrimage to the mountain back in May had done a considerable amount of work on the trail. Now you could ride the whole way to the top without dismounting. The pilgrims were accompanied by a contingent of lamas who performed an ovoo ceremony in honor of Chingis. Which brought up the reason for our luncheon date. I showed Tuya the *Atlas* and explained to her that there was now a question as to what mountain was actually Burkhan Khaldun. She too was mystified and agreed that we better meet with the compilers of the *Atlas*.

The Geographical Research Institute of the Mongolian Academy of Sciences resides in a two-story building tucked away in a cul-de-sac directly behind the United States Embassy. Dambyn Bazargür, Ph. D., in his sixties, silver-haired, distinguished-looking, cordially invites us into his cubbyhole office where we are soon joined by fortyish, bookish-looking Dambyn Enkhbayar. I explain that the summer before Tuya and I had been to Khentii Khan Uul, which according to our guides and to various other sources is also known as Burkhan Khaldun, the mountain which Chingis Khan had worshipped. But according to their *Atlas*, the mountain known as Erdene Mount is actually Burkhan Khaldun. I am confused. Can they offer some clarification?

Bazargür explains that as one of the maps in the *Atlas* shows there is more than one Burkhan Khaldun. Originally, the name itself was not so much a geographical designation as a description of certain activities centered around the shamanistic worship of deceased ancestors—as I understand his rather tortuous explanation and Tuya's even more tortuous translation. Thus several places where these activities took place became known as Burkhan Khaldun. One of them was the mountain known as Erdene Mount. After a thorough study of all the geographical clues in the *Secret History* and other texts, it is his considered opinion that it was Erdene Mount on which Chingis escaped from the Merkits. It was also on Erdene Mount that the brothers Dobun-Mergen and Duwa-Soqor first spied Alan-qo'a who, it will be remembered from an early episode in the *Secret History*, was the ancestress of Chingis's own clan. I point out that the *Secret History* says Burkhan Khaldun is at the source of the Onon, while Erdene Mount clearly overlooks the valley of the Kherlen. There is no clear explanation for this discrepancy, but the researchers allow that perhaps "source of the Onon" means the general area of the Khentii Mountains and not the actual beginning of the Onon River.

In any event Khentii Khan Uul was also known as Burkhan Khaldun, and according to Bazargür's interpretation of the *Secret History* it was here that Chingis later went to perform ceremonies before going into battle. Thus it was this mountain that his followers began to worship. And, Bazargür admits, it is this Burkhan Khaldun which Mongolians, in accordance with Chingis's famous injunction, continue to worship down to the present day; witness the over 300 people who went there the previous May.

At this point I pull out of my briefcase the book *Chinggis Khaan* by D. Bold and N. Ayuush. I get the fleeting impression that Bazargür and Enkhbayar aren't too thrilled to see this book. I show them the photograph of Erdene Mount, which is described as the "Sentry Post," with no mention of anything about Burkhan Khaldun. Then I show them the photograph of the mountain identified as Burkhan Khaldun. As alluded to earlier, it's a very poor photograph, but they allow that it is the mountain also known as Khentii Khan Uul. The caption, I point out, reads, the ". . . mount which Temüjin reached safely uncaptured after escaping from Merkits."

"You may have noticed," Enkhbayar says after about fifteen seconds of silence, "that Bazargür and I are listed as the editors of that book." I had noticed. "Although that is the case, I must respectfully point out that we do not agree with all the opinions stated by the authors." Enkhbayar adds with just a hint of resentment that the book *Chinggis Khaan* was a commercial venture and thus had been lavishly printed in Korea. He and Bazargür are poor, state-supported researchers and they had to print their *Atlas* in Mongolia on very poor-quality paper, he notes.

Pressing on, I point out that our guide to the upper Onon had once guided some Mongolian researchers who had told him that Botoqan Bo'orji was at the beginning of the Onon River, at the confluence of Tsonj Chuluu and Ongoljin creeks. Again they respectfully disagree. To this day, as they have indicated in their *Atlas*, there is just north of the Russian border a small tributary of the Minj River called Botoqan Bo'orji. This, they maintain, is also the Botoqan Bo'orji where Chingis met with Jamukha and To'oril to plan his campaign against the Merkits. I mention that as with Burkhan Khaldun the *Secret History* says that Botoqan Bo'orji was "at the source of the Onon." If it was in the valley of the Minj River why didn't the *Secret History* simply say so? Again, it appears that the "source of the Onon" may just refer to the Khentii Mountains in general. So again we are back to differing opinions. Enkhbayar allows, however, that on their way to the Botoqan Bo'orji on the Minj the Mongol chiefs would have passed right by the confluence of Tsonj

Chuluu and Ongoljin creeks and indeed might have stopped and camped there.

There is one last point I want clarified. Had the temple at the base of Burkhan Khaldun (Khentii Khan Uul), the ruins of which we had seen when descending from the mountain, actually been built by Zanabazar? Happily, both men agree that Zanabazar had ordered its construction, and it was here that pilgrims on the way to Burkhan Khaldun stopped to make offerings. With that Tuya and I bowed our way out.

I can't say I was all that satisfied with the interview. All said and done the locations of many of the places mentioned in the *Secret History* remain open to interpretation. Barring the miraculous appearance of the original Mongol language version of the *Secret History*—the existing version has actually been transliterated back into Mongolian from the Chinese, which accounts for a lot of the confusion about name places—or of some new, previously unknown source materials about the early life of Chingis Khan, it seems unlikely that anyone can determine beyond a shadow of doubt the exact location of, for instance, the mountain where Chingis sought refuge from the Merkits. And it might be argued that only hopelessly pedantic antiquarians need concern themselves with such issues. By hallowed tradition Khentii Khan Uul has become the Burkhan Khaldun to which Mongolians go when they want to honor the spirit of Chingis, and where they no doubt will continue to do so in the future. I myself hope one day to return there and pay my respects to the World Conqueror. And just to be on the safe side I also plan to climb Erdene Mount.

References

The Source of the Ider

[1]   Pozdneev 1971, 157
[2]   quoted in Grousset 1994, 528
[3]   Ossendowski 1922, 104
[4]   Ossendowski 1922, 116
[5]   Ossendowski 1922, 160
[6]   Ossendowski 1922, 163
[7]   Ossendowski 1922, 165
[8]   The story is recounted in Ossendowski 1922, 128. I have changed some of Ossendowski's spellings and added some dialogue.
[9]   Pozdneev 1971, 244
[10] Ossendowski 1922, 130

In Search of Zanabazar

[1]   Pozdneev 1971, 17
[2]   Pozdneev 1971, 333
[3]   Pozdneev 1971, 333
[4]   Pozdneev 1971, 335
[5]   Pozdneev 1971, 338
[6]   Pozdneev 1971, 338
[7]   Pozdneev 1971, 22
[8]   Pozdneev 1971, 24
[9]   Pozdneev 1971, 28

10   Pozdneev 1971, 367

11   Pozdneev 1971, 325

12   Bawden 1989, 53

13   Bawden 1961, 39

14   Pozdneev 1971, 323

15   Pozdneev 1971, 318

16   Bawden 1961, 39

17   Bawden 1961, 40

18   Pozdneev 1971, 323

19   Bawden 1961, 42

20   Pozdneev 1971, 324

21   Pozdneev 1971, 322

22   Pozdneev 1971, 328

23   Pozdneev 1971, 329

24   Pozdneev 1971, 330

25   Tsultem 1982, 7

26   Berger 1995, Introduction

27   Pozdneev 1971, 303

28   Pozdneev 1971, 282

29   Philips 1943, 18

30   Bawden 1961, 37

31   Pozdneev 1971, 283

32   Bawden 1989, 77

33   Bawden 1989, 366

34   Several sources refer to Gombodorj (1594-1655) as the son of Abudai. Since Abudai died in 1587 this hardly seems possible. Presumably Gombodorj was the grandson of Abudai, and thus Zanabazar would not be Abudai's grandson, as stated in numerous sources (and by tour guides at Erdene Zuu Museum) but rather his great-grandson.

35   Pozdneev 1971, 289

36   Pozdneev 1971, 290

37   Tsultem 1989

38   Choinkhor 1995, 3

39   quoted in Bawden 1989, 262

40   Bernbaum 1980, 4

[41] Lattimore 1982, 133
[42] Roerich 1931, 132

The Birthplace of the Mongols

[1]   Onon 1990, 3
[2]   Onon 1990, 5
[3]   Heissig 1980, 14
[4]   Onon 1990, 36
[5]   Onon 1990, 1
[6]   Barfield 1989, 183
[7]   quoted in Ratchnevsky 1991, 9
[8]   Onon 1990, 15
[9]   quoted in Ratchnevsky 1991, 23
[10] Onon 1990, 22
[11] Onon 1990, 32
[12] quoted in Ratchnevsky 1991, 34
[13] quoted in Ratchnevsky 1991, 35
[14] Onon 1990, 52
[15] quoted in Ratchnevsky 1991, 68
[16] Ratchnevsky 1991, 78
[17] Ratchnevsky 1991, 86
[18] Ratchnevsky 1991, 87
[19] See Morgan 1986, 152; The *Secret History*, para.201
[20] Ratchnevsky 1991, 109; Grousset 1994, 219
[21] Ratchnevsky 1991, 123

Bibliography

BAWDEN, CHARLES. 1961. *The Jebtsundamba Khutukhus of Urga*. Weisbaden: Otto Harrassowitz.

Bawden, C. R. 1989. *The Modern History of Mongolia*. London and New York: Kegan Paul International.

Berger, Patricia. 1995. *Mongolia: The Legacy of Chinggis Khan*. London: Thames and Hudson.

Bernbaum, Edwin. 1980. *The Way to Shambhala*. Garden City, New York: Anchor Press/Doubleday.

Choinkhor, J. 1995. *Undur Geghen Zanabazar*. Ulaan Baatar: Mongolian National Commission for UNESCO.

Grousset, René. 1994. *The Empire of the Steppes: A History of Central Asia*. Translated by Naomi Walford. New Brunswick: Rutgers University Press.

Heissig, Walther. 1980. *The Religions of Mongolia*. Berkeley and Los Angeles: University of California Press.

Lattimore, Owen, and Fujiko Isono. 1982. *The Diluv Khutagt: Memoirs of a Mongol Buddhist Reincarnation in Religion and Revolution*. Wiesbaden: Otto Harrassowitz.

Onon, Urgunge. 1990. *The History and Life of Chinggis Khan (The Secret History of the Mongols)*. Leiden, New York: E. J. Brill.

Ossendowski, Ferdinand. 1922. *Beasts, Men and Gods*. New York: E. P. Dutton.

Philips, G.D.R. 1943. *Dawn in Siberia: The Mongols of Lake Baikal*. London: Frederick Muller.

Pozdneev. 1971. *Mongolia and the Mongols*. Edited by J. R. Kreuger. Uralic and Altaic Series. Bloomington, Indiana: Indiana University.

Ratchnevsky, Paul. 1991. *Genghis Khan: His Life and Legacy*. Oxford: Blackwell Publishers.

Roerich, George. 1931. *Trails to Innermost Asia*. New Haven: Yale University Press.

Tsultem, N. 1982. *The Eminent Mongolian Sculptor–G. Zanabazar*. Ulaan Baatar: State Publishing House.

Tsultem, N. 1989. *Mongolian Sculpture*. Ulaan Baatar: State Publishing House.